BRONX FACES & VOICES

BRONX FACES & VOICES

Sixteen Stories of Courage and Community

Edited by
Emita Brady Hill and **Janet Butler Munch**

Foreword by **Fernando Ferrer**

Preface by **Ray Bromley**

Photographs by **Georgeen Comerford** and **Walter Rosenblum**

Texas Tech University Press

This book is typeset in Minion Pro. The paper used in this book meets the minimum requirements of ANSI/NISO Z39.48-1992 (R1997). ♾

Designed by Kasey McBeath
Cover photographs by Georgeen Comerford

Library of Congress Cataloging-in-Publication Data
Bronx faces and voices : sixteen stories of courage and community / edited by Emita Brady Hill and Janet Butler Munch ; foreword by Fernando Ferrer ; preface by Ray Bromley ; photographs by Georgeen Comerford and Walter Rosenblum.
pages cm
Includes bibliographical references and index.
ISBN 978-0-89672-888-2 (hardback) — ISBN 978-0-89672-889-9 (e-book) 1. Bronx (New York, N.Y.)—Biography. 2. Bronx (New York, N.Y.)—Biography—Portraits. 3. Bronx (New York, N.Y.)—Social life and customs—20th century. 4. Bronx (New York, N.Y.)—Social conditions—20th century. 5. Community life—New York (State)—New York—History—20th century. 6. Urban beautification—New York (State)—New York—History—20th century. 7. Community development—New York (State)—New York—History—20th century. 8. Courage—New York (State)—New York—Case studies. 9. New York (N.Y.)—Biography. 10. New York (N.Y.)—Biography—Portraits. I. Hill, Emita Brady. II. Munch, Janet Butler, 1950- III. Comerford, Georgeen. IV. Rosenblum, Walter, 1919-2006.
F128.68.B8B78 2014
974.7'275—dc23 2014024580

14 15 16 17 18 19 20 21 22 / 9 8 7 6 5 4 3 2 1

Texas Tech University Press
Box 41037 | Lubbock, Texas 79409-1037 USA
800.832.4042 | ttup@ttu.edu | www.ttupress.org

This book of stories is dedicated to my sister,
Virginia Brady Calkins,
who loves a good story.

Emita Brady Hill

And also to all those
whose "voices" helped us
know and apprecciate the Bronx.

Janet and Emita

History is not a record of what really happened
but of what men believe really happened.
For without witnesses, history becomes
a victory of the imagination over actuality.

Author unknown

CONTENTS

ILLUSTRATIONS

PHOTOGRAPHS

BLACK AND WHITE PLATES, FOLLOWING PAGE xxiv

BLACK AND WHITE PLATES, FOLLOWING PAGE 54

BLACK AND WHITE PLATES, FOLLOWING PAGE 182

FOREWORD

From the time of its first European settlement when Dutch was commonly spoken until its polyglot present, diverse people have come to the Bronx—the only one of New York City's five boroughs attached to the mainland United States—to make a better life for themselves and their families. They have come, they have flourished, they have made unique contributions, and they have made a way for others to come and, in succession, do exactly the same thing.

Historians have told those stories, selecting swaths of time, digging deeply into records, journals, accounts, maps, drawings, photographs, and registries, reconstructing what living in those times was like. Some of the most engaging histories of the Bronx have been authored by Lloyd Ultan and Gary Hermalyn (Bronx borough historian and executive director of the Bronx County Historical Society, respectively). From early settlements to great farms; old colonial homesteads to Revolutionary War battlegrounds; from creating centers of commerce and manufacturing to founding and building great universities; from a building boom that saw the borough swell to one and a half million people by 1960 only to see the population drop to slightly over a million two decades later, as Bronxites fled abandonment, arson, and eventually the rubble that used to be their neighborhoods, the Bronx has had an almost Shakespearean past.

But some of the richest depictions of the borough of my birth come from first-person, twentieth-century accounts. If the story of a place is best told by its own people in their own words, then the Bronx's recent story is best told by Bronx faces and voices.

Emita Hill, herself an important part of the Bronx story, carefully and thoughtfully curates the oral artifacts of formative Bronxites and bestows them upon future generations of Bronxites as well as on those who seek a deep understanding of what the Bronx is and how it got that way. More fundamentally, you will feel, as I did, that you were right there with these Bronxites as they reminisced about the old farms and movie theaters, and going to school and the street games, as well as their home lives, the obstacles their families overcame, the battles to maintain vital public services in the wake of blight, and the unmistakable feeling of optimism shared by all, even in the face of adversity.

I grew up on Fox Street, just off the corner of Avenue St. John. My world growing up encompassed just a few blocks going in any direction. We had everything we needed right there in the neighborhood: school, church, stores, and parks (except for Orchard

Beach). My maternal grandmother lived in our building, and my paternal grandmother lived several blocks away on Tinton Avenue. It wasn't until I took a scholarship exam for high school that I first saw an apartment building with elevators (we lived in a five-story walkup). I shined shoes on the corner of 149th Street and Southern Boulevard. Soon I graduated to stocking groceries (and delivering them to those same five-story walkup apartments) at the grocery-deli across the street from my building. On Sundays after church (St. Anselm's) we would all go to my paternal grandmother's apartment on the first floor of 768 Tinton Avenue, where I consumed some of the greatest meals of my life (still) and played with my growing army of cousins.

My younger sister and I walked to elementary school every day (about nine blocks each way) at a time in the Bronx and the city when about the worst thing that could befall young kids on their way to school was a fight (or two). Stickball on Fox Street, 52 Park, the Ace Theater's double features (with free comic books!)—my universe was small but fabulous.

Life was indeed good . . . that is, until it wasn't so very good anymore. We couldn't see the early signs. Only the occasional mugging or burglary by a drug addict. And then, the days and winter nights without heat or hot water (tenants, in those days, didn't have the use of an intercom to communicate with the superintendent and were moved to send him angry messages by banging on the iron radiators, which became an almost unbearable but still irresistible cacophony of clanging metal), and the leaks and ceiling collapses and the inevitable "We've got to move!"

I came to take personally the loss of my and so many other neighborhoods in the Bronx. I couldn't understand why it seemed that no one could stop this. In later years, I was even more baffled at some leaders' seeming belief that the barrenness of block after block had no apparent antidote. I couldn't and wouldn't accept their acceptance as our fate.

The fires, crime, and consequent wholesale abandonment of my neighborhood seemed to come in a great tsunami, sweeping away irretrievably almost everything we knew and loved. The devastation was nearly metaphysical, crushing not merely physical buildings but also people's spirits. Nearly a decade after Howard Cosell in Yankee Stadium announced to his World Series audience that "the Bronx is burning," the embers cooled long enough for a serious effort at revival in the Bronx, but nothing came easily. A friend of mine called me in the late eighties, as I was beginning my work as borough president, to say that he had heard that Mother Teresa was coming to the South Bronx.

"Wonderful," I said. "What a great feather in our cap!"

"Not so fast," the friend cautioned. "Mother Teresa only comes to the most hopeless places." Yeah, wonderful.

On reflection, however, the seeds of the South Bronx's destruction were sown well before fire consumed nearly everything in its path. Policies that redlined certain neighborhoods from top-tier credit in order to invest in renewal set the forces in motion. Contractions in public spending resulting in budget cutbacks for hospitals, parks, and infrastructure accelerated decline and undesirability of once-thriving middle- and lower-middle-class neighborhoods. Most politicians and government leaders not only failed to see the early signs but seemed incapable or unwilling to muster the political will to mount a counteroffensive. The fires could be seen burning in broad daylight. Disinvestment, arson, abandonment, and decay became the Four Horsemen of the Bronx's apocalypse.

Halting attempts at community renewal were made but seemed to run out of steam until then-mayor Ed Koch, the city council, and the board of estimate finally got serious about allocating the money necessary for an effective undertaking. Moreover, the last few years of life for the old board of estimate proved a very good thing for the South Bronx in that the pipeline for new housing was stuffed so tight with new projects that they survived three mayors. I'm proud of the role that I played in aligning communities with the city government. In truth, the revival of the South Bronx came only when petty rivalries were set aside and we worked in partnership with communities, acting in concert and with common purpose. Like an orchestra, we all made beautiful music! In any case, the rest is, as they might say, the story of one career in public service and a great and challenging time in the Bronx, ending, for me, in nearly fifteen exciting, eventful, and deeply satisfying years as its borough president.

In the years leading up to the last day of my service as leader of the Bronx, I have known and worked with nearly every one of those interviewed in *Bronx Faces and Voices* (including its author). I can still hear their voices, and many of them inspired me and others. They were characters, to be sure (some, with the passage of over thirty years and the verdict of history as well as some courts of competent jurisdiction, might even be considered something worse), but Bronx originals all. Love them or loathe them, these voices were here and made their own unique contributions. The Bronx would not have been the same without them. And neither would this great assemblage of oral histories and images that Emita Hill has so thoughtfully served up to all of us.

Fernando Ferrer
Bronx, New York
January 2014

PREFACE

The first edition of Jill Jonnes's classic book, published in 1986, was very aptly titled, *We're Still Here: The Rise, Fall, and Resurrection of the South Bronx*.[1] The title perfectly portrayed the notoriety of the South Bronx and the almost biblical drama of decline, crisis, and revitalization. It also underlined the crucial fact that in the midst of white flight to the North and East Bronx, the New York metropolitan regional suburbs, and many other parts of America—and of considerable churning of low-income and minority populations, as they moved from place to place in search of affordable housing and accessible job opportunities—many people stayed. They endured the rising crime rate of the 1960s, the abandonment and cuts in public services of the 1970s, and the Koch-era apartment-building rehabilitations of the 1980s. They witnessed the peak population period between 1950 and 1970, the sharp decline in population of the 1970s, and the gradual resumption of growth from the 1980s onward that was fueled by an upsurge in immigration from a very broad range of countries.

The South Bronx crisis of the 1970s led to a population fall in the area west of the Bronx River and south of Fordham Road from over 760,000 to little more than 450,000. This dramatic loss caused a fall of more than 20 percent in the borough population, even though the neighborhoods of the North and East Bronx did not experience significant losses.[2] The South Bronx crisis was dramatic, especially because the whole area was just five to ten miles from Midtown Manhattan, but the same type of crisis was occurring in Harlem and in northeastern Brooklyn, including areas even closer to Manhattan's corporate headquarters and elite neighborhoods. The New York metropolitan region was, and remains, a world-famous center of socioeconomic inequality, of wealth and poverty and of growth and decline, in close, interrelated proximity. As a world city, New York attracted global attention and millions of visitors, who saw crisis neighborhoods and socioeconomic inequalities far beyond anything found in Canada, Europe, Japan, Australia, or New Zealand. The inequalities had a third-world feeling about them, but the destruction in the most deprived neighborhoods had an aura of war damage or collective insanity, very different from the underlying upward mobility of most third-world shantytowns.

Nevertheless, the crisis extended beyond New York City to many other urban areas in the U.S. Northeast and Midwest and to a few cities of the American South and West. If population decline, arson, and abandonment are the hallmarks of crisis, the decline of the

South Bronx in the 1970s was smaller and shorter than the corresponding declines of cities like St. Louis, Cleveland, and Detroit, and much less dramatic than the crises of smaller rust belt cities like East St. Louis, Illinois; Youngstown, Ohio; Gary, Indiana; Flint, Michigan; and Utica, New York. Many northeastern and midwestern U.S. industrial cities peaked in population around 1950 and have been declining ever since. Over sixty years of decline led Detroit to its record-breaking municipal bankruptcy of 2013.

By using *We're Still Here* as her title, Jonnes emphasized that the South Bronx had *not* been abandoned, and that for every picture of vacant buildings, rubble, and empty lots, corresponding pictures could be taken of ordinary people living in their neighborhood and going about their daily lives. In many cases, if the photographer had simply pointed the camera in the opposite direction, a much more "normal" scene of daily life would have been portrayed.

Because of its reputation and proximity to Manhattan, the South Bronx was a mecca for photographers seeking images of the 1970s U.S. urban crisis. The abandoned and burned-out five- or six-story apartment buildings of the South Bronx looked more eerie and forbidding than the abandoned two-story row houses of Baltimore or the burned-out single-family homes of Detroit or Youngstown, but they were manifestations of many of the same processes. The list of interrelated causes, varying in significance from city to city and from decade to decade, included redlining, disinvestment, suburbanization, overzealous urban renewal, blockbusting, insurance fraud, arson, cuts in public services, rising crime rates, racial discrimination and prejudice, deindustrialization, overambitious planning schemes, rapidly escalating fuel costs, and rising interest rates. Explicitly or implicitly, city administrations often engaged in a form of planned shrinkage, cutting services and investments in neighborhoods that were officially deemed to be blighted, unstable, or scheduled for renewal. Many of the most negatively affected neighborhoods had high percentages of African American or Hispanic residents.

This book focuses on the people who stayed in the Bronx—South, North, and East—and the crucial role they played in ensuring that the crisis of the South Bronx was relatively short by national standards, and that it did not spread to the whole borough. The subjects are primarily ordinary people—the everyday heroes who stayed, worked, and lived by maxims like "Don't Move, Improve!" and "Nos Quedamos, We Stay!"—along with some of the local politicians and institution builders who represented the Bronx in its dealings with city, state, and federal governments.

The Bronx is special in many ways, but not because it is uniquely poor, depressed, or devastated. In per capita terms, it is the poorest of the five boroughs of New York City, but it includes prosperous neighborhoods like Riverdale and Fieldston; a grand system of parks and parkways, recreational areas like Orchard Beach and City Island; several major hospitals, universities, and colleges; and major regional attractions like Yankee Stadium and the Bronx Zoo. Because many of its inhabitants organized to confront the South Bronx crisis of the 1970s, it has a broad range of community organizations, including well-known community development corporations

(CDCs) like Banana Kelly, Mid Bronx Desperadoes (MBD), the Northwest Bronx Community and Clergy Coalition (NW-BCCC), Nos Quedamos, and the Point. In *We're Still Here*, Jonnes gave us a graphic picture of the community revitalization process, based on community organization; community pressure on city, state, and federal authorities; and the blending of government and corporate funding. As investment increased in the South Bronx from the late 1970s onward, all neighborhoods improved to some degree, and some CDCs won international renown for their achievements. Most of those who stayed, worked, and invested their lives and savings in the South Bronx were committed supporters of community development and neighborhood revitalization. Nevertheless, the Bronx had its share of slumlords and racketeers who sought to make a quick profit out of neighborhood decline, and poverty pimps who sought to profit from new construction and from job creation and social services programs. Community development was a contentious process, confronting apathy, greed, and powerful interests within and outside the borough. Several of the more successful CDCs have survived crises and changes of management, while many incipient organizations failed to build the momentum to establish themselves on a long-term basis.

So if the Bronx is nowhere near having endured America's worst urban crisis, and its record of revitalization is bright but not unsullied, why is it so well known, and why is it still useful to publish this book of oral histories of Bronx residents covering the periods of "life, death, and resurrection"? There are many good reasons.

First, of course, the Bronx is both a county and an outer borough of New York City, and New York is arguably the best-known city on Earth. For much of the twentieth century it has been the greatest metropolis: a mecca and gateway for immigrants to the United States, and a global center for finance, publishing, broadcasting, and the arts. New York may be the most photographed and filmed city on earth, and its images and major events are known worldwide. It has had a tremendous influence on global culture, developing and diffusing many forms of cultural syncretism. Jazz, doo-wop, salsa, and hip-hop are vibrant forms of music with strong New York City ties and special links to the Bronx, and New York City has a leading role in the development and diffusion of many forms of drama, dance, and fast food. Though the city is not even the capital of New York State, inhabitants of New York City often refer to it as the capital of the world or the capital of capitalism, assertions that ring true because it is the seat of the United Nations and home to Wall Street.

New York City is the only U.S. city that is made up of counties, rather than simply being a municipality within a county. The five boroughs form a municipal juggernaut, with more power and a much clearer identity than any other municipality in the United States. The city of Los Angeles, the nation's second-largest city, is one of 88 municipalities within Los Angeles County, and the city of Chicago, the nation's third-largest city, is one of 132 municipalities within Cook County. Governmentally, the Bronx, Queens, Brooklyn, and Staten Island are unique—boroughs and counties with their own borough presidents, county courthouses, representatives in the state legislature, and other instruments of government. Unlike neighborhoods, whose boundaries are "fuzzy," with no lasting long-term definition or guarantee of identity, the boroughs have clear, legally defined territories and boundaries.

All four of the outer boroughs of New York City contrast sharply with Manhattan, "the inner borough," the center of global capitalist activity and the focus of most domestic and international tourism. Though the portion of Manhattan (New York County) that stretches from Harlem northward to Inwood and Marble Hill often feels like an outer borough or a part of the Bronx, this area receives little consideration when New Yorkers compare Manhattan with the Bronx. As exemplified in one of Tom Wolfe's classics, *The Bonfire of the Vanities*,[3] the Bronx is a distant and very different world for Manhattan sophisticates—a world they rarely visit, unless it is simply to pass through quickly by car or train on their way to elite suburbs or to Upstate New York and New England mountain and lake resorts. Elite Manhattanites occasionally behave like adventurous foreign tourists, making a trip to witness poverty and destruction, but rarely staying or returning regularly to observe daily life and neighborhood change.

Though New York City is, in many senses, the quintessential world city, some New York scholars turn this cosmopolitan virtue into a parochial vice, ignoring other American cities, other world cities, U.S. government policies, and New York State government policies—all of which have some independence from the internal processes of New York City. Powerful New Yorkers are magnified to become masters of the universe, and New York's most spectacular buildings, events, personalities, triumphs, and disasters are presented as if nowhere else really mattered. Most of the writers who exemplify this tradition are Manhattanites, and the outer boroughs play modest roles in their narratives, portrayed simply as areas to be crossed to reach airports, suburbs, and recreational zones, locations for specific projects that cannot be fitted into Manhattan, areas inhabited by "ordinary people," and sources of rank-and-file workers, consumers, and votes.[4]

Of the four outer boroughs, the Bronx is, in many ways, the most exceptional. It is the only borough on the U.S. mainland, and it has by far the most memorable and peculiar name. Generations have puzzled and discussed why it is "the" Bronx, and what on earth the name "Bronx" signifies.[5] While Brooklyn had a clear municipal identity before fusion with New York City, the Bronx was the result of railroad- and subway-driven outward expansion from Manhattan, and the annexation of neighboring villages and farmlands, separated from Westchester County. It was the fastest-growing borough from the consolidation of Greater New York in 1898 until Queens achieved even higher rates of growth in the 1920s. Its mainland location made it crucial to the city's water and food supplies, and from the 1920s until the 1940s it was very important in Democratic Party politics. Many immigrants from different parts of the world lived their early or middle years in the United States in the Bronx, and many white and minority Americans lived the first part of their lives in the Bronx before migrating to other areas of the country.

The Bronx has one of the most vibrant nostalgia industries of any city in the United States, as exemplified by the ongoing success of *Back in the Bronx* magazine, which has now published over eighty quarterly issues celebrating such bygone delights as egg creams, movie matinées, and stickball in the street. Also notable are the Bronx County Historical Society and the Bronx Museum of the Arts, substantial and enduring institutions when the Bronx is compared with other counties across the nation. Nostalgia sells newsletters, books, and memorabilia, and it generates some return tourism, but its primary significance lies elsewhere. It represents Americans of European descent who look back on their lost youth in the Bronx as "the good old days" of socializing, flirting, and sport—a simpler life in a bygone era, now remembered in a world clouded by aging and often also by illness, divorce, and financial difficulties. The Bronx is romanticized as a happy place and a simpler world, where young people had fun together despite relative poverty, and where everyone's primary identity was the high school they graduated from and the year they graduated. *Back in the Bronx* nostalgia stretches across America, with distant concentrations in California and Florida, and it carries fairly strong ethnic overtones. Its focus is on white Irish Americans, Italian Americans, Jewish Americans, German Americans, and others who left rather than integrating with the rapidly increasing in Hispanic population and the significant growth in African American population that occurred after World War II. It is the nostalgia of those who went, rather than those who stayed, and comparison with the oral histories of those who stayed provides many insights on American society, ethnicity, migration, and identity. Both those who left and those who stayed made choices, took or rejected opportunities, and can sometimes claim that they had no alternative.

When those who left say, "I'm from the Bronx," many thoughts come to the minds of non-Bronx listeners. First and foremost, Bronx birth and upbringing combined with migration elsewhere tends to symbolize upward social mobility. Whether true or not, Bronx origins are often perceived as humble, and Bronx residents are seen as possessing strong ethnic identity as hyphenated Americans, as well as worldly knowledge of gangs, slumlords, racketeers, machine politics, graffiti artists, and hip-hop. The listener's mind fills with images of the Bronx, some derived from history, many from popular news, and some from media portrayals, novels, and movies. On radio from 1929 until 1946, and on television from 1949 until 1956, *The Goldbergs* provided America with soap-opera-like portrayals of working-class Bronx Jewish life. *The Goldbergs* movie (1950) initiated a long sequence of movies set in the Bronx, including such classics as *Marty* (1955), *The Wanderers* (1979), *Raging Bull* (1980), *Fort Apache, the Bronx* (1981), *The Bronx Warriors* (1982), *Escape from the Bronx* (1983), *Five Corners* (1987), *Billy Bathgate* (1991), *A Bronx Tale* (1993), *Rumble in the Bronx* (1995), and *Dead Presidents* (1995). Some feature Bronxites like Chazz Palminteri, but most are outsider impressions of a fictional Bronx—folksy, negative, violent, and often surreal. Hilarious examples are the "Spaghetti-Bronx" epic *Escape from the Bronx*, directed by Enzo G. Castellari, and the Jackie Chan classic *Rumble in the Bronx*. Castellari's film is a sci-fi portrayal of urban renewal and gangland resistance, with avaricious Manhattan speculators paying a squad of "disinfestors" to drive the last residents out of the Bronx so that it can be redeveloped as a city of the future for Manhattanites. Jackie Chan's *Rumble in the Bronx* is an action drama of gangs and crime syndicates, filmed in Vancouver, but set in the Bronx because "Rumble in Vancouver" would not appeal or seem credible to an international audience!

The media image of the Bronx tends to focus mainly on "the South Bronx," even though it makes up only about 27 percent of the borough's land area; since the early 1970s it has not had the majority of the borough's population.[6] Though it was always possible to refer to the southern Bronx from the creation of the borough onward, the term "South Bronx" did not acquire widespread use or significance until the 1960s. The area stretched from Mott Haven, Port Morris, and Hunts Point to University Heights, Belmont, and West Farms, and it included about twenty distinct neighborhoods. Nevertheless, many recent arrivals seemed unfamiliar with the neighborhood names and identified themselves more with street addresses and nearby subway stations, or even with Catholic parishes. As crime rates, building fires, and building abandonment rose in significance, and as public services were cut, the ratio of newcomers to long-term residents increased, and middle-class outsiders visited less frequently. The old neighborhood names were used less, and more and more people adopted "the South Bronx" as a generic term for the whole area south of Fordham Road and west of the Bronx River. Like the South Bronx, North Philadelphia, the South Side of Chicago, and South Central Los Angeles, all have undergone severe urban crises and rapid turnover of residents. Though much of Harlem and northeastern Brooklyn went through similar dramatic transitions in the 1960s and 1970s, those areas of the city retained their separate neighborhood names and identities (East Harlem, El Barrio, Flatbush, Brownsville, Bushwick, East New York, etc.), thus avoiding the national and international notoriety of the South Bronx.

When viewed from an urban studies perspective, the New York metropolitan region is America's largest and most heavily studied metropolis. It is part of the archetypal "megalopolis" centered on what may well be the world's best-known and most-studied city.[7] A good urban studies library of New York runs to thousands of books, articles, and periodicals, and material can be added daily from the intense reporting of the world and local media, most of which view New York–based reporting as essential to their trade. Though some authors and reporters ignore the Bronx, the borough still receives much more global attention than most of the world's cities with populations in the 1- to 2-million range. The depth and variety of New York research creates publishing opportunities that do not exist in smaller and less-studied cities. Los Angeles, Chicago, Boston, San Francisco, and other major metropolises have substantial published literatures, but the available material on America's small cities rarely extends beyond a handful of books and articles, and microfilm of one or two local newspapers. Presses are rarely interested in scholarly monographs on smaller and less-well-known cities, publishing only occasionally on such places and mainly catering to the nostalgia industry by producing local guides and albums of historic photographs. For New York, however, embracing all five boroughs, rich, intertwined histories are continuously reinterpreted as newer and more specialized publications become available. This very welcome collection of Bronx oral histories should be viewed in that context—as an important addition to a rich literature that provides a springboard for more discussion, debate, and research.

Bronx Faces and Voices will help generate a better understanding of the twentieth-century Bronx and its twenty-first-century future, and of the dynamics of a New York metropolitan region that is still heavily focused on Manhattan. Though much has been written on the Bronx devastation-resurrection theme,[8] much more analysis is needed, and the testimony of those who stayed through the crisis period is especially valuable. Many factors and issues are intertwined, and oral history is a rich source, both to generate questions and to develop explanations.

Ray Bromley
Albany, New York
January 2014

Emita Hill interviewing Alice Kramer, 1982
Photograph by Georgeen Comerford

Edna Grzetic with family photos, 1984
Photograph by Georgeen Comerford

ACKNOWLEDGMENTS

I am indebted to the librarians of the Leonard Lief Library—foremost among them my coeditor, Janet Munch, special collections librarian, and an active participant in the Bronx Regional and Community History project since its inception. Under her guidance, interviews taped thirty years ago on mini-cassettes were digitized to be instantly accessible. Photographs, vintage and contemporary, were carefully catalogued. Janet helped me locate several of the interviewees still resident in the Bronx when I had lost all record of where they might be, even whether they were still alive. Most importantly, Janet has provided the meticulous endnotes and bibliography, a labor of love and of long hours. Her invaluable research has greatly enriched this oeuvre. Janet's assistant, Mariela Galarza, managed the challenging transcription of the almost inaudible interview with Carmen Bermudez and patiently copied documents and photographs from the BRACHS Archives. Mariela and also Wayne Halliday, electronic information systems librarian, provided significant help with technical problems. I am indebted to Tabitha Kirin, whose expert knowledge of the techniques of oral interviewing, of the protocols of preserving and archiving such materials, and whose knowledge and love of the Bronx and local history guided all of us engaged in this oral and photo history project in the early 1980s. Edith Litt, Anne Perryman, Ann Ives, Paul Hohenberg, Madeleine Vedel, Virginia and Evan Calkins, Joan Lipsitz, and Peggy Miller each read portions of the volume, and their encouragement helped me to persevere. The daughters of Ada Quiñones and Raquel Flores provided information about their mothers and helped me locate Susan Boyd. I am grateful to all of them and also to Susan's son John Rivera. Gary Greenstein, Moe's son, told me stories about Moe's artistic abilities that he had never mentioned. Moe was a man of many parts but modest, not one to talk about himself, only about the borough he loved.

I am grateful to photographer and associate professor of photography at Brooklyn College, CUNY, Georgeen Comerford, for allowing me to include some of her stunning black-and-white portraits of several of the interviewees and of residents young and old of the South Bronx, and also for her re-creation of vintage photographs, some of which were in the exhibit *Childhood in the Bronx*. I am beholden to Nina and Naomi Rosenblum, daughter and widow, respectively, of Walter Rosenblum, noted Photo League photographer and onetime president of the 1940s Photo League, for allowing me to include a selection of Walter's South Bronx portraits taken in the early 1980s under the auspices of a prestigious

Guggenheim award. Walter and Georgeen from the outset shared their artistry and their passion for the integrity of the black-and-white photographic image with those of us engaged in this project of documentation and discovery. Walter delighted in showing his images to student audiences at Lehman College and recounting the stories of friendship, love, loyalty, and loss that lay behind each image. Fordham Hospital no longer existed when he was working in the South Bronx, but his portraits of patients and staff at Lincoln Hospital document the emotions and relationships in a similar setting. Georgeen lovingly bonded with her subjects young and old.

Because the oral interviews were conducted separately from the work of the photographers, the images in our book only rarely document the narrators. Rather, they complement the narratives by illustrating a comment or a situation or an emotion. Georgeen's photographs of children and also her re-creation of the vintage photo of immigrant children crowded into an auditorium at P.S. 8 capture the feelings expressed by several of our narrators recalling their childhoods in immigrant families where German, Spanish, or Yiddish was spoken at home. Ignorant of English until they entered school, they were then confronted with tough Irish teachers and mocking peers who made them feel lost and inadequate. Rae Flores spoke about taking a wheelchair-bound woman in an ambulance to a hearing to lobby for home health care, a woman who then had to sit patiently for many hours before being heard. Walter's beautiful image of an elderly woman in a wheelchair speaks to that situation, that helpless patience many of us can relate to.

Fernando Ferrer, former three-term Bronx borough president, graciously and enthusiastically agreed to lend his own voice through writing a personal foreword to this volume, sharing his perspective on where the Bronx has been and how it has evolved in the thirty years between the time when the interviews were conducted in the 1980s and our present post–9/11 era. Born in the Bronx, Freddy still resides in the Bronx and can speak for it with the authority born of deep knowledge and love for his borough. His friendship and his partnership in this publication honor me. In this year of centennial celebrations for the Bronx—first established as an independent county in 1914—I am delighted that Freddy will be the honorary chairman of these activities. No one would be more deserving of this honor. Ray Bromley, a distinguished scholar of urban history at SUNY/Albany, has enriched *Bronx Faces and Voices* with his preface, providing a solid scholarly context for the stories and images. I am grateful to Jane Dieckmann for lending us her expertise in preparing the invaluable index.

Without generous support—two grants in the early 1980s—from the National Endowment for the Humanities under the leadership of William Ferris, an oral and video historian of southern culture now at the Center for the Study of the American South at University of North Carolina, none of this could have taken place. NEH inspired, monitored, and funded everything we did, from training us in oral interviewing, to providing other models and consultants, to giving us the funds to pay additional interviewers and transcribers and acquire the essential archival materials to preserve our taped interviews and the transcripts. I have also to thank Theodore Dürr, who headed up an oral history and theater project in Baltimore, Maryland, who became an advisor and mentor to our project and who assisted in the training of interviewers. I acknowledge the support of the late Leonard Lief, president of Lehman College, who encouraged every entrepreneurial initiative and supported us whenever we applied to NEH or the New York Council on the Arts or the Bronx Council on the Arts, and who believed in any venture that enhanced the image of Lehman College and of the Bronx.

Emita Brady Hill
New Rochelle, New York
January, 2014

INTRODUCTION

More than thirty years ago, in 1982, when I first encountered the men and women whose personal stories are presented in *Bronx Faces and Voices*, another title came to my mind, but John F. Kennedy had already used it, namely, *Profiles in Courage*. We had received a grant from the National Endowment for the Humanities to create a Bronx Regional and Community History Studies (BRACHS) Project at Lehman College, drawing on the expertise of a number of faculty but to be implemented primarily through conducting interviews with what we then termed—in our innocence—Mr. and Mrs. Everyman.

Lehman College is the Bronx senior campus of the City University of New York. Most of our students have been residents in the Bronx. They and their parents and grandparents have represented in their different backgrounds the many waves of immigration and migration that had taken place in the Bronx since the late nineteenth century—first, the Europeans: Irish, Italian, and Jews from Russia, Poland, and Germany; later, the Hispanic groups, predominantly from Puerto Rico but also from other Caribbean Islands; also a diversified black population, some migrating north from southern states like Georgia, Alabama, and the Carolinas, others immigrating, like the Hispanics, from the West Indies. Each group had its distinct experience of the Bronx and made its distinct contribution to the history and shaping of that borough, but their stories share common threads of discovery, alienation, rejection, and then acceptance through accommodation and compromise—with the discovery, as one woman eloquently said, "We realized that there really isn't much difference under the skin."

As Irving (né Itzhak, but the name change was part of the accommodation) Bick told me, and it was echoed by many others, "The Bronx was up." Unlike Harlem or the Lower East Side of Manhattan, where many of these families first lived, the Bronx promised space, light, safe streets, an almost rural environment. Stanley Friedman wrote of the goat farms in his childhood. Morris (Moe) Greenstein described the pride that owners and supers took in the buildings they managed, including polishing the railings and brass plates so that they shone—until, that is, life changed and the brass plates were stolen, replaced, stolen again, and then not replaced anymore.

Even as America in its totality represented hope, upward mobility, a chance to escape repressive forces in other countries—whether king or church in the eighteenth century or the toxic ideologies of fascism and communism in the twentieth century—the Bronx held out the same promise to those who came to it. It was a promise that initially was fulfilled and only in the mid-twentieth century was broken. In the 1970s the Bronx that had been "up," a borough of open parklands and gracious homes and spacious apartments, became the international icon for urban decay—in particular, for drugs and arson. The Bronx burned until, as one man said, "there was nothing left to burn." By then President Kennedy had been assassinated, as had his brother Robert, as had Martin Luther King, Jr. Our entire country was overshadowed by a sense of loss and shame. We were a fragmented people, and the Bronx epitomized this fragmentation as banks redlined most of its neighborhoods. Janet Munch, librarian at Lehman College's Leonard Lief Library and my coeditor, told me of promotional literature sent by banks to her parents' home in the Parkchester neighborhood offering real estate deals in Florida, urging long-time Bronx residents to leave, to abandon the borough as it burned. Robert Abrams, former Bronx borough president, tells of a building project in the center of Lehman's campus that was stalled for four long years after state funding was lost. Some Lehman students spent their entire undergraduate years walking around construction barricades, with no construction taking place behind those barriers.

In the course of our Bronx history project we conducted many interviews, some of them done by students with their own parents and grandparents. The range of stories is quite extraordinary. During those years people brought us their albums of family photographs to copy and preserve in the library. Churches brought us their records to copy and preserve. The fear of arson was still omnipresent, although the fires had subsided by the early 1980s when we were working. Those interviews and vintage photographs remain in Lehman's BRACHS Archives open to all scholars or interested citizens.

The men and women I personally interviewed—those profiles in courage as I thought of them—were active in the preservation of the Bronx. I was guided from one source to the next, simply following the thread they laid out for me. I met community organizers, program developers, property managers, and religious leaders. Later, moving away a bit from the anonymous Mr. and Mrs. Everyman, I interviewed politicians who had a broader mandate to act on behalf of their borough.

For *Bronx Faces and Voices* I selected sixteen stories of individuals who made a difference through their commitment to a building, a block, a neighborhood, or the entire borough. Because many of them lived long lives, they saw the full cycle—from the early green, partly rural, and very neighborly Bronx—to the horrors of the crime-ridden, arson-threatened decade that left in its wake the rubble-strewn lots that both Irma Fleck and Eae Mitchell eloquently describe. They survived the desperate years from the late 1960s to the late 1970s and then witnessed the revival, the rebuilding, and the reaching out and across lines of demarcation to what Jill Jonnes aptly chose as the title for her book: *We're Still Here*. Good times and bad times, these men and women are still with us. Their stories are here, and what they accomplished to preserve their community and their borough is still here. Without their lives and their service, much more would have been lost.

Because these are personal memories, this book is neither history nor fiction. The events and the protagonists in these stories—and they are stories; oral history is the telling and retelling of stories—all happened. But it is possible, more than possible, that they happened a year or two earlier, and more than possible that the actions and motivations attributed to others by our narrators might be framed differently if those individuals could speak for themselves. We feel we know the narrators, our storytellers, because they speak freely and openly to us of memories good and bad, from childhood and their adult years, memories of events that affected their lives, but also—since most were engaged in shaping their communities—memories of events where they played significant roles. Historians will note the actual events—a hospital that closed; public housing that was or was not built; structures, including churches, that burned, sometimes by accident, sometimes by deliberate arson.

The population of the Bronx was changing continuously throughout the twentieth century. Where it had been mostly white—Irish, Jewish, Italian—it became predominantly black and Hispanic. Where English had been the primary language in the streets, in the churches, in the schools—English with many different accents, to be sure—now it was Italian, Albanian, and increasingly Spanish, a change that many found disconcerting. The individuals interviewed here came at different times and at different ages, some born in the Bronx, some only moving there as adults. A few—Irving Bick, Irma Fleck, Moe Greenstein—came early. Their families were already in the Bronx in the 1920s, and stayed. Many former Bronx residents—long after leaving—retain their nostalgia for the borough and return for reunions from their new homes, often in Florida. The voices included here are from those who stayed and were active, whether they came early or late. Some of the voices are from individuals who held elected office while others were only known locally. Several of them—for very disparate reasons—spent time in jail. Each man and each woman at one time played a positive role in the community. Each had a powerful story to tell. Some of them are no longer alive, but all of them deserve to be remembered and to have their voices heard.

Moreover, these stories of poverty, of waves of unemployment and home foreclosures, of public funds flowing and then cut off like water from a spigot, resonate today as we slowly emerge from a deep recession and are, once again, a people fragmented over the benefits of taxing the wealthiest among us versus cutting human services like food stamps, Medicare, Medicaid, and Social Security. Listening to these Bronx voices and reading their stories reminds us that there is no straight line in history. The future is always uncertain, and as surely as what goes up will come down, so also what goes down—even what crashes down—can rise again provided that individuals like the ones here work and fight and organize to make possible a better future. To borrow the title of Alexander von Hoffman's magisterial study of urban housing, rebirth comes "house by house, block by block."

Several events stand out as life-changing or neighborhood-changing in these stories: the Great Depression and World War II, of course; but also, in later decades, came the closing of Fordham Hospital and the shaping and reshaping of neighborhoods through public housing created by the early antipoverty programs, as well as the seeming overnight evacuation of entire neighborhoods when Co-op City became an irresistible magnet. Most of our narrators were personally involved in some form of community development. They bore witness to the conflict and also the cooperation among different nationalities and ethnic groups as they moved into or out of these neighborhoods. The Bronx was an obvious focus for many of the antipoverty programs, and along with early enthusiasm and unprecedented funding came mistakes, some easily corrected, others leaving permanent scars on the landscape and on individual souls.

Many histories of the Bronx in the twentieth century are available. I recommend Jill Jonnes's solidly researched study *We're Still Here: The Rise, Fall, and Resurrection of the South Bronx* (Fordham University Press, 1986, rev. 2002 and retitled *South Bronx Rising*); Alexander von Hoffman's *House by House, Block by Block: The Rebirth of American's Urban Neighborhoods* (Oxford University Press, 2003); and Constance Rosenblum's *Boulevard of Dreams* (New York University Press, 2009), relating the extraordinary history of the Grand Concourse from its inception in the late 1880s to the present. The Bronx County Historical Society continues to provide and also promote accurate histories of the Bronx, its neighborhoods, and its residents.

The heart of this book, *Bronx Faces and Voices*, and its appeal lie not in its historical accuracy but in the texture of the stories themselves and the emotions triggered in these retellings. Taken together, these different "voices" and different perspectives play like a set of variations on the theme of the rising and falling tides in the Bronx, the one mainland borough of New York City but still bounded by water on both sides: the Hudson River on the west, Long Island Sound on the east.

In preparing these narratives for publication I have edited with as light a hand as possible, seeking to preserve the words in which they were told, complete with any grammatical errors. Because they were spoken narratives, the punctuation and the division into sentences and paragraphs is my responsibility with the aid of editorial consultants. The primary change from the original consists in the elimination of the interviewer—me—in order to give free and uninterrupted rein to the interviewees' stories. On a few occasions I have shifted the sequence of paragraphs when the narrator digressed and returned later to a theme discussed earlier in the story. I have also tightened a few of the narratives where the narrator's stories repeated. The entire original text of all the interviews and also the recorded voices are preserved in the Bronx Regional and Community History Studies (BRACHS) Archives of Lehman College's Leonard Lief Library.

Recognizing that many readers may be unfamiliar with Bronx history and with the many sung and unsung heroes whose names occur in these pages, my coeditor, Janet Munch, has performed extensive research to provide generous explanatory notes and a bibliography of works consulted. Her notes in a number of instances provide the corrective to errors of memory on the part of the narrators. Ray Bromley, director of the Urban and Regional Planning Program at SUNY/Albany, has contributed a solid prefatory essay that fills in the historical background against which these stories were told and lives lived. Jane Dieckmann, author and scholar in her own right and an experienced indexer—having provided the index for numerous major publications from the Cornell University Press—has created our index. For those readers who lived through the 1980s and earlier decades in the Bronx, the names will already be familiar and will conjure up welcome memories. For further research I refer the reader to the BRACHS Archives, to the bibliography of works consulted in the preparation of this book, and to the ongoing publications on many disparate topics under the mantle of the Bronx County Historical Society.

Emita Brady Hill
New Rochelle, New York
January, 2014

PART ONE
THE FIRST WAVE

I. Looking Back over a Century of Change: The Overview

Morris (Moe) Greenstein, oldest of the sixteen storytellers, was born in the Bronx in 1911 and lived until 2010, the span of a century. A property owner and landlord, Moe's narrative covers both world wars and the Depression of the 1930s, significant periods of growth and expansion in the postwar twenties and again in the postwar forties when soldiers returning home to work and raise families created housing shortages that led to housing booms. His tale also deals with the blight—drugs, crime, vandalism, and arson—in the sixties and seventies. Central to his narrative are the buildings that he loved and their furnishings—whether exterior, like cornices or doors and brass plates, or interior, from tubs to elevators to boilers to light fixtures. Moe's influence was pervasive and benign over decades. By making it possible for Bishop Ernest Crooms to acquire a home for his church, Moe helped improve the lives of several generations of young people. On his recommendation, his brother Sidney sponsored Eae Mitchell for the training that qualified him to manage apartment buildings. Moe helped stabilize many buildings that otherwise might have been abandoned. Moe brought Mike Nuñez his first "venture," the first company in which Bronx Venture invested. These were three positive interventions among many.

II. One Small Business at a Time

Irving Bick's is the classic Horatio Alger story of a self-made man. Born in 1925, the child of Russian/Polish immigrants, moving up to the Bronx at a very young age, Irving observed at close hand his father and his father's friends, most of whom worked in the garment industry and were involved with the Amalgamated and its internal conflicts. He didn't want to follow his father and grandfather into the garment industry, didn't want another man as his boss, but instead for years had his own beauty parlor with a half-dozen employees, rising to the presidency of the New York State Hairdressers' association, and then sold that business to start an insurance business, which he ran for another two decades until retirement. The troubled Bronx of the 1970s and 1980s was served and even saved by the community organizers and the neighborhood associations they created, but the Bronx was also built and preserved by small-business people like Irving Bick.

CHAPTER ONE
MOE

Morris Greenstein, 1911–2010
Interview: February 10, 1983

"When they did windows, it's like you were painting the Mona Lisa."

I was born on Simpson Street in the Bronx, which is about two houses from the famous Fort Apache police station,[1] and when I was born it was a cobblestone street. It was during the administration of Woodrow Wilson, so it's a long, long time ago. And the house I was born in didn't have heat. We heated with a wood and coal oven. We had coal in the kitchen that heated our apartment, and eventually my father did put heat into that building. The landlady of the building was a woman by the name of Gisela Klinko, who had been in the Bronx since the year one, probably. And her son, who's ninety-five, is still alive. Today he's in St. Barnabas Hospital where we keep him in the Fairfield Nursing Home.[2] The rents were seventeen dollars a month. We had a ground-floor apartment, and my family was in real estate.

So I witnessed the phenomenal growth during the 1920s when the Bronx expanded so rapidly. As you drive around the Bronx you can easily distinguish those buildings that were put up in the twenties by their exterior appearance. They lacked cornices. In about the year 1921 they stopped putting in cornices. It was better design. There was no need for a cornice. In a sense it was economy because cornices were very expensive to build, very ornate and hard to paint, and you had to maintain them. If you went inside the building you could easily determine the age. We had a very simple rule of thumb. Either a property had recessed tubs, which meant it was built after 1924, or it had tubs on aprons, which was sort of like a little base underneath the tub. We knew that was built between 1920 and 1924. It was tubs on legs which meant it was prior to the First World War.

My father was a plumber who went to work on a bicycle like everybody in the Bronx here. He did the typical thing. When the Bronx was built, everybody followed a certain path. You could actually spot it on a map with an arrow. When the immigrants came here around the turn of the century their first stop was the Lower East Side. The second stop was Harlem, and then they branched off into two directions. One branch went to the Bronx, and one went to Washington Heights. You could follow the path. It's beautiful.

The Bronx was a strange borough. First of all, we're prefaced with the article "the." You don't say "the Manhattan" or "the Brooklyn." We are "the Bronx," and if you look in the dictionary, "the" signifies something unique. The Bronx was a borough that never had a teenage. It just went from its infancy into the twentieth century. The Bronx was always big estates. You had the Faile Estate. You had the Gilbert Estate, the Barretto Estate, the Richard March Hoe Estate, the Fox Estate, the Simpson Estate. They never broke them up, and the Bronx was very provincial. We had no population up until 1880. I don't think there was forty thousand people here, where Manhattan was close to a million and Brooklyn was completely settled. Staten Island was settled. Jersey City was settled. We never really grew up here.

The thing that opened up the Bronx was the building of the subways. First came the subways, then came the housing, and, really, the development of the Bronx started in 1905 when they broke up the estates.[3] Of course the First World War interfered with all the development. And the first people that came here were very much surprised that they could rent these beautiful living quarters that had inside bathrooms because where the immigrants came into the Lower East Side, that was the Black Hole of Calcutta compared to this.

My mother came from Russia, and my father came from Romania. Of course my mother went through this also. My mother did come very early to the Bronx, before my father. And my mother of course worked in the garment industry. She was a sewing machine operator, and my father was a plumber. And my uncles all were plumbers and things of this nature. Everybody who came here got into real estate when they discovered that they can find apartments, delightful apartments with foyers. You didn't have to walk room to room like you did in a railroad flat or what we called the dumbbell buildings.[4] There are very few dumbbell buildings in the Bronx, only a handful. There are only a few toilet-in-the-hall buildings in the Bronx, only a handful of those. So when they say in 1932 they came out with the statement that the Bronx is a borough without slums, they were 1,000 percent right. There wasn't one single slum in the Bronx because everything was new. It wasn't like Manhattan where you had buildings from the 1860s and 1870s and 1880s. We didn't have those apartment buildings. Sure, we had mansions here, but no multiple dwellings. Anything that was built in the Bronx came under the new tenement housing laws,[5] so they were built well.

In the twenties, after the First World War, there was a tremendous housing shortage. Now, they did have rent control for a very short period of time during the First World War. In order to induce a builder to build in New York the state legislature passed a law, and it was called the tax-exempt law. And they said to a builder, "If you build an apartment house with no ifs, ands, or buts, with no strings attached, we'll give you a ten-year tax exemption."[6] This started the wave.

The only place where they could really build was in the Bronx, where there were vast areas of land available. The people that came up from 1905 to the First World War, that was the first wave of immigrants that came here. The immigration laws were amended sometime around 1920, and the immigration tapered off after 1924. I mean, I did see immigrants coming in those years. As an individual moved to the Bronx, he would tell his friend living on the Lower East Side how much better the Bronx was. They even had apartment houses in the Bronx here where part of the superintendent's job was to have his daughter sit in a hallway at a telephone exchange because some people had telephones. And she would operate it. Well, they came up, and they looked at this, and they even found buildings with elevators. The first elevators started to come in, and that was over on Boston Road and over on Longwood Avenue. The big wave started in Hunts Point when the huge estates were broken up. Henry Morgenthau's grandfather was the first of the land speculators who came up here when the estates were broken up,[7] and he said, "Gee, there's a subway on this corner," which was the Hunts Point subway. "I want to buy everything around here." And they organized the syndicate, and they bought the Edward G. Faile Estate for one million dollars. The speculators started to come in. Everybody in the Bronx became a land speculator. In other words, who were these builders, these real estate people? The first people that went into it were those people who had been working on the jobs—carpenters, plumbers, roofers. You didn't have many electricians then because they were still talking gas, but a few electricians and ironworkers. They used to love this. They would work on a job and they would say, "Well, we'll build also." The other advantage that they had, in addition to having the tax-exempt law, was the fact that mortgage money was available, was being thrown at you to such an extent that if you were a builder people would approach you and say, "Well, what are you paying? Five and a half percent? We'll do five and a quarter percent." Or they'd say, "What are you getting, two hundred thousand? We'll get you three hundred thousand." And they created monstrous mortgages, and they created a plan called the certificates. They were selling mortgage certificates in those days.[8] So mortgage money was available. The land was available. Properties were built. Every single day you would hear of another plan filed in the Bronx or three plans or five plans, and you could say 70 percent of the Bronx was built in the twenties.

There was some two-family houses and some four-family houses went up on the old Ward Estate. In those days they even called it Westchester because that was part of Westchester up until around 1895, so they still referred to it as Westchester. Hunts Point became the focal point of new industries coming in. Buildings were built there, garages were built, theaters were built by very famous people. We had a theater in the Bronx called the Benenson Theater.[9] The Benenson family is very active in Manhattan today. And you had the Minskoff people who were the biggest.[10] He was a carpenter down the street here. So that's how they got into it. These buildings filled up.

Now the builders discovered something. The larger apartments were hard to get rid of. You'd have five or six rooms, you couldn't get rid of it, and people moved around a lot. There was an interesting theory then which was referred to again a couple of years back. It was called the "filter-down theory," and it worked. Filter down meant as follows. If you lived in the Bronx, for example, on Kelly Street—because I remember people that were on Kelly Street that did this—and you had a four-room apartment and you were paying, in those days, thirty-one dollars a month rent. You knew that over on Bryant Avenue they built a brand-new house with a recessed tub and an elevator, and you can get an apartment there for forty-two dollars a month. So, if you were established already, you took that new apartment, and a fellow who came from the Lower East Side took yours. Now your next step from Bryant Avenue is when they built the new buildings on the Grand Concourse. If you could afford that, you went there, and the fellow in your old apartment on Kelly Street, he moved into yours on Bryant Street, and someone else moved up to Kelly Street. So this filter-down process worked perfectly. For many, many years the filter-down process worked, and people were always moving around, they always improved themselves, they went a step higher.

And this is the interesting part. None of these people worked in the Bronx. With the exception of a merchant, a grocer, or a butcher, the interesting thing about the Bronx in those days and into the thirties, you never saw a man on the streets here, never. You would say, "Well, something's wrong if you saw one. Either there might have been a death in the family, that's why he's home." And that went on into the Depression. The filter-down process was beautiful. If a guy were to build a six- or a seven-room apartment he'd be hung up with it. I know that in my own family—of course I never figured out why, maybe because I was a child—we'd always be moving.

Only lately I asked my mother, who's in her nineties, I said, "Mom, why were we moving so much? I can't understand it."

She said, "Well, Poppa always felt sorry for his friends who built a house and they couldn't rent the six-room apartments, and he said, 'Let's take the apartment.' " And she told me a story the other day. She said one apartment that they took, which is opposite Father Gigante's church, the man had a six-room apartment, and when my father said "let's take it," my mother found there were two boarders. Boarders were very popular in those days in a large apartment. So my father said, "Let them stay." My mother let them stay a couple of weeks, but then she couldn't take it, and they moved out. I had often wondered why we were moving so much, but that was the reason for it. My father would say, "Gee, so and so, he's got a seven-room apartment, let's take it to help him." That happened in the twenties.

All the men worked in Manhattan.

They'd take the subway. Subways were very important. You had to live close to a subway. In other words, when our family would buy properties, one of the first things they'd say is, "It's a two-fare zone; we can't buy it."[11] Okay. Two-fare zones; I remembered that. You wouldn't buy a building with a two-fare zone. Most of the people were in the garment trades. Almost every person that I knew, they were a blocker. I remember they were a blocker or a cutter or things of this nature.[12] Or they were in the fur trades. And they worked in Manhattan, and they lived in the Bronx. It was very, very pleasant.

The other problem that they encountered in the Bronx was education. They weren't prepared for this phenomenal expansion of population which started to hit a million in 1926. They just couldn't keep up to it. The schools couldn't keep up to it so they decided to open a new high school, James Monroe High School. And in the first year of operation in 1925 they had fourteen thousand students. They couldn't accommodate them so, of course, as kids we also thought it was normal that you never went to your high school, that you went to your annex first. And your annex would be usually the top floor of a public school building or, in my wife's case, she went to a wooden building, a little wooden building out in Clason Point. And you would go there for the first year or two, and then you would go to the high school. The other thing we didn't know was that schools had to be far away. You had to walk two or three miles to school. We never thought anything of it. Today if somebody says your child has to walk . . . And we thought it was normal to go in snow. Schools didn't close for snow days. Also we thought it was normal to walk two miles to a library. Even as a child in the early twenties when I lived on Faile Street the nearest library was the Woodstock Branch. And the older children brought us there. The older children brought us to the Woodstock Branch over a mile away. There was no Hunts Point library. These were the difficulties we had in those days.

The schools in those days put a tremendous emphasis in the early twenties on patriotism. Every classroom of course had to have a picture of George Washington, and you had to have a salute to the flag and the oath of allegiance. And of course you'd always be reciting poems like "In Flanders Field" or "Barbara Fritchie." I didn't learn till fifty years later what they were doing, never realized it.

In those days everyone I knew, with a few exceptions, only very few exceptions, were either Jewish or Italian immigrants in which the parents spoke no English. The mother spoke none and the father may have spoken some because he was out in trade and he had to learn a little English. I look at my yearbook in Monroe, and we were 99 percent Jewish and Italian, really almost all Jewish. The things we were afraid of—we were very much afraid of our teachers because in those day, in the early twenties was before the Jewish teachers came in—it was all Irish teachers. And we were afraid that they would ask our mother to come to school. The worst thing they could say to you is—if you chewed gum or you spoke out of turn—they'd say, "Bring your mother to school." And it wasn't as much bring in your mother as you were afraid to bring in your mother because your mother wouldn't understand what the teacher was saying. You didn't want anybody to know that your mother couldn't speak English. I used to witness a kid whose mother would come to school and he'd warn her, "Mama, please don't say anything, make believe you understand, okay?" And the mother would come in, and they would go out in the hallway—this was the routine—and the teacher would say, "Your child chewed gum in class," or "He didn't bring a handkerchief," or something like that. And the mother didn't know what the teacher was saying, but she would take her hand and whack the kid across the head. That's what every mother did, whacked her kid across the head. Those were our schools in those days.

My daughter happens to be a teacher and she showed me some literature that she had found. It was very interesting that they were instructed in those days to take these immigrant kids—and they used to call us "incorrigibles"—and turn them into Americans. Now I think back, geez, every day we had all these patriotic things, and I enjoyed it.

The expansion of the population and the building continued right up to the Depression. At the Depression many houses weren't finished, but the money dried up, the people weren't able to pay the rent.[13] Foundations remained of unfinished buildings. We used to play in these foundations. So the Depression brought a complete halt to housing. There were some jobs that were finished in 1929. There may have been one or two, I recall, in 1930, even in 1931. When the market collapsed in housing the rents were reduced. The landlord would chase you to rent an apartment. In those days the rents were around eight dollars a month for a room. If you moved into an apartment they'd give you a brand-new toilet seat. They'd give you your choice of window shades. They'd scrape and shellac the floors and give you a paint job according to your desires.

By then we were landlords, and as landlords we would "remove." We used to remove all the fixtures in the apartment and take them over to Harris the plater and have them plated. Everything was plated. If you had a shower, which was great in those days—we used to advertise showers—we'd take the shower bar off and plate it. We would give you a shower curtain. We would take your washtub—we had washtubs in those days—we would take the washtub cover off and take it over to Third Avenue. We had a fellow who used to porcelainize them. When a person came in and they would bicker over the rent—they would bicker over fifty cents—we would do all these things for them. And we would rent the apartment. Then we knew that in June, the end of June, we knew they would leave. June was a popular moving month, May and June, because the school ended then, and many people had a very good system. They would leave and go to Coney Island or to the country for the summer, come back and get another apartment, and repeat this process every year. But everybody counted their dollars.

One of the things about those days is that there were no window gates in the Bronx. You never saw that. There was no crime, none whatsoever. Now you see metal gates in front of all the stores. We didn't have that. In the thirties when the housing mortgages collapsed here—the market collapsed and mortgages were all in jeopardy—every one of the mortgages was in jeopardy, especially the large mortgages that were put out. Again, the legislature—in those days they had pretty good statesmen—they created with a simple law the rebirth of the Bronx insofar as housing is concerned with the tax-exempts. They formed a commission which was called the Mortgage Commission, a very, very wise thing. And they said, "Let's try to save the housing here, let's not foreclose." Everything was in default. And the commission was formed, and they passed certain laws that were called the mortgage moratorium.[14] They put a moratorium on foreclosures. As long as you maintained your 4 percent or your four and a quarter percent interest payment, they couldn't foreclose you. Now that saved thousands and thousands of buildings. The Mortgage Commission then took over all the defaulted mortgage companies like the Guaranty Title Company, and they had names for them, F-1 series, F-2 series. As a matter of fact right around the corner here they were handling the F-1 series, and they administered these mortgages on behalf of the thousands of people who had invested in them. Thinking that they were going to realize 5 percent, a market developed in these mortgages, and we used to trade, and then we used to buy them for sixty cents on the dollar, sometimes sell them for seventy. If we bought a building we would attempt to buy up the certificates. The strange part about these certificates is this: Any individual who would have sat with his certificate would not have lost one penny, if he could have waited. The Mortgage Commission ran through the Second World War and well into the fifties and sixties until it was discontinued. And these certificates still fall out of bank vaults, but they can't be redeemed these days. So, our statesmen were great in those days. They formed the Mortgage Commission, and they had a moratorium.

The people like my father who were in the real estate business during these years were very remarkable people. Being people who were in the trades, they could do what we could never do, and we couldn't know what they knew. They took such great, great pride in these apartment houses, it was a matter of pride with them. To them it was an honor to go to the building. The buildings were really maintained. The superintendent every day would scrub the marble. On every hallway every door had a curtain. The halls were freshly painted. There was no such thing as graffiti. One other thing that they did, there's a thing called "deferred maintenance," which is in every building in the Bronx today. Of course the rent control people never took cognizance of it, that there was such a thing. But if my father and his people would go to a building—they would visit a building—they would call me in and say, "Do the roof." Nobody had to tell them, "Do the roof, it's nine years old; do your windows, they're six years old." When they did windows it's like you were painting the Mona Lisa. They always wanted two coats on there. And they wanted every one glazed. In order to assure that two coats were put on you didn't use the same color. You'd say, "Make your first coat brown and your second coat green," so you knew that it was that way. The other interesting thing about those days, the supers were phenomenal. The supers were mostly Polish and German, absolutely the greatest, and they also took great pride in the apartments. Every house had brass kickplates and they were shined every day and polished. Noxon was one of our big items of expense, to send Noxon to a building.[15] Every building had awnings, and the superintendent, as part of his job, every spring would take the awnings out of the cellar and put up awnings in the building. The superintendent did the minor repairs. In apartments that didn't have clothes poles in the backyard, every kitchen had a clothes rack. And the super was an expert at putting the cords on those. The other thing they didn't have in those days was a heat-complaint bureau in New York. You didn't need it. Every building ran on coal, except in the early thirties we put in our first oil burner, and we were always sorry we did. We used to love coal.

The buildings had central heating, and the superintendent was responsible for firing that furnace. The only time you didn't have heat in a building was if your superintendent was sick, in which event you tried to get a neighboring superintendent. But usually it was the wife who fired the furnace or he got drunk and something went wrong or something happened to the furnace where the grates fell down. You very seldom had problems with tubes because coal heat was a constant heat; it wasn't like an oil burner going on and off. So there was no heat-complaint bureau. The only time I ever remember a problem with heat in a building was one time we had dirty water in the boiler and we could not pick up heat. My father went over and he said, "Well, that's the problem." He said, "Blow it off." And that solved that. And one other time I had two buildings with 124 families that we were managing, and both superintendents were in the hospital and the wives couldn't fire those furnaces. They were very huge. So what I did was I went down and fired them up. I would go at five in the afternoon, leave the office, go home, and fire the furnaces.

The population went on growing. It always grew. It grew in the thirties. The filtering-down process kept going beautifully. Some people who had acquired land in the twenties, then around 1932, '33, '36, even '37, all the way up to the forties, started to build. Those are the art deco buildings.[16] There was always somebody who could afford a better apartment, and they started to build the art deco buildings with a new style of casement window with a light-colored brick. And in those apartments they had step-down living rooms, and everybody wanted a step-down living room. So there was a lot of building of those. And that went right up until 1940. Right opposite Lehman College on Reservoir Avenue,[17] that corner building was put up in 1940, and then during the Second World War the WAVES took it over.[18] That was the last building that was built there. I think the population had increased to about a million and a half. All those art deco buildings were built in the thirties on the Grand Concourse. The popular thing then was casement windows, which everybody is sorry about today. They hate them now.

Meanwhile there were a couple of other strange developments that happened here in the Bronx. The Astors built a building on the Grand Concourse because they were always very severely criticized for their housing policies, and then John D. Rockefeller, Jr. built 840 Grand Concourse.[19] He built what is still a beautiful building. The other one, the Astor, is in pretty sad shape. It's called the Astor Gardens.[20] The population in the part of the Bronx with Taft High School was still all Jewish after the war in 1950. Taft, Morris, Monroe also was almost all Jewish, with some Italian in Monroe.[21] The change came later.

And still the men took the subway to work in Manhattan. With the exception of people like myself—I had an office here and worked in the Bronx—you never saw a man during the day. Even if the husband was unemployed, he would get up every morning and you would see him catching the train at seven-thirty or eight in the morning, go to Manhattan, and stay down there for the day. He didn't stay in the Bronx. You never saw a man here. I used to drive all over the Bronx in those days and never saw a man. The fellows who graduated high school in those days, it took them an average of two years to find a job. And you know some guys would get jobs at ten dollars a week, or twelve dollars a week, they thought that was great. So the Bronx was a quiet place. We had our trolley cars. You could go any place for a nickel, any place. The theaters were a dime. It was tough years. I mean, there was no money, but people kept themselves busy. There was no television.

The Second World War really created the big change in the Bronx. The first unit that left the Bronx was the 105th Field Artillery. It left out of the Franklin Armory when President Roosevelt federalized the National Guard.[22] That was September 16, 1940. Up until that point it was very interesting, but some of the factories in the Bronx started to get more work. I was just watching a play called *The Winds of War*, and they mentioned Roosevelt asking for fifty thousand airplanes.[23] I think that was in 1939. Triboro Foundry was already getting war work—Triboro Brass Foundry—and Ex-Cell-O Brass was making parts for pursuit planes.[24] There was the Hoe factory already started doing some kind of work making some sort of artillery,[25] and there was a company down off Spofford Avenue that was making slot machines that changed to make something for machine guns. So we started to see this little by little. The Bronx started to become involved in the war.

I happened to have left. I was called to active duty in 1940 so I missed the war years, except I knew what was going on for a couple of reasons. If a tour of duty brought me to New York I always came into the office. And the other thing that happened was that during the war we would receive a certain ordnance, and I would see "made in the Bronx, this and this company" on it. Like, for example, the invasion money for the Philippine Islands was printed here at the American Bank Note Company.[26] It said so on each bill.

Very early in the war, when the first troops left here and the first what they called the "selectives" left the Bronx, they were sent to Fort Dix. In those days it was called Camp Dix,[27] and that was in November of 1940. And the only quarters available to them were tents. It was called "tent city." It was all New Yorkers down there except for the contingent that left earlier that went to Camp Rucker in Alabama—Anniston, Alabama.[28] That was the 258th Ordnance out of Kingsbridge,[29] the 105th Field Artillery, they were part of the Rainbow Division. When all the New York boys were sent to Fort Dix they built barracks down there for them, and this was about March or April 1941. And the Bronx did a very nice thing for them. I happened to mention to some of the businesspeople on the street here, "Gee, they have all these day rooms, and they don't know where to outfit them." They wanted furniture for the soldiers to sit on, and the people on 149th Street here got together and they said, "Listen, if you send us a convoy, we'll outfit a battalion." And they did. I went to the commanding officer, Colonel Schwarzkopf, and I told the colonel, and he says, "Gee, what a nice gesture." He says, "Take all the trucks you want." And we came from Fort Dix with a convoy to 149th Street. They hadn't seen soldiers here before, and we brought the convoy here, and they went into the stores on Third Avenue and they loaded the trucks up, and they outfitted a complete battalion, which is five companies. So I thought the Bronx was in the war very early, and they did a very nice thing.

As the men left to go in the war it was incredible. There were no men here. I was gone for six years, but I came back except for when I was overseas. If I was stationed in the United States I would come to New York, and you never saw a man here. Manhattan was always full of soldiers but not the Bronx. The women were doing everything. Matter of fact the girls that I knew here were all actively engaged in all sorts of civil defense. I really admired them because I'd want to go out on a date with a girl, and she'd say, "I'm sorry, I'm a watcher tonight. I'm an airplane watcher." They'd watch from roofs, from every rooftop and every top landing. During the war years every building owner cooperated. They asked every building owner to provide a shovel and pails of sand for the top floors, and they had them on the top landing of every roof. I wasn't here during the scrap drives, but I had heard about it, and of course I was always getting reports from the office. We maintained contact all the time.

I was very well aware that the Bronx became a ghost town, which brought up a very serious complaint later. When rent control came in, in 1943, they set the rents as of that date, which was at the lowest ebb in rents in the Bronx, and that was one of the things that hastened the decline. When I came back and saw the rents they were absolutely absurd. The

Bronx was a ghost town. There were no heavy industries here. People followed the industries. The welders went out to New Jersey and other places where they were getting one hundred dollars a week. Our war plants here, R. Hoe & Company and some of the other companies, worked full blast. That's all they did. When I got back here in 1946 it was like I'd never left. I had my office, and I was right in business the first day. My father had his real estate office, and I was with him. The first thing I noticed—a very strange thing—is that there was a tremendous shortage of apartments. The soldiers all started to come back, poured back. I noticed on every store regardless of how small it was—it could be a five-hundred-foot store—it was rented and in that store was a machinist. Everybody was doing things for the war effort. Every inch of space was occupied, and that lasted for a while because as the industries converted to peacetime—first of all filling up their own filled orders as they converted to the huge demand created by the shortages during the war—they immediately went into consumer things. They kept very busy. The stores stood for about five or six years. Every little store was a machinist—it was crazy; even the basements had fellows down there grinding optical lenses, anything you could think of. They were very exciting years with a tremendous housing shortage. The soldiers came back. The soldiers were doing two things. First of all they all got jobs. That's the nice part. And just like before, they always lived here, but they all worked in Manhattan, everybody worked in Manhattan, except for people like me who had our businesses here.

The marriages started, and you would go to a wedding every week. Everybody was getting married, and the first thing they did was to try and find an apartment. Rents were controlled, you couldn't increase the rents, no way. And I helped out a lot of guys with the apartments that I had—areas that today you would say nobody would live in, Hoe Avenue, Vyse Avenue, Southern Boulevard—anything that could rent. You could rent the closet. The men started to move, and that was their first apartment, and they used to fix them up nice. They were all young, they were full of vigor.

But they had discovered one other thing, another strange development. They had been out of New York. In the Depression nobody moved around much out of New York. It was a rare thing. I remember when we once went to Florida we thought it was like going to the ends of the earth. Of course we drove, and we took twenty-five dollars along for spending money. But these young men had discovered California; they had discovered the Midwest. From the particular group of boys I'd run around with we had one fellow who married a girl from Charlotte, North Carolina. Another fellow married a girl from Washington, DC. Three of the guys immediately headed off for California. One went to Florida. Others went to Texas. They discovered the United States. All of their parents were immigrants, and this was the first generation of children of immigrants, so for the first few years after the war they remained in the Bronx.

The government did another

marvelous thing here in the Bronx. They built temporary houses for the veterans, Quonset huts.[30] And they built those on Story Avenue near Bruckner Boulevard, and they were very nice. You'd go over there, and they enjoyed it. They'd have little gardens, and they lived in these Quonset huts. Then another development occurred. All of a sudden you had Levittown,[31] and that was the dream. For six or eight thousand dollars you had a home. Many of the fellows would sit me down and say, "Moe, how do you carry eight thousand dollars? What would it cost you to carry an eight-thousand-dollar home?" And I'd say, "Gee, it's gonna run seventy-five dollars a month for the mortgage and interest." And they'd think very hard.

But this was the first generation that had discovered the United States, and even around New York they had other options. A lot of them moved to Stuyvesant Town.[32] They wanted to be involved in Manhattan. Then Long Island beckoned, and everybody moved to Long Island. I'll bet that almost three quarters of Long Islanders now came from the Bronx. Some went to Westchester, but their prices were a little higher. Suddenly toward the end of the fifties we discovered that we had no more tenants for apartments. The housing shortage was over. With rents controlled, the only other people available are other immigrant groups coming later.

The only way to get around rent control in those days was if you owned a property and could show that you could increase the number of units. Then that was decontrolled. It didn't take long for some of the owners to discover that if you were able to buy, or if you already owned a dumbbell building with the two five-room or two six-rooms on a floor, with an expense of maybe five or six thousand dollars you can convert that into twenty units. They were getting rent of maybe five dollars an apartment, but with smaller units and five dollars a room you could get twenty-five dollars rent for the same space. That became very popular, and loan money was available to do it at 5 percent interest. The difficulty was to get that building emptied.

Some owners were fortunate. They'd already have one floor empty, and they'd start developing, and eventually the other tenants would move. In order to get these high rents the owners had to attract tenants from Harlem. They would advertise in the various newspapers. In the early days they would say "interracial apartments." I recall those ads that said "interracial." And then that was stopped. It started in the South Bronx, around here, because that's where the dumbbell buildings were located. So it started around here, and I don't think it ever went as far as the North Bronx. I had never seen it, but I recall the fellows who were doing it around here. At first they would advertise "interracial," until that was stopped, and later they would say "for all." They would use all sorts of crazy things. But nevertheless people started to come up here, and for a two- or three-room unit they would get fifty or even fifty-five dollars a month, whereas for the entire five or six-room apartment they used to get thirty dollars.

I remember the first newcomers.

They were absolutely marvelous. I really thought in those days, "Gee, this is a great thing for the Bronx, it's a new wave of immigrants." And the first black families that I saw come in always fixed their apartments up far superior to the white apartments. I remember one fellow tiled his whole kitchen. I walked in with amazement. I said, "Gee, I can't believe this," I was so proud of it. And prompt rent, the most satisfactory people you've ever seen. Some of the old-time people still lived there with their furniture from before the First World War or from the twenties, and these people came in and outfitted these apartments beautifully. The old-timers resented it and would complain to me that it was horrible, but it was really nice.

It's hard to put any dates to when the different groups moved into the Bronx. I recall a Hispanic family over on Barretto Street that owned a bakery, Los Tres Mosqueteros Bakery, the Three Musketeers Bakery. I remember a house occupied by blacks in the Melrose section. They were Pullman porters for Penn Central. I know there was a house on Coster Street going back into the thirties that was occupied by black postal workers. I know this, but it doesn't pinpoint the date when really the influx started. I've tried to do this through school yearbooks with names and pictures. For example, the 1937 Monroe High School book has four blacks in it, but when I looked at the addresses I said, "Well, I know those buildings, and these were the superintendents' kids." I knew the buildings so when I looked at yearbooks I could tell if they were tenants or if they were superintendents in those early years. But later, in the fifties, I don't know.

Meanwhile, as time went by, there were none of the first-generation soldiers left in the Bronx, a few in the North Bronx, but here in the South Bronx they were all gone. They moved out to the suburbs wanting that little plot of ground, a yard, a garden. They weren't fleeing the newcomers, not back then. The parents of course remained for a while, but some died off, some moved to Florida, and some moved to Co-op City.[33] But the change kept accelerating and the deterioration. Banks up until 1964 granted mortgages on multiple dwellings in the South Bronx. But the last mortgage I ever heard given was in 1964. Prices peaked in 1964. We had a rule of thumb that worked with multiples of rent. A building with tubs on legs was worth four times the rent. A building with recessed tub was five times, with an elevator was six times. That determined the loans.

It peaked in 1963 and 1964. From then on in it was a downhill slide to where today I've sold properties for very astute investors—I'm talking about banks—for one quarter of one year's rent. That was the slide. The other thing that hastened the slide was that an astute investor—a reliable investor—the people that I knew who took great pride in these buildings suddenly discovered a thing called vandalism which they've never had before. It started in 1964 and 1965 when the brass plates stated to disappear. A superintendent would call up an office and tell the managing agent, "Somebody stole our brass plates." You'd wonder, why would anybody steal a brass plate? And he would order a new set right away, and then that was gone. They said, "Let's put aluminum plates on." They put aluminum, but finally that was gone. The other thing that happened is that no longer could the owners predict in advance what their operating costs would be and what their net would be because they started to raise the taxes. The tax rate went up. We used to have something called a water charge here, and now it was water and sewer, another way of saying, "We're raising it." Insurance rates went up. The other thing that came were fires. In all the years we had to do with property, going back in my family before the First World War, I never saw a fire in a building, never.

The other thing that happened—I think it was 1963 or 1964—the city passed what was called an all-night heat law.[34] And the theory was that if somebody wanted to watch television at 3 a.m., let's give them heat. This was at the same time that they were screaming "air pollution," so I never understood it. When the air pollution laws came out and they mandated a reduced sulfur content on fuel—at that time I was appraising a lot of properties and doing some management—I said to my people, "I can no longer manage." They asked, "Why?" and I said, "Well, with the new sulfur fuel, low-sulfur fuel, the oil price went from five to seven cents and that's a 40 percent increase in fuel cost. In addition to that it doesn't have the BTUs that the old fuel had." And I said, "Look at this building here where we used for twenty years an average 99 to 101 gallons of fuel, now we're using 120 gallons." My suggestion was at that time to sell the buildings. I said, "You can't afford to run these buildings." I was a scaredy-cat then because the numbers frightened me. The big thing that hastened the decline was deferred maintenance. No longer were the owners able to go to a building and say, "Let's paint our fire escape, let's replace the boiler." You couldn't do that any longer. The buildings worked strictly on a cash flow. You never replaced a roof, you patched it. You didn't paint your windows or your hallways.

So the old-timers left when the prices weren't stable any longer, where you never knew what to expect. For twenty-five years they knew that your oil price would be about five cents a gallon. Now you didn't know if tomorrow it was gonna be eleven cents. I always said, "What if oil went to a quarter?" There are some good owners here today who are really trying very hard, but the odds are very great, I think, with the expenses on these buildings.

The vandalism was terrible and was resented by everyone whether they were black or white or Hispanic. The first time I became aware of drug problems was in the sixties,[35] when superintendents started to leave because they didn't want to work in those buildings anymore. They knew there was a tenant in the building dealing in drugs, stealing the lightbulbs out of the halls. I never knew there was such a thing as drugs until in the sixties I became aware of that. But when you talk to people about the stealing of all the stuff, the tenant will tell you it's the landlord; the landlord will tell you it's the tenant; the storekeeper will tell you it's crime; and another one will tell you it's drugs. And one owner will tell you it's the courts, and another one will blame the politicians. They'll blame everybody up to the president. I don't know the answer. Maybe I'm too close to it to have seen it. And then there were fires. The only fire that I remember in a building was an oil burner fire. It's the only one I remember. We never had a fire in any of the properties we ever managed, and we managed for different people, for different estates, mostly in the East Bronx.

The Bronx is interesting. Until a few years ago there was no such thing as the South Bronx. Matter of fact, the crazy part, this area instead of being the South Bronx was always called the North Side.[36] So if you say the Bronx is peculiar, it is. We used to distinguish, to differentiate the parts of the Bronx as East Bronx and West Bronx. That's all we knew, East and West, and Westchester. We would call what is now really the East Bronx the Northeast Bronx. But starting with the housing decline in 1963 and 1968, there was an absolutely incredible decline started in 1968. From 1968 to 1978, 40 percent of the manufacturing jobs in the Bronx were lost; one after another company moved away or closed. I still drive around every morning now—Hunts Point, Port Morris, Oak Point, Mott Haven—and I see where the companies left. And it wasn't from something in the Bronx, but in the economy. A lot of the companies just folded in those ten years. But now it's turned and there's hope again. There's hope again.

CHAPTER TWO
IRVING

Irving Bick, Small Businessman, b. 1924
Interview: May 18, 1983

"Moving to the Bronx was moving up."

I was born on the Lower East Side in 1924 and moved to the Bronx in 1934 when I was ten years old. We moved directly to Charlotte Street,[1] and my mother moved to three different buildings in the same block, first 1511, then 1509, and then we moved to 1513. It was Depression years, and you could save a month or two in rent when you moved.

Interestingly enough when we moved we went over the roof rather than coming down into the street. It was easier to carry all the furniture over the roof and down than to carry it up. I had one brother and one sister. My brother has since passed away, but my sister is alive and well.

My grandfather came from Poland, which was Russian Poland. At one time it was Poland, at one time it was Russia. When he lived there and when my parents lived there, it was Russian. My grandfather was in the Russian army. He had something to do with the Crimean War. And my father came to this country to escape from serving in the Russian army. He didn't want to fight for the czar, so he came here as a stowaway on a cattle boat. He was down in the hold with hay and cows or horses or whatever. It was around 1914, a really bad time in Russia.

My grandfather (my mother's father) was already here. My father came here and started working, and he saved his money so that he could bring his brother and his sister here. They were orphans. His father had died of starvation, and his mother passed away when he was eight years old. He saved up his money, but my grandfather, although he was a very religious man, was a bit of a gambler. We weren't supposed to know this, but I found out by accident as we were growing up, as I got older. Then I heard stories from people who knew my grandfather in those days before I was born.

I learned about it from the woman I worked for. I got the job as a hair stylist for Sarah Tushinsky, and in those years she had a house in Coney Island. Coney Island was the place to be in the summertime, and so she rented out rooms. And strangely enough this woman was the landlady of my grandfather and my father when they were young men.

My grandfather was already married, and he came here alone but wanted to bring his wife and children. He and my father were uncle and nephew. My father had enough money to bring his brother and sister here, but my grandfather, who was a bit of a con man, persuaded him to give him the money, which he will pay him back ultimately to bring his sister and brother over, but that he would like first to bring his wife and two daughters here, and my father would have the pick of his daughters for a wife. And in those days the father of the house—the Orthodox house—picked the husbands for their daughters, and there were no questions asked. That's what Papa says, and that's what is done. So my father, remembering the beautiful girl he'd known and left behind, agreed to this. And it was my father's money that brought my grandfather's wife and daughters here. My mother was born in 1900, and she came here when she was twenty and married my father.

Things moved fast after they got here. My brother was born in 1922, I was born in 1924, my sister was born in 1926, so my brother and I were twenty-two months apart, and my sister and I are eighteen months apart. And that was on the Lower East Side.

My mother and her family experienced hard times during the First World War before they came here, 1914 to 1920. She told me there were times they were digging in the soil for potato stubs and roots to keep alive and prevent themselves from starving. And when they came here my mother was absolutely overwhelmed by the food that was available to her. She saw a pushcart with fruit on it, with oranges and bananas. She didn't remember what that stuff looked like. And the first thing my grandfather gave her was an orange from the pushcart. She hadn't eaten an orange since before 1914 until she came here. She hadn't even seen an orange.

When I started sixth grade I couldn't speak English. All my conversation as a child was in Yiddish. When I got into sixth grade it didn't take too long. I caught on and was playing with the kids. My parents started to make a little money in 1932. In 1933 my father was working steady. So in 1934 we were ready to move to the Bronx. When we were moving to the Bronx my mother sat the three of us down and started to give us an orientation.

Many years later when I was in World War II and we were leaving our ship to go to Liverpool—we docked in Liverpool—we had an orientation as to the language when we got off, because there were certain things that we said and they said in England that were very different in meaning. And they told us, "Don't use the word 'bloody' because 'bloody' is a curse word in England." And other things, like, "Tinkle you on the blower" was a telephone call. Really funny. But when they gave us that orientation it brought back when my mother moved us to the Bronx. She told us "*pishe* from now on is the number one." And so on and so on, all the different things we said as children.

My name in Yiddish was Itzhak, so she says, "Itzhak, you're now Irving." Esther was the same in Yiddish as in English, so my sister's name was no different, but my brother's name was Asher, and she says, "Your name now is Arthur." And so we moved to the Bronx with English names, English expressions, and a mixture of Yiddish and English. Even though the neighborhood in the Bronx where we were moving was still mostly Jewish, they had been there longer and their English was more advanced than the families on the Lower East Side.

Moving to the Bronx was moving up. My mother said, "We're getting an apartment where everyone is going to have their own bedroom." My brother and I would share, and my sister would have her own room. I had visions of grandeur because we had lived in a railroad flat. Our new building was not a heated building. There was a coal stove in the kitchen to keep the apartment warm. We were on relief, what today you call welfare. At five o'clock every morning my mother was on line for food. In those days the winters were very cold, not like today. We have a much warmer climate now than when I was a little boy. There was never a moment in Crotona Park that the lake during the winter was not frozen. We could always say, "We're going ice skating," not needing to check, because it was always cold enough for the lake to be frozen.

So we had a big apartment in the Bronx, and we had a park to climb rocks and go rowboating. There were old retired seamen in Crotona Park who made model sailboats, and their sport was to sail the boats across the lake and to have races, and they were fine instruments, magnificently done. One fellow had made a schooner with three sails, and everything on it worked—I mean the steering and everything. It was fantastic what they did. They used to show us children and explain things to us. It was a marvelous time. I don't see that today. Maybe in some places in the country where there's a pond and an old retired seaman, maybe. It was tough times economically, but from the standpoint of making lasting friendships and loving each other and playing with each other and enjoying our lives, it was a marvelous time, I would say far superior to today.

Families were very strong and tight. If my father said something, it was law. If my mother said something, it was law. I've raised two kids—my daughter who is twenty-nine and my son who is thirty-one—and we're all together, we're not apart, we don't hate each other. There's a little friction between my son and his mother, normal, I think, but also strong love and devotion. I think by today's standards it's pretty good.

Even when I was very young, if our peers wanted us to do something bad, the first thing I would say in my mind was, "It would hurt my mother if I got caught. I don't want to hurt my mother." And so I didn't do it, not because I had a fear, but because I didn't want to hurt my mother. And that's why I kept pretty straight. And we stayed close to home. We never moved anywhere and never went anywhere. The only place we went was downtown to the Lower East Side on holidays to be with our grandparents, and that was very familiar to us because we were born there and we knew the area.

My father worked in a factory in Manhattan. He was what they called a pocket-maker. He was a tailor, but they were specializing then. Each one made a different part of a garment for mass production, and he was a member of a team of five who did one operation all day long to create the pockets for a garment. He never complained except sometimes about the other four men if one was faster, or slower, that kind of thing. They got twelve cents for each operation that they did, and it was piecework at the time, no hourly wage, no minimum wage.

Our neighborhood was mostly Jewish. I had some friends that weren't Jewish, but most of them were. I was an oddball because I had friends all over the place. Most of the people I knew on Charlotte Street only knew everyone on Charlotte Street, but I ventured elsewhere. I knew everyone on Wilkins Avenue as well as Charlotte Street and 172nd Street, and we had a rivalry between the Whippets and the Comets. The Comets were from Vyse Avenue, so I also became friendly with a lot of people up in that area. We played every sport—basketball, football, softball, and stickball. Stickball was really the main sport at that time. A good hitter's prowess was measured by how many sewers he hit. First base was the fender of a car. Second base was the second sewer. Third base was the fender of another car, and home plate was a sewer from which you batted. There was no pitching, no pitcher.

My mother worked as an examiner for a sportswear manufacturer who was a distant cousin. This was unusual, because most women were at home and we all had our chores. We rotated the work in the house. My brother did the cooking because my sister was too young. And then when my sister was old enough she took over the cooking, so I was bypassed in the kitchen. As a result, I did most of the cleaning, so I'm a very good cleaner.

There were some small businesses on Charlotte Street. Directly across from the building I lived in there was a large building, and that building had a candy store and a grocery store. Originally there was a large market in there, but they moved down to Jennings Street leaving just the grocery store and the candy store. No one had a phone in those days, so the candy store had two pay phones, and if anyone had to be reached by phone they called the candy store, and a kid hung out in the candy store waiting for the phone to ring, so they could run and call something, and then get a two-cent or five-cent tip with which to buy something in the store. The candy store didn't just have candy. It had sodas, ice cream, newspapers, and school supplies like pencils, pen and ink, pads.

Two brothers, Sam and Abe Fier, were partners in the grocery store, and they were wonderful people. When families or their customers didn't have any money to come for food, they would have a running charge, and everything would be on charge with them. I don't think that exists anymore today. I haven't seen it anywhere. I recall that as I grew older and matured and recognized some things—things I took for granted as a child—I realized that these two brothers were godsends to the community because they kept food on our table when we didn't have any money to pay for it. They were really like good Samaritans.

Most of the fathers worked in the garment district in Manhattan. Most of the Italian people were pressers, and the Jewish people were tailors, and my grandfather, when he came here, was a presser, so all his buddies were Italian. He was a religious man, very orthodox, with a beard, and he learned to speak English with an Italian accent. My grandfather was one of the founders of the Amalgamated Union. There's no record of him being a founder because there was political feuding going on between the leaders. My grandfather and two partners of his had organized 770 workers back in the 1920s. They were all brought to the headquarters, Sidney Hillman's headquarters. I'm not accusing Sidney Hillman of anything because I don't know the details. I'm giving you vague memories of what I recall happening. It could have been someone else—I don't know—because Sidney Hillman's name is revered in the labor movement. Whether it should be or not, I don't know. But at that time there seemed to be some ruthless people afoot, and my grandfather's partner came in to a meeting, and he sold out. He took a big union's position, to give the 770 workers over to the Sidney Hillman group. My grandfather's name was Sam Spector. And then they called in my grandfather, and my grandfather said "no." And his other partner said "no." The other partner was murdered on the street. He was shot down on the street. And because the third partner had sold them out and the other was killed, my grandfather didn't have control over the whole 770. So they called him in and they blackballed him, and my grandfather couldn't work for two years because of not wanting to cooperate with them. And then he came back as just a worker after two years. Whatever the history is of the Amalgamated Union from then on, this is just family knowledge, never published, and no one knows about it. A lot of people died in the early labor movement. Maybe the name of my grandfather's partner who was murdered is in the history, but I don't know.[2] I was very young when it all happened.

Then my father was a member of the Amalgamated Union. "Clucks" was a word that was used by Jews to express "cloaks and suits in the ladies' line, not the men's line." Anyone who clucks would be a member of the ILGWU, International Ladies' Garment Workers' Union.[3]

I lived on Charlotte Street until I was eighteen, at which time I was drafted into the army. My brother was already in the service. He was a little older and had a better realization of what was going on in the world than I did. And when the Japanese attacked Pearl Harbor he enlisted the next day. And of course I was only sixteen or seventeen at that time. But at eighteen I was drafted, before I could make up my mind whether or not to enlist. I was in the service from age eighteen to twenty-one, for three years. I left in 1943 and came back in 1946 and still lived on Charlotte Street.

I was married in 1948, and at that time there were no apartments available. Families were moving into Quonset huts, temporary housing, for lack of housing. There were some Quonset huts located near the Soundview area—Westchester and Soundview. Housing was bad, and you had to pay under the table to get an apartment, and we didn't have the money, and also we resented that. So we wound up living with my mother on Charlotte Street in a little room, and my wife and I lived there for three years.

My first job was selling appointments for photographers to come and take pictures of babies in the homes. We had to take a three-dollar deposit, and that three dollars was ours to keep, and we brought in the appointment, and that was the end of it. We didn't know what was going on. My first day on the job I came in with three appointments, so I got nine dollars for that first day. When I brought it to my manager, he was shocked, because usually the first day on the job before you get experience you flop. And I was bringing in orders. I was really bringing in orders. I worked for him for about two or three weeks, and one woman, one mother, said, "It would be nice if we had samples." I agreed with her. I said, "I don't have any samples, but I'll ask my manager for some samples, and I think it would be easier to sell if I had some samples." So I asked him for samples. He said, "We don't have any samples. No samples. You sell without a sample just like you've been doing." So I said to myself, "Sounds like a crooked operation," and I decided to chuck the job. I says, "I can't be a party to this. I think you're ripping off people." And I walked out.

I was in a quandary. I didn't know where to go. What to do. I had graduated from Roosevelt Evening High and I'd gotten a diploma, and I had taken three more courses in business law and advertising, and they helped me later in my business. But I didn't yet know what kind of business. I went to visit a friend of mine who's still my friend. He was engaged to be married. He said, "Come over to my girlfriend's house on Jennings Street. We're getting married, and I want you to meet each other." So I went over. I really was in a quandary. I didn't know what industry to go into, no idea what I wanted to do with my life.

The rehabilitation from army life to civilian life was difficult. We used to hang out in bars, close up the bar, get home at four o'clock in the morning. I was not happy with my life. I didn't realize that what I was doing was not the greatest thing in the world at the time. We did a lot of drinking, learned from the army, and we'd close up the bars in the neighborhood just hanging out. Didn't go home to go to sleep or get up early. We went every week to the 52/20 Club to sign for checks. "52/20" meant that all veterans were entitled to twenty dollars a week unemployment insurance for fifty-two weeks. So we were all signing for checks. There weren't that many jobs.

When I went to meet my close friend's girlfriend, her brother Bobby was there, and Bobby had enrolled in beauty school to learn to become a hairdresser. And when she told me that, it sort of rang a bell. "Gee, that's a good idea. Why don't I do that?" So when I went to get the authorization and subsistence from the Veterans Administration—before they would invest in my education which they paid for—they sent me to Columbia University for aptitude tests. And it came out that I should follow a vocation that would require me to more or less use my artistic inclinations according to the aptitude tests. So they were happy with that report. It wasn't my own idea, someone else's idea, but it rang a bell, and I went to school and became a hair stylist. And they weren't wrong in the aptitude tests. I was a very fine hair stylist. I was very well known. I became president of the New York State Hairdressers' Board of Trade. If I'd wanted to I could have been the leader of the whole national organization, but I chose not to. As a hairdresser I was very good, and I was doing platform demonstrations for other hairdressers. I'd get good applause, spontaneous applause, and I'd be shocked that it happened.

I realized that when I was on platform there was an imaginary screen between me and the audience. I didn't feel a part of it. While I was good enough as far as my speaking was concerned, and the audience wasn't aware of any lack, I was. So in 1954 I took the Dale Carnegie course in public speaking,[4] and the result was that I was better able to understand the role of being a speaker and making presentations and being president and what have you. I did a much better job as a result of the course.

Then I joined a book club, a self-improvement book club, and I used to get a book each month—how to talk well, how to speak well, successful human relations—which was one of the best books I ever read. I still have the book. It helped me greatly in my profession, to advance in my career. Finally I sold my business. I left hairdressing and went into life insurance and health insurance and employee benefit plans and pension trusts and so on. I've been in that since 1970.

I also left Charlotte Street in 1951 and moved to University Avenue in the West Bronx. I lived there for three years. I had been working for five years on Wilkins Avenue, and then I bought my own business, which is where I live today, on Broadway and Arden Street in a section called Inwood. I've been in that area ever since. I got an apartment in the same building that my store was in, and I went into business there. When my children were born we often took them to see their grandparents on Charlotte Street, and we took them to the playground in Crotona Park where I grew up and played. Crotona Park was a place where all the Jewish people that came from Russia and Poland would meet and have hot political discussions and have a crowd of twenty or thirty men standing around arguing. And some, of course, were Democrats. Many of them were Bolsheviks. My father couldn't say a bad word about Russia or craftsmen in Russia. A man who made a boot made a boot, and he was proud of his work, and he produced something fantastic. My father didn't understand the Industrial Revolution and mass production, although of course he became a part of it when he worked here in this country.

Charlotte Street where I grew up so happily has become a name for something ugly, urban decay at its worst. But I think now that Charlotte Gardens will be the answer to this problem. I think that if people will own their own homes they'll take care of them. I think that the idea of a high-rise putting a lot of low-income people in it together has proved to be wrong. And I hope that our politicians and our real estate people and what-have-you now realize it and understand that it was the wrong move. But we learn by mistakes. It was very difficult to realize that they would be so destructive. I think that because of having their own home and owning their own property the parents will wind up being a little stricter with the children to respect the property that they own. And as a result of respecting their own property they will respect others' property. And I think it's the right route to take. And it will increase the tax base. Building the communities will create jobs, and the communities will need businesses to shop in and places to buy, and so there'll be new businesses that will come up, and businesses will need people to work for them. I think it's a slow process. I don't think it's going to turn around overnight, but I think it will lead towards a steady improvement. Much better than a big building, a panacea, that gets to deteriorating before long. A panacea doesn't work.

I don't think the people who lived there in my time will be moving back, but I think the people who will live there will be better people than those that destroyed it. It's a shame that it was destroyed the way it was. I couldn't believe it. I drove my car into the old neighborhood, saying to myself, "Let me see what the old neighborhood looks like." It had been years before I went there. When I came into the area and saw that I could see from Boston Road and 173rd Street straight down to Freeman Street Station and no buildings standing, it was really a shocker. I must say I got chills. I get chills thinking about it and talking about it. It was a horrible experience to realize what had happened. And then coming home I went into the road that goes through the park, from Wilkins Avenue to the other side of the park—I forget the name of the street on the other side of the park. It was like a dumping ground for discarded vehicles. It just broke my heart, knowing and having such fond memories of the area.

PART TWO
COMMUNITY ORGANIZERS

One Neighbor and One Block at a Time

Ada Quiñones, Rae Flores, Carmen Bermudez, and Susan Boyd—none of them born in the Bronx but moving there by choice as young adults—dove into community work like children into a pool, responding to needs all around them in the then predominantly black and Hispanic South Bronx. Carmen was born in Puerto Rico in 1918; Ada and Rae in Harlem in 1925 and 1926, respectively; Susan in Massachusetts in 1944. Ada and Rae were sisters, and through them I met Carmen and also Susan. Theirs was a close-knit world where many of the same people joined together first as unpaid volunteers, later with antipoverty government funding, in different organizations like the Federation of Puerto Rican Volunteers or the Tremont Health Planning Council—to help neighbors in their community with key issues like housing, health, English-language skills, and navigating the welfare system. As an adult helping her community, Ada didn't hesitate to write to her congressman and even to the president of the United States to call attention to the plight of one Bronx citizen. And she got a response. Mario Biaggi, a four-term congressman, talked in his interview about phoning presidents, several of whom he knew personally, and he too lobbied on behalf of individual constituents. Ada, with no elected title before her name, felt the same empowerment to go to the top to help her community. These four women understood the power of collective voices, of the press that Susan worked most effectively, but they also understood the power of one and never hesitated to speak out as individuals to protest or prevent abuses in the domestic sphere and in the public domain.

CHAPTER THREE
ADA

Ada Quiñones, Community Organizer, b. 1925
Interviewed on May 11, 1982

"It's that one candle. If a few of us have that little candle it makes the world brighter and brighter, until it really sparkles."

I used to live on 113th Street in what you now call Spanish Harlem, El Barrio. I went to school in Junior High School 101 and went on to Wadleigh High School on 114th Street and Seventh Avenue. We used to walk from Fifth Avenue and 11th Street to 114th and Seventh Avenue. We couldn't afford trains and buses. Mami worked very hard in the laundries and cleaned houses. My father used to be with us. When jobs got bad, President Roosevelt brought the WPA, and this gave my father a job. But he froze his ears working on the street. He couldn't cope with the cold, being that we come from a warm climate. When I was about eight years old he abandoned us.

We were three girls and there were also two boys from my father's former marriage. Those two boys were always coming to stay with us. They felt that my mother was their mother. To this day as grown men they still consider my mother their mother. So she raised five kids in times when they were very, very tough. Life was different when we were growing up. Nowadays, even the poor can go to movies, have a TV. Not when we were growing up. I used to sell shopping bags. My brother used to shine shoes. Movies cost ten cents, and he would give me his ten cents so I could go to the movies. We'd see a chapter of a movie every week and wait to see the next one. It was very exciting.

It wasn't easy feeding five children. There were pushcarts then, and in the afternoons or at dusk we'd go pick up after the pushcarts and bring home the discards, things they would throw away, lettuce, tomatoes, a few times *plátanos*, sometimes things that were already beginning to rot. I remember once we picked up a whole lot of tomatoes that were kind of raw or a little damaged, and my mother put sugar in it and made us tomato candy. It was delicious! With this and my mother earning whatever she could and any extra pennies we could earn we managed to survive. We ate a lot of rice and beans. With a nickel we used to be able to buy milk, *leche*, and bread and coffee. As a treat we'd buy chocolate and at night have a big cup of chocolate with some big crackers they used to sell for a penny.

When my father lived with us he was very strict, but there was a lot of love too. Even after he abandoned us he would show up because he still loved my mother, and she loved him so much that she would forgive and forget. He'd call her or write a letter, or he'd even come by, but as a surprise. One day out of a clear blue sky he came around three in the morning, to check and make sure that my mother didn't have any other man in the house. My mother told me stories about him, that he would hide in the closet to see whether she'd come home with a man. My mother was a one-man woman; she always loved my father, only my father.

So I wasn't born in the Bronx, and I didn't grow up in the Bronx but in Spanish Harlem. I moved up (and to us the Bronx was "up," high up in society) after I got married and had my first daughter. That was in 1951. We felt we had a real opportunity to buy a house, a real house, but I hate to tell you the condition it was in! It was a three-family house, and in one of the apartments there was a big hole. The house was cold; it had no heat and no hot water. In fact, I think that's where I developed the crippling arthritis that I now have. But we were happy. My husband was good at fixing things and was sure he could fix this house. The down payment on the house was seven hundred fifty dollars. My mother loaned us three hundred and I sold our furniture and that's how we managed. There was a tenant on the third floor who paid us eighteen dollars a month, and we lived in the middle floor because we felt it was in the best shape. We started fixing the place and made it livable. Then we moved downstairs so that we could rent out the second floor as well as the third floor. With the rental money I bought my first car. It was a red and white 1955 Ford. We were proud of that car.

Only after we had lived there more than two years did our attorney tell us we could put in heat. You see, the man selling these houses, Samuel Hurwitz, bought up a lot of houses, sold them for a down payment, and then would find a way to get people out again, to take them back after they'd been partly fixed up. Our attorney didn't want this to happen to us after we'd invested a lot of money. So we waited for two years without heat until he told us it was okay. We used kerosene heat and there was a stove in the kitchen that burned coal, so we used that. Our house is gone now. Lots of the neighborhood was torn down later. It was on Alden Place, right about 178th and 179th and Webster and Park Avenues. When the houses were torn down there was a McDonald's on that little street. Then McDonald's went out of business, and it changed again.

After I got the car I went into business selling fresh fish and vegetables. My husband's been crazy about fish all his life. He went across to Webster Avenue between 180th and 181st to sell the fish. We'd sell the raw fish, then whatever remained on Friday we'd sell fried. But business wasn't good. I was working as a bookkeeper for a truck firm, and my husband used to take care of the business. When I got home at night my husband would be so discouraged that I told him, "Look, go back to work." He used to work for the city, and he'd taken a leave of absence in order to run this business, with the understanding that if it went better he'd stay there. But he went back to work and stayed in that job for twenty-seven years until he retired in 1976. He was the foreman of a laundry department, the washing department. He started off from the very bottom as a laundryman and worked his way up. He used to work in the summer programs for the city giving out lunches. But he wasn't satisfied with that. The laundry work suited him better.

I owe my own business to a Jewish fellow. God bless him, wherever he is. I haven't seen him for many years. He insisted that I go into real estate. He said, "Ada, that's the type of business you have to get into because that's where the money's at." I used to have an accountant, her name was Stern, and, boy, was she stern! She also used to get after me, and she used to say to me, "Well, you know, Ada, you have to get into real estate because, look, I have second mortgages." She used to have Dun and Bradstreet check out the people. Then she would take the second mortgages, and she was making good money out of it. So they both insisted, "You've got to get into real estate."

So I went to school. I went to the Eastern School for Real Estate. I took the test and passed; then I became a saleslady. Then, this Jewish fellow again, Fred Klein, he decided I should go into insurance because "that's where the money is at, and you have to get it." Again, I went into studying, and this time I went to Fordham University, and I became an insurance broker. The first time I failed my test, but the second time I passed it. It was funny, because my husband was driving. He had picked me up and was bringing me home, and I made it sound like a very long story. I said, "You know, Ralphie, I got this call from Farleigh, and Farleigh told me I had received a letter, and . . ."—a whole long story to tell him that I had finally passed and I was now an insurance broker. He's still driving, and listening, and all of a sudden he stopped and said, "What, you passed?" He turned around and told his cousin, and then another man who was with us, Johnny Morales, an Italian, and he said, "Now we've got another broker in the family, now we have an insurance broker." He was so proud. I'll always remember that. He decided that I had to go into business even though I had just had my last baby. My Ada had just been born.

I've always been a coward, afraid to take chances, but Ralphie decided for me. "By hook or by crook," he said, he was going to get me into business. Somehow he heard that a jeweler had been held up and robbed in his shop on 183rd Street. He was a stout man, and the robbers had grabbed him and locked him in the bathroom. Now he was giving up the business. He didn't want any more trouble. He took all the jewelry with him and left. Then Ralphie called the landlord and said he wanted to rent the place. Ralphie made me shelves, desks, everything—he made it for me. The next thing you know, June eleventh, I was in business, starting from scratch, but it wasn't just insurance, it was travel.

I had started selling insurance in my apartment, in a little room that I had. I used to make income taxes for people and things like that. Ralphie said, "You got to sell travel." I said, "Ralphie, I don't know nothing about travel." He said, "You're going to sell travel." So, a few days before I opened, he took me to a Mr. Dave Kaplan on Tremont Avenue. His wife and I had taken classes together at Fordham University. Ralphie said, "Let's go see Kaplan." Kaplan said to me, "I don't have anything on travel, but I have a friend who does." He took me over to this friend, and this friend helped me enter the travel industry. In one day he showed me everything he could, and that same week I went into business. Any time that I had problems I would call him on the phone, and he would help me. I've been very grateful to him. I love helping people; I love working with people. And because of the businesses I was in, a lot of people came to me. I helped them with welfare problems; whatever it was, I helped them. I would charge them if it had to do with travel and insurance. If it was something on the side like explaining tax forms, I wouldn't charge them.

On the basis of the work I was doing to help the community, I was funded to become a Federation of Puerto Rican Volunteer.[1] This let me hire one employee to continue helping people in the community. This Puerto Rican organization called PRCDP used to get funding from the government. In turn they would take this into different community organizations, and I was one of them because we helped people pay the rent, the light, the phone when they couldn't do this without help. Then, on account of everything we had done, the Community Development Agency gave me money for another place, this time with six employees. I'm very proud of what we have done. Now, it doesn't exist anymore. When President Reagan started cutting budgets, this was one of the programs that went. But over time we helped a lot of people. I believe in helping people.

Even without funding, I just managed. I used to have a friend, Bertha, and I used to say to her, "Bertha, I have this or that problem; how do I go about solving it?" She'd say, "Ada, if you have to write to the president of the United States to get that problem solved, you write to him." And that's just what I did. I had one case where this fellow was hurt in Korea and then sent back to the front. His mother felt he should not have to go back while he was still recuperating. I didn't know who else to write to, so I did write to the president of the United States. Hubert Humphrey was vice president at that time. I'm not sure about the president, but I think it was Johnson. I'll always bless Humphrey, and I always ask God to give him, like we say, "light," because he's dead now. But in my way of thinking I will always be grateful to that man. He wrote me a letter. He also wrote to the marines, because the boy was in the marines. He wrote to the head man in the marines. He got that boy out, until the boy really got healed. This is the way I found that powers what may would help.

You know, if you wrote to them and told them.

There was a congressman named Jacob Gilbert. I had another case with him helping. This was before we had any funding. After I showed some of these cases, we were able to get money. I had this lady who had been trying for over two years to get benefits for her children. She had been married, had three children with her husband, and then was divorced. He married somebody else and then he died, and after he died, this woman he was then married to got money as well as her children, but the other three kids didn't get any. Their mother, his first wife, had been trying for over two years, she said, and she couldn't get a penny. I got on the case. I wrote to Congressman Gilbert. Congressman Gilbert went to Commissioner Ball. The woman got a check for her kids and continued receiving benefits until they were of age.

I also had another case where this man had been trying to get into the projects for the longest time, and he wasn't able to do it. His son had been in the service. I wrote a letter and I explained to them that the boy was good enough to give part of his life for our country, and yet the father only wanted to get in the projects, and was having difficulty. Needless to say, the man got a call from the Housing Authority. They sent him a telegram, telling him to come down and get the keys. They processed him through in such a way that he was so happy. As a matter of fact, I'll always remember the house; it was at 2625 Third Avenue that they gave him the apartment. He was so thrilled. He kept coming to me and kept bringing everybody who had problems. He would bring them to me so that I would help them. This is how we started the Federation of Puerto Rican Volunteers.

At one point the schools were on strike. At the federation we had a school where we used to help mothers get their high school diploma. As a matter of fact, when the first woman graduated from our school the mayor—it was Mayor Lindsay at that time—sent her a letter, and to this day she has it. It inspired her so that she went on from her high school diploma to become a nurse's aide and then a practical nurse. She's now a practical nurse at Lenox Hill. She used to be on welfare; now she owns her own house. One of her kids is a meter maid. They have all got into higher learning, and it has increased their stability.

We had this school where we were teaching these mothers how to read and write English. Some of the mothers didn't even know how to write their name. We still have mothers now. We have an elderly woman who is in her seventies who is still associated with us. She was one of the ones who learned how to write. It's so funny, because she didn't know how to read or write in Spanish, but she learned in English! She used to write her last name first and then her first name.

Because of the school, we brought in the kids during the strike. We would bring them to study at our school. The teachers from the school would come in and teach them in our school. We would break the strike, because we wanted our kids to learn. The teachers would come in from P.S. 59. They would come help teach the mothers as well as the children. We were very involved. We had one lady who used to come and teach us about weights and measures and how we were being cheated. At one time she was Miss America, Bess Myerson.[2] She came over and all the teachers were there, and all the people from the community came. She spoke to them, taught them, and showed them. She even brought scales with her to show them, and she brought brochures.

Oh, we were very, very involved. You could say that our community was the envy of the world. The churches, the schools, the hospitals—we were very involved with Fordham Hospital—everybody in the community, even the Police Department, we were all one family. The Police Department used to bring us funny books, comic books, for the kids in the community. They would bring us ropes and arts and designs. They would come out and help us and call us at all hours of the night, whenever there were fights between the gangs. We would come out, people from the community, blacks, Puerto Ricans, all of us to try to quell the fighting. There were a lot of gangs and a lot of fighting between blacks and Puerto Ricans. Herman Badillo was the borough president then;[3] that's how long ago it was. I remember how well we used to all work together.

Then it changed. Everybody started moving. The churches started closing their classrooms. It's not the same now as it was then. We all tried, we all strived, we all fought to make it better for the next generation. I think there was more love for mankind in those days. It was like a little family, a little community. We had Theresa Montioni, who was the deputy commissioner from the Police Department. Her office was on 12th Street, and she used to come up to the Bronx. Everybody loved that woman. May God bless her wherever she's at. She used to really knock herself out, trying to make it a better world. Then there was a patrolman; he died of cancer of the eyes. His name was Andrew Giannone. As a matter of fact, there's a center now on Webster Avenue and 183rd, a PAL Center.[4] It was named after him because he was a policeman who gave his all. When you least expected, he was there.

We used to have Puerto Rican parades.[5] And I pride myself that I was the only woman that I know of who had seven different gangs from different parts of the Bronx and Manhattan who marched with us. We had a dance and they helped me clean afterwards, at ten o'clock in the night. I really feel very fortunate. The cops were all over the place because they were sure that a fight was going to happen. Thank God, nothing, nothing. They had motorcycles all over the place. But they got along well—for that party, that one day, the Commonwealth of Puerto Rico, July 25. We even had newspaper coverage, we had television. I used to bring in from PRCDP, they used to have these people who acted. They were theater; they would come in with the props and the lights and all that, and they would give plays in the street. Everybody in the community, whether they understood it or not, would come out and look at the play and applaud. If they didn't understand, they'd dance to the music, and they'd shake their hands. They were so happy with everything that was going on. They'd look through the windows. Then, at 10 p.m., everybody would clean up the streets, and everybody would go home. It was like a little family.

In the sixties we were going strong, but towards the end of the seventies we started changing. I started losing my love of what I was doing because people were not working together. They started slacking off; different elements were coming in. They weren't showing the love and affection that we had towards the communities. I don't know. I do know that I stopped giving parades. Everybody would come and ask me, "come on, Ada, give that parade, because you can't allow that to happen." I was unhappy with some of the employees in my organization, and I lost a little affection for it. But I went back. I'm still doing my job. I still help the community. A lot of people come to me with problems, and I still help everybody that needs me. I'm there.

The kids that come around me from different ages and different levels, they come in and they ask me about helping other people. If they have to take them to welfare, they go with them. I would say the growing generation is oriented towards loving their fellow man. There used to be a lot of break-ins on the block where I have my agency, but now we've all taken different measures. As far as the people in my area now, the store owners, we all are like brothers and sisters. We all take care of each other. As a matter of fact, we have to buy each others' articles. We give each other discounts. Like me, when my son-in-law goes to the motor vehicle bureau, I stay by myself. My neighbor, Al, who sells the bikes, he goes out of his way to make sure that I'm okay. If I need coffee, he goes out and buys me coffee. Or, if he goes and buys coffee for himself, he comes back and brings me coffee. The boys in Webster Locksmith, they all come out to watch me and take care of me. We're like a big family. Alan Hochberg, he was an assemblyman, used to say, "If we can light one little candle, it would be a blessing, because it would be one more candle to make it brighter." In this way, I think of these little kids that are beginning to try to help people. They try to go with them, try to help them, translate for them, or just help them cross the street, or whatever. It's that one candle. If a few of us have that little candle, it makes the world brighter and brighter, until it really sparkles.

CHAPTER FOUR
RAE

Raquel Flores, Community Organizer, b. 1926
Interview: May 28, 1982

"We would go whether it was snowing or raining to fight for their rights and fight for some survival for these people in that area. Some of us got hurt, some got arrested, but it was quite an education."

My parents came here . . . my father in 1922 and my mother came towards the end of 1923. They didn't know each other; they met here. There were very few Hispanics or Puerto Ricans at the time in New York City. My understanding was that my aunt who was already here had sent for my mother. One of the main reasons that she said she was anxious to get to the United States was because her sister had written that over here in New York you can get good jobs, and not only that, it was to get away from a man out there in Puerto Rico who wanted to marry her. In those times, whatever your father decided, that was it, so she really had to leave to get away from marrying this guy. She said that she could never stand a man who wore his pants below his belt, and this guy did! She just couldn't deal with that. Her father kept telling her that "a woman makes a man, and a man makes a woman." But she said that any man she saw with his pants hanging down, his balls are too big or something to that effect.

Anyway, she came here, and she began to work the very next day in a laundry. I think it was at the Biltmore Hotel. She worked all her life in laundries. In fact, she had a million burns on her arms from laundering. She met my father. I think he had come with my aunt to pick her up at the dock. The next day my aunt took her to where he lived at, because they were having a party. Then she started going out with him. What happened is that my mother was already about twenty-six, not very young—by Puerto Rican standards like an old maid already. She became pregnant from my father, and her sister threw her out. My father had been married previously. His wife was in Puerto Rico and refused to come to the United States. Therefore, my mother couldn't marry him, so she ended up living with him. She had Ada and then, eleven months later, she had me, and a year later my brother. Then after that my mother kept working, even though she had three children. She would drop us off at a babysitter and go to work.

My father was a very good-looking man. Valentino looked like nothing next to him. He was a cigar manufacturer because he came from a town, Cayey, in Puerto Rico, which manufactured cigars. Afterwards, he decided to become a dancer. He started taking lessons, and he became a dancer. He was a good-looking guy and a dancer, so every partner he had, he would end up sleeping with her. My mother was always a good old soul who allowed him to do whatever he wanted, and she would keep supporting the family while he would do his thing. He would leave but always came back. Finally, I remember, when I was about four years old and my mother pregnant with my younger sister Olga—by that time my brother had died, about a year after he was born—my father had impregnated this black woman. At that time it wasn't like now when if you get pregnant they accuse you: "What did you open your legs for?" At that time they would actually put the man in jail, and he was jailed.

I was two when my brother died, but I remember it. When he died, there wasn't enough money to rent a car. I remember they put the coffin on my mother and father's laps in the limousine in the back, so vivid in my mind. Anyway, then they jailed my father, and then we really were in trouble. We went to court. We had to appear in court, and when we went there we saw my father coming. The two detectives were bringing him in, and they had him handcuffed. My sister ran up to him and threw her arms around him, and the detective pushed her on the floor and said, "Get away from here." My father wanted to bend down to pick her up, but they pulled him away. Afterwards, I remember, in court, that I had to stand up with my mother. I guess they wanted to see the family. The court was filled, crowded. My mother was crying. I remember all these things even though I was only two.

I remember when my mother was unable to work, we were going to be evicted, and at that time she had a friend of hers move her into a basement. It was at 114th Street. At that time those basements were used just for supplies and storage. Since the Park Avenue Market, which now is enclosed, was an open market, the people used to bring the stuff and leave it in the basement. We put everything in there. The food attracted rodents. I remember, oh, do I remember, I was bitten by a rat.

When my father came out of jail, he was put on probation or something like that. He had to send this woman money when she had the baby. I remember, while she was pregnant, she came to our house. She came to the basement where we were living. She came in, and my mother was sitting on the bed, and she came in to talk to my mother. My mother was sewing a pair of pajamas for my father. The woman picked it up and said, "Ahh, feel it." She started kissing them and smelling them. I don't know how my mother put up with it. Now that I'm older I say, "Why didn't she punch her in her mouth and throw her out?" The woman was pregnant by my father, but she never let him see the kid. She used to tell the judge that the kid would be at this spot, but when my father got there, no kid and nobody who knew the woman. Eventually, in order to get away from all this, since he was still a dancer, when my father saw an ad in a Philadelphia paper about a woman who needed a dancing partner, he left.

When he left, my mother didn't have her job at the Biltmore anymore because he'd told her to go on welfare so she could stay home with the kids. Welfare was very bad because the investigators used to come to the house and check your closets, drawers, everything. If anyone was visiting they would ask, "Who are you? What are you doing here?" and all that kind of stuff. Because it was so hard trying to make it, my mother used to make lampshades and other things at night, together with her sister and some friends. Everyone in the area was on welfare because it was right during the Depression, right after the thirties. They had to do it on the sneak, make lampshades at night and hide everything during the day, 142 lampshades for maybe two dollars, and then deliver them somewhere else. Everybody sewed, even us kids. We used to put on the ears. There used to be those lamps that used to hang on the back of the bed, and we used to put on what we called "ears," the hooks that would go on the bed. Finally, my mother was able to start working again, and she always kept pushing us to continue our school.

My father kept coming back and going away again. He was a very strange man. Apart from the fact that he never supported you he gave you so much love and attention that you really couldn't feel hurt about the things he had done or hadn't done. The thing is, after I grew older, I used to blame my mother for the things that happened to her. I didn't understand that he really was a bad man. He used to beat her, and she used to accept it and let him keep coming back. I guess a lot of people were going through that at that time, during the Depression. I remember living in a building where there were other men that beat their children, or they'd throw them against the wall. I remember one kid falling unconscious on the floor. The men used to beat their wives. It was an ongoing thing in the neighborhood.

My father would go out with his women or whatever and then come back the next day, and if he had had a fight with that other woman, he would take it out on my mother. The thing is that she was a type of woman who had it instilled in her by her mother that you stick to your husband no matter what. If you had daughters, it was better for you to remain with your husband no matter what, rather than have another man come into the house who might rape your daughters. This was always in her mind. My mother never looked at another man. She never smoked; she never went out dancing.

But our father gave us so much love that we all kind of worshipped him. He was an attentive father. He never hit us, or if he did . . . it wasn't so bad. His first wife divorced him when she found out what kind of woman my mother was, so pure. She said, "I'm never going to go to the United States," but she had sent her son here when he was about ten or eleven and giving her lots of problems. When he went back he told her how good my mother had been to him, and that's when she decided to divorce my father so he would marry my mother, but he never did. She died with that in her mind, that he had never married her. Meanwhile he ended up marrying a woman who had been a prostitute. I said, "Well, these are things that maybe you have to pay for something that you did." And that's the way it was.

I think I was my mother's favorite. Except when we were little and all of us were sewing, I never worked. I was the brains in the family, and school was what mattered. Also, I look a lot like my father, even have some of his mannerisms, and so she favored me over the others. Another thing too, my mother had a thing about being black. She was the only one in her own family that wasn't born with straight hair. The rest of them all have straight hair. Three were white, and three darker. Her mother was part French and was a real dark woman with very keen features and straight, straight black hair. Her father was the son of a Spaniard who was a white man with straight hair. So when this kinky-haired daughter was born, she was treated like Cinderella, really. Listening to my mother tell me her stories about what happened to her, I realize that this was it. She really was Cinderella. Her sisters used to do all that neat sewing, beautiful sewing, to sell. She was told that her hands were too rough, she was only good for the stove, the coal stove. That's another reason that she didn't want to marry anybody that was black or had kinky hair. So she chose my father who was white and good-looking. But look at my sister Ada, the first baby. She's as black as can be, like God punished my mother. I said, "You know, he was telling you something." My mother's whole thing was about black, and then Ada came out dark.

I think my mother suffered even when she was a little girl. She lived with her stepmother from the age of eleven or twelve, and the stepmother mistreated her very badly. Also, she wasn't able to talk to her father. If she wanted to talk to him, she had to pass him a note on the sneak. He was very henpecked. Her father was a policeman, so they used to move around a lot. Even before her father left her mother, since he was a policeman, each one of her sisters or brothers was born in different towns.

Not only that, her mother was a very cultured woman who read a lot and never read novels because she said that was trash. She read philosophy and things like that. They spoke French in the house, except they would speak Spanish to the kids. I understand originally her grandmother came from Haiti during the revolution, and they had been a high-class family down there. They had migrated to Puerto Rico during the revolution. The mother, even though she was dark, had straight hair. She considered herself white, but treated my mother as black. My mother really had a bad life all her life. I think the best years of her life were after we were all grown up. I think only these last twenty years that she lived with me before she died, she finally had what she wanted, everything she wanted.

She was proud of me. I went to Brooklyn College when I graduated from high school,[1] and then I got married. I started with real ambition to be a lawyer, but I found out something hard. College was very difficult for me at the beginning because of the schooling I had had at P.S. 111 and then Wadleigh High School on 114th Street. Those schools weren't the best schools because they were in poor and minority neighborhoods. Consequently, when I went to college, I found out that I was way behind other students even though I had had good marks in high school. My father had pushed reading on us. Even though he wasn't there that much, he pushed us on education. My mother wanted us to aspire to be something, but it was my father who kept on pushing. "You got to be a lawyer, Rae," and "Ada, you got to be something big." You know, he pushed each one of us. He had books, and even though he didn't have much schooling, he spoke beautiful Spanish. He was involved in a lot of political clubs. Whenever he was in the city they would call on him to make speeches on account of his beautiful proper Spanish. He was a very intelligent man, and he was very much into poetry, Spanish poetry. He used to read poetry in different places, and people liked it.

At home we started by speaking Spanish, and then later on we learned English. By the time I was four I knew English. What is now Spanish Harlem was Jewish at that time. You had to learn English because you were playing with kids who were Jewish. There was a black lady living next door who used to take care of my younger sister. We started school early, age four, because that was a kind of babysitting. I remember being in kindergarten for almost two years. I think at that time kindergarten was all day long. I always had a key hanging around my neck because I was better than my sister at not losing things and better even than my half-brother when he came to live with us. My mother gave me the money, and I would go pay the grocer at the end of the week. All week long he would take credit, and I would go and pay the balance. There would always be a balance. Then I would buy big groceries for the whole week. I had more responsibility than all of them, even more than Ada, who was older than me. Ada changed a lot after she got older, but she used to be quite nutty, running around and everything. She and my brother were both the same. I used to take care of my little sister when I came home from school, pick her up so my mother wouldn't have to pay too much for a babysitter.

We lived on every block in The Barrio. The Barrio started at 110th Street up to 116th and from the east side of Fifth Avenue to the west side of Park Avenue. We moved because it was easy to find apartments and because you used to get the first two months rent-free. So if you were stuck for the rent where you were, you just moved in the middle of the night with pushcarts. You would pile everything on a pushcart. Your neighbors would always help you, and you would move. My mother always moved to the top floors or the third floors because they were cheap and nobody wanted them. It was different from now where everybody wants to live up high so they can see the view. At that time, nobody wanted to see the view.

Also, on the top floor during Prohibition, they had stills. We used to go up there. They used to leave them open, and it was a model of honesty. Nobody would steal from the gin mills. We'd go up there, we kids would watch what they did and what was happening. Sometimes we'd go up there alone when no one was there. Times were tough. We learned how to steal from Con Edison to have light and electricity. One of the fellows that worked in the building showed me how to put out a little wire so the light wouldn't register, and we wouldn't get charged for it. I used to be able to get up there. It was high up, but we had something I could jump on to reach it and put the wire on. One time we almost got caught by a man coming in to check the meter. But I think they were aware that most everybody was doing this because the times were so hard.

There was a Jewish bakery around the corner, and the rolls we got would be a little green with mold. My mother would cut the green off and wet the hard rolls and put them on top of the stove to make toast. Until I was thirteen I didn't know that the tomato jelly she made from rotten tomatoes wasn't really jelly. We would bring in tomatoes from the open markets that had been discarded, and she would make jelly with them, cutting off really bad pieces, putting in some sugar. We always kept this constant pot. We were the most popular kids on the block. They'd come in and spread this jam or jelly on the stale toast or just eat it plain by the spoonful. The first time I really tasted a jar of jam or jelly that wasn't my mother's I couldn't believe it. I didn't know there was any kind other than tomato. My mother was a very economical woman who made ends meet. And she was always there for us, all of us, her own children, our father's sons from his wife in Puerto Rico. Most people don't even know this; they think we're all hers. My father also had other kids; in fact, I raised one of his daughters, and nobody knows that. We were always close, and he wanted to make sure we knew each other. This was very important to him. You weren't supposed to say "half brother" or "half sister," just brothers and sisters, one family. We had lots of fun. My mother would always make sure that for Christmas we would have a special dress, even though every Sunday we'd use the same dress, and that we had a pair of shoes.

She used to do a lot of things to earn money. She used to go clean people's houses for maybe two dollars a day, come back home at midnight. Sometimes we used to go help her. She always did something. Even when we were on welfare, she always did something to enhance whatever she could. When times started to get better around 1940 or '41, she started working steady, and then she got off welfare. I was in high school before that happened. Both Ada and I, even Olga, my sister, we went to school and finished.

We all went to college as my father wanted, but Olga went later in life. She even has her master's. In fact, she just now got her master's. Ada went to college, to City College,[2] for about a year, but then she quit. I went to Brooklyn College for close to two years. But my husband, a seaman I had married, he didn't particularly care for it. So every time he'd come home, I'd have problems. I kept giving it up, and it wasn't until I was forty-five that I went back to college and finished. Prior to that, even without the degree, I was able to do a lot of things. The first job that I had was with the Immigration and Naturalization Service. Ada was working there, and that was during the Second World War, and they needed people. I had taken the Civil Service Exam, and when she told them I had taken it, they took me in right away. I started working as a messenger, and I was promoted to a file clerk in the "lemon department" because I was able to find things that nobody else could find. I was promoted, I did well. Then I stopped working. By that time I was married. I went back and forth. I worked in credit mostly, and I became very adept at that also. I was a good skip-tracer. I could find the people. I spoke two languages; that helped me. Even in French, I was able to get across.

All this time I still lived in Manhattan. When mostly everybody had moved from the Barrio to the Bronx, we moved from the East Side to the West Side. I didn't move to the Bronx until I had been married, separated, and was on my way to getting divorced. I was already thirty years old. I lived in the Bronx for a while, but I found that the Bronx was backwards in education. I had come from Brooklyn. When my husband and I were still together I had bought a house in Brooklyn. When we broke off I left him the house, and he sold it. My kids were very much advanced, and when I moved to the Bronx there was only half-day schooling. So I stayed there two and a half years and then moved back to Brooklyn. I was living on Eagle Avenue and 158th Street. That's a very strange street because it's one street on top of the other. It's like a railroad. You walk up to 161st and there it is, another street underneath, and you walk down. It's very strange the way that it's made. When I moved, there was a two-story house that belonged to my *comadre*. From there I started going out with my present husband. I moved to Brooklyn because he was living in the Bronx, and this was a problem. His mother really didn't want him to go with me when she saw we were talking about marriage because, she said, I had children. So I moved to get away from him, but when I moved to Brooklyn he followed me, and we got married. But I didn't stop working in the Bronx until the end of 1976.

Before the antipoverty programs began, Ada already had the Federation of Puerto Rican Volunteers, only it had another name at that time. It was just a social club. She used to help all the Puerto Ricans in the area, and she was one of the first people to move into that Tremont area. Her block on 186th Street was mostly Italian and Irish. When the Hispanics started moving in there, Ada had gotten her notary public stamp, and she used to help people with a lot of problems. Then, when the antipoverty programs came in, the club applied to them. They needed somebody with college experience or a college degree. They couldn't get anyone that would be willing to take a chance and go into this particular thing. I was working for a television repair place. They used to repair TVs, and they also used to sell TVs, and I did well in that. When I first started working there, there were six women in the office. They ended up with all males except for me. I could sell the TV repairs as good as the men did and maybe better. I was doing very well, and I was disappointed that because I was a female they didn't feel that I should earn the same that the men were earning, even though they came into the business later. When Ada spoke to me and also my brother-in-law, they kept saying, "You got to try, why don't you go, you're going to earn fifty dollars more." I figured out, fifty dollars, but minus carfare, because the TV job was near my house. My husband said, "Take it, because here you're not being considered where you are now, and you don't know what you may gain out of this other job." So I did that.

I went for training, and the fellow training me was a Vista volunteer. He was very radical. I had mixed feelings about the people in that area being on welfare, and this was a welfare advocacy program that we were beginning. Because I knew that my mother had made it out of welfare by working—she never stopped trying. So I kind of criticized a woman that sat back and had children and didn't do anything except welfare. But when I started working I realized that these women really needed help. They really needed someone to advocate for them and to help them to beat the system. The money they were getting was so little. It's true that there were a few women that had a husband hidden underneath the bed somewhere. But 95 percent of the women really needed what they were getting. They didn't have a husband. And those that did, the husbands were abusive, but when they beat them, the wives didn't dare report them. And if they did report them, and the man was supposed to give ten dollars a week, he would never give it, and welfare would cut them off. So I got really involved, and I saw too, when I used to take people to the welfare, the way that the investigators, even ones of your own kind—black or Hispanic—would look down on these people, treat them like dirt, and make them wait interminable hours.

These were people that hadn't been here too long and had language problems. But in fact the ones that had been here longer and spoke English were abused also. If you knew English, if you had had an education and fell on bad times, they figured that you were too slick for them, and they didn't want to help you. That happened to me when I got separated from my first husband. I was pregnant, and I was bleeding. The doctor from City Hospital had told me to stay in bed. When I went to welfare they refused to help me. They looked at my education, and they figured that I could make it. They said, "Why don't you work until your stomach shows?" I said, "But I have a letter from the doctor stipulating that I am in a bad way and need to stay in bed." I weighed ninety pounds then. I'm five foot four. I was having a very hard time. Finally, I entered the hospital with a very severe hemorrhage. The investigator came to investigate again, and when she found out I was in the hospital they reopened the case. They were giving me twenty dollars every two weeks, telling me that my husband should give me the balance, but my husband refused. I went back to work before I should have. I just couldn't deal with that situation. It was too hard. So I knew what these women experienced, but I had forgotten in a way until I went back there, back to the Bronx.

When I started working in the Bronx I was still living in Brooklyn, and even though I still live in Brooklyn, I know more about the Bronx than I know about my own neighborhood. I know the politicians in the Bronx. I know the different people that I have to know in the Bronx. I love that area of the Bronx, and I feel for it. I think that if it hadn't been that we had bought a house twenty years ago, my husband and I, I probably would have ended up back in the Bronx. When we first started working in Tremont–West Farms there were still a lot of whites in the area, in all the areas, Tremont and particularly West Farms. It was mostly Italian and Irish. The Puerto Ricans started coming in, little by little, and the blacks then followed. People started moving out. I guess once you opened the street to a Hispanic or black, people started moving out. When my sister moved to 186th Street she was the only minority person on the block. Before you knew it, the whole block was minority. That usually happens everywhere. In some areas the people remain and fight back by staying, like in Belmont. In that particular area it was more of a mixed area, it wasn't just one ethnic group. I really don't know, because I never went around asking them, but I think it was very mixed.

It was difficult at first for the families moving in. Kids wouldn't play with the new kids. Shopkeepers watched you a lot because they figured you were going to steal. That happens wherever you go. Now we have Asians coming in, and when you walk into the store they're looking at you like you're going to steal. All these new Asians do it. So when I first started seeing what was happening, when I was being trained to work with welfare, then I really got involved and tried to help people. The federation had even started a school with help from the welfare, a program to get people to learn English. Teachers would volunteer to come there.

There were two churches in the neighborhood, Mount Carmel on 187th Street and Our Savior on 183rd Street. Mount Carmel was Italian and was going to remain Italian and is still very prejudiced against Hispanics even though as the neighborhood changed they did admit them. Our Savior had an Irish priest who I felt was very discriminatory. He refused at all times to allow Spanish language in the church. He was older, and he was adamant at only allowing Latin and English and no Spanish. My sister had a lot of dealings with that church, Our Savior, which, by the way, now has a Hispanic priest. Before that, Father Banome was the one who brought in some Spanish. He only came around 1968, and because he spoke Spanish and could understand, he brought in some Spanish, although the service was still mostly in English.

Mount Carmel had a school, but if they could help it they wouldn't take the Hispanic kids. The priests were rude and not friendly, to me very unreligious. A new priest came from Puerto Rico who had just finished his training and was working out of the Archdiocese of

Mayaguez, in a little town outside of Mayaguez. He came to the federation and said he had come because his father was dying and he wanted to take him back to Puerto Rico to die and to be buried there. His mother was still there; she had been unable to come. His sister was in the parish of Mount Carmel, so I called up the priest that was there then because Ada had a working relationship with him—also because he was from Mayaguez. I called him and said, "I have a priest here who needs help. He's here in his sister's house and he's from your archdiocese. He needs help in getting back, and I was wondering, is there anything the church could do to help?" He told me to send the man down there and asked where he was from. I told him, "He's from Mayaguez Archdiocese."

When the man got there, the priest at Mount Carmel asked for his ID, and when the man showed it, it named the small town, not the bigger city of Mayaguez. Well, if you are from Puerto Rico, you know that the small town is under the Archdiocese of Mayaguez. But this priest called me up and cursed me out. He told me that I had a nerve sending this priest to him, that they had their own to take care of. The priest who needed help was dark; he was darker than I am. The priest at Mount Carmel said he'd never heard of me. Who the hell was I? He had heard of Ada Quiñones as being the federation's president, but who was I? I said, "I'm the director." He wouldn't let me talk. When the priest came back that I had sent there he was in tears. He said, "I have never experienced such humiliation. I'm sorry that I bothered anyone, but I had to come and tell you what happened." What we did was that I called my sister Ada, and she then gave them the two tickets out of her travel agency for him and his father's body to go back to Puerto Rico. The thing is that when the priest got here the father hadn't died, but by the time we got the whole thing together he had died. So he went back with his father's body to be buried, thanks to Ada. So that was some of the kind of discrimination that you could see in the church. But it happens everywhere. When I lived in the barrio the only Spanish church was the Miraculous Medal up on the West Side. Because they were white Spanish they discriminated against Puerto Ricans. So it's the same thing. It boils down more to a question of color than of language.

The federation tried to help everyone. We started giving dances to get money together. We used to help people that were bad off, who were sick, or they needed money for burial. We got some money from the federal government, but we used to do a lot of things on our own. I did a lot of going to welfare hearings for the people. I got to be so well respected by the welfare centers in the area and also in Brooklyn that a lot of times when I went there I didn't even have to appear before a hearing officer. They would just take care of me and my client because they developed confidence in me, and trust. I always went with everything documented, what was said, what time, everything, so I won most of the cases. After a while the federation got so important that people would be standing on line. They used to come from all over the city just to have me represent them. They used to call me "Missy Flores."

I used to teach them how to deal with the bureaucracy. I ran two classes, one for the blacks, one for the Hispanics, in English and in Spanish, all at the same time because the store was very large. Also, I tried to teach them how to start getting on their feet. We were able to put some people into different types of classes to help them begin making a life for themselves. We would then try to place them because the welfare wouldn't do that. We had to fight welfare to do this. If someone wanted to go for training, the investigators didn't want to deal with it because they said it was a lot of paperwork. We had to force them to do the paperwork. Here you see what it was, people trying to do for themselves and get off welfare, but the system would not allow them to do this. That's what we learned.

Our store started off on 183rd Street between Bathgate and Washington. From there we moved into Washington and 187th Street. We were the first ones who started taking care of the Italians, because they had no agencies—also the Albanians. A lot of Albanians were living in that area too, among the Hispanics. Eventually, the Italians started bringing them to their side because they figured they were white. But before that, the Albanians were living among the Hispanics, and the Hispanics would help them out a lot. They were very proud people, and they didn't like needing any kind of help. You really had to instill in them some kind of confidence, otherwise they wouldn't come to you. We started getting them jobs, even though they couldn't speak the language. We would call up an Italian construction worker and we'd call the Albanians and they would accept them. The Italians wouldn't accept Hispanics, but they would accept the Albanians. I tried to help everyone that needed it. Nue Kola, the president of the Albanians for Foreign Nationals,[3] heard about me and came to see me, to see who was this woman who was doing this for his people.

We became very friendly, and the Italian people too. They started the Belmont Association around 1970 after I had left the federation and was working at Fordham Hospital. The Italians were proud, and they felt that their people weren't on welfare so they didn't need help, but there were a lot of people, Italians, that did. The first time I went to speak to them was around 1974 when Fordham Hospital was going to be closed. We were trying to fight for the hospital, but when I went to speak to them I was treated very cold and told that that hospital was for the blacks and the Hispanics, not for them, so they didn't see why they had to get involved in this struggle. But they were wrong. A lot of Italians were going to Fordham Hospital, but not the ones who were better off. The first time I was supposed to go speak before them they cancelled the date. They told me they had cancelled their meeting, but I found out it was a lie. The second time, I had made a date way in advance to speak at their meeting and they forgot about it.

When I appeared I went in with this fellow from the Albanians, and I sat down. They treated me very cold. First, the guy that was the president of their organization started talking at me from across the room to kind of belittle me. He's now a judge. He tried to belittle me. By that time the welfare had given me such experience at handling people who thought they were better than I was or better than the client. One of the things that I taught my personnel was you don't yell, you don't scream, you speak in a normal voice, but don't belittle yourself, and, at the same time, make them have to listen to you. Because when they're yelling, if you speak in a normal tone, they have to stop to hear what you're saying. Plus, the first thing I always tell them is, "Look, a little courtesy costs very little." So I had adopted—even though I have a fast temper—I adopted this real easy method of talking to them. So I answered his questions. Then he said, "Look, we're going to have to leave you for the last." I said, "I'm willing to wait." I found out that the reason he wanted to leave me for the last is because they were talking about the houses that were being built, one on Fordham Road and the corner of Southern Boulevard, one for senior housing at 187th Street. These two houses were coming up, and they were trying to make sure that no Hispanics or blacks went into them. It was subsidized housing, not public housing, but it was sponsored by the Belmont Organization, COBO,[4] and that was Italians.

After that, I got up and I spoke to the people. I said that I was glad they were taking a stand to try and save their neighborhood. I could understand their position, because if other ethnic groups came in, it would destroy the beauty that they had in there. So I could sympathize with them and agree with them. I would help them in any way possible to keep their neighborhood pure. I also said to them that I was glad that finally COBO had come. Prior to that, there was a lot of problems there and no one to solve those problems for the Italians. I had been taking care of them for quite some time with my half-bad Italian, and using Spanish. By the time I got through talking and I had pointed out that even though Fordham Hospital was a city hospital, and many of them felt that they were above that, that if any of them got hit by an ambulance, or anything else happened to them, no matter how much green they had in their pocket, it was Fordham Hospital that was going to pick them up. And it was important to have a nearby hospital that could take care of this problem so that they wouldn't die. We were so adept at emergencies, in more than 95 or 97 percent of the time, the person would be saved. When I got through talking, they started applauding. And before I left, people were clapping me on the back and telling me to come whenever I felt like coming. So I established a rapport with them. It's not what you'd call a real close one, but I think that they respect me, and I respect them, and it's been like that for a long time. It's true what I said about their keeping their section pure. The director that they have now of the COBO organization and I talk to each other.

When we opened the Bronx 2000,[5] I took David Muchnick over there. We were trying to start an economic development program. We had a conference at Fordham University: Phipps Houses[6] and T.I.P. Neighborhood House[7] together. This was later. Back when the hospital was going to start closing we were working very hard to keep it alive. It so happened that we had a community board, which was something that came out from the Health and Hospitals Corporation because they wanted the community to be involved in the health processes for their own. When the community board first began, I was on the planning council that set it up. There was an advisory board prior to the community advisory board. They were supposed to have been disbanded, but the people refused to stop meeting. It was mandated by the Health and Hospitals Corporation that a new planning committee come in. I dealt with that, and I had a lot of back-flack from a man who sat at Fordham Hospital, was extremely rich, and felt this was his baby. He couldn't understand that this was something new that was coming, a new regime.

We had set up a group of community people as the Tremont Health Planning Council.[8] It was a very knowledgeable group. It was a mixed group—black, Hispanic, Italian, everything. We felt that we wanted to control the help that came into our area, to see that it would be adaptable to our people and could do things for our area. A doctor at Einstein or Bronx Developmental Center,[9] I forget which, wanted to bring in a group of students to study the community, research it, and give them some services. Then after two years they would pack up and leave. We had a group of people that were very concerned about people researching us, killing us with this kind of thing, and then leaving us. So a bunch of us opposed it unless we had involvement in it. We formed the Tremont Health Planning Council with the help of Fordham Hospital, which at that time had a man named Tom Butler, a director of community affairs, and a woman named Blanche Sanchez. Blanche was involved with the mental health hospital—Bronx State, we used to call it, Bronx State Hospital. We all got together with their help, and we formed a planning council. Then we met with these people from Bronx State Hospital, and we said, "No, you cannot do it this way, unless we have an agreement worked out that you're going to at least service us here after you've stopped training your students. And you're going to give community mental health services, and it has to continue." That's how the Tremont Crisis Center began,[10] but we were also on the Tremont Health Planning Council.

First, Cynthia Rowe was president for two years, then it was Susan Boyd, then Albert Rivera. By the time Father Banome became president it was beginning to fall apart because a lot of people had moved out of the area. But we controlled a lot of the help that came into the area. We got very involved both in mental health and regular health. We were involved also in Fordham Hospital's community help. That's how I ended up working for Fordham Hospital. Since I was on the Tremont Health Planning Council, I became chairman of the planning committee trying to set up the guidelines for the board that had to come in. Finally, after much bickering back and forth over a year, the whole thing fell apart, and we began again. We had people who refused to resign from the old advisory committee. We started again. One lady, Frances Stark, worked very good with us. She was from the Department of Health. She gave us a lot of help. Also Tom Butler and Blanche Sanchez. I became again chairman of the planning council to set up the board. From there, we had the guidelines; then we started the voting procedures on how to get people onto the board. We had the community coming in to vote on that. After the board was all established I went on vacation. When I came back, the director of community affairs for Fordham Hospital was leaving for another job. The administrator from Fordham had called me to come in for an interview. He asked me would I like the job, and I said, "Well, I don't know if I'm capable of doing it." He said, "There's nothing different from what you're doing now." So I took the chance and I took the job. I worked there for five years until the hospital closed, roughly 1971 to 1976. It closed in July of '76. The community said to me, "Go out there and bring people to take over the hospital because we don't want it to close." But I had always told the board and the community, "Look, you can't keep the hospital open because this is a political move that no one can do anything about. Because North Central Bronx Hospital is going to open, Morrisania Hospital will close, and so will Fordham. But you must fight to keep some kind of services here."

The community figured that they didn't want to fight for it. But I went out and I got the top leaders of the community, and I talked to them and convinced them to get their people into the hospital. The next day people started coming in, one by one. Consequently, it was a takeover of Fordham Hospital. I also fought very hard to keep the hospital open. One of the things I did, which now I know better than to do, I took a woman with me who was in a wheelchair. Her leg had been amputated. I called her. She was an Irish woman with a real heavy Irish brogue. I also called this other man who I knew was being taken care of by home care. This kept him out of having to live in a nursing home. I asked them would they be willing to come to the board meeting downtown at the Health and Hospitals Corporation office. They said yes. Then I called up one of the local hospitals which I had a good rapport with, and I asked the administrator to give me an ambulance. He gave me an ambulance and a driver, and I got them through the takeover people. At the last minute the man couldn't come because he had an appointment, and I didn't want him to lose it. So I took the lady. We took her on her wheelchair, and we laid her on the bed inside the ambulance. I had talked to the guards at the Health and Hospitals Corporation. I knew them all, and I explained that I was coming in, so that they would let me in. They not only let me in, they made a space for me to be able to park the ambulance in front. And they watched so that we wouldn't get into trouble. I took the lady upstairs in her wheelchair. The board purposely kept us waiting, and they wouldn't let us into the room. Finally, towards the end of the day, this woman wouldn't eat or drink because she didn't want to have to go to the bathroom. All day long all she did was sit there and smoke cigarettes.

Finally, they allowed us in because I went in the back and I spoke to Dr. Holloman. I said, "Listen, this is not fair. We're community people, we do pay your salary, and blah, blah, blah." Then I went in. By the time I went, most of the community people had left. There was a group, but some had to go home to cook, some had to go to work at night. The group that got left behind said, "Oh, we can't talk." They didn't want to talk, so I became their spokesman. I went before the board and I identified myself, even though a lot of them knew me. I said, "I know that I get paid by the Health and Hospitals Corporation. But my first priority is to the community and to the people we serve. I've come here to speak to you about the problems that we're having up there. The people have asked me to be their spokesman." So I explained the problems, and I explained that even home care was going to be closed. And I said, "Most of the time you look at papers, they are black and white. But I've brought you real, live-flesh, white-and-red person, with red blood, for you to see for yourself." I told that doctor that was in charge of the board, "I want you to tell this lady that she's going to have to go into a nursing home because she can no longer get home care. And I want you to look at her and tell her in her face that she's not allowed to live a normal life like anyone else." I made a nice speech, then I asked her to speak, and she spoke. The woman was practically hysterical because she knew it was true, she was going to have to go into a nursing home if she didn't have home care. Then he, the doctor, promised her—that's the first time that they actually promised her—they would leave the home-care department open, and that Misericordia would start taking care of it.[11]

So I was able to accomplish that and I felt good about it. And the home care has lasted. But I figured later I had done something crazy. What would have happened to that woman with her wheelchair if we had had an accident? Because the ambulance driver bringing us was going so fast. I figured there was no indemnity for me. We did a lot of crazy things.

During the time we were there I used to get people to go to Washington and to Albany. They had so much faith in my agency and the work we were doing that if I said, "You have to be here at 6 a.m., when I got there at five-thirty or five, to be there before them, they were sitting on the ground waiting for me outside. If it was in the wintertime, they would be huddled at the door. People would bring whatever they could bring, and I would buy chicken and somebody would cook it. We took a whole bunch of kids, and we would go whether it was snowing or raining to fight for their rights—and fight for survival for these people in that area. We did a lot of things. Some of us got hurt, some got arrested, but it was quite an education.

Our area goes from Tremont over to West Farms. But in reality, it's Tremont, then there's the Bathgate area, then where Lambert is it's called the Bronx Park South, then the West Farms Area. So it engulfs all of that. Everybody from the four areas knows each other, back and forth. When we first started out there were thirteen delegate agencies. These were antipoverty agencies that later on got called Community Action Programs.[12] Some of them are still there but very little. It was very difficult. We had gotten people off welfare to work with us and they were getting paid one hundred dollars a week, and years later they were still getting paid one hundred dollars a week. They had never had an increase, at least my agency never did. People worked because they wanted to do things. You had to be very dedicated. We ran programs for kids at night, and we weren't paid. We taught kids, then we sent them to different kinds of involvement.

When I went to work at Fordham Hospital, one of the guys that came to work for me, a CETA worker,[13] had been a junkie and had been in every jail you could possibly think of. I got him to teach the doctors and the nurses how to deal with junkies and how to deal with the medication. They would give the methadone medication. They would break it up into three or four parts, and it wasn't helping the junkie that was trying to get off it. We told them that it has to be done in one. We developed a lot of respect for my department, again in the Community Affairs Department at Fordham.

They had a language bank, but it wasn't really any good until I got involved. I did the translating. We had some Haitians. I would do the French translation, Spanish, English, and even Albanian. When we printed something out, we would put it in Albanian, English, Italian, Jewish. I made sure that I got all kinds. When we were forming the community board I made sure that the thing was circulated in all the languages that I thought we'd use in the hospital so that people would come and sit on the board.

There was a big conflict among the Albanians. Two factions developed up there among the Albanians, one who represented the foreign nationals and the other a priest, a monsignor that had come in. Both of them wanted to sit on the board, and it almost came to bloodshed. Again, we had to deal with that. I guess I did a lot of mediating back and forth. After the hospital closed, people still looked out for each other, and they still do in a way, but a lot was lost.

When Fordham closed, and even before I left the hospital, I knew that I wasn't going to the new hospital because all the administration had been ousted by the community. I had kept peace between the community, the nurses, and the doctors that were there, although most of the doctors were already on the side of the community. The nurses were, at the beginning, but then we had a woman, Norma Noriega, who was a director of nurses, who kind of turned them around. She was very false to the community; until this day the community hates her. People wish her the worst luck in the world. She was second in command at North Central, and now she's over at Woodhill, the new hospital that's being opened. It was very bad because she was

Puerto Rican, and the people felt that she should have had a little compassion for them. It's true that we understood that the hospital had to close, but compassion was something else. She didn't give it. She feels that I'm her enemy, and she doesn't know that I did her a lot of good because a lot of times when the community had been after her, I used to intercede. When she became director of nurses, the community people felt that that was done wrong, and the community board should have been consulted. Again, I interceded. At that time I didn't know her well, although I worked in the hospital. I said, "She's a good person, I hear, and she does well, so why don't we leave her? Why should you antagonize the nurses by trying to push her out?" But she'd been a vicious woman; she was vicious even to one of my children. When my son graduated and went to apply for a job, she was at Lincoln because she ran Lincoln on an interim basis. She blocked him. So there's been a lot of animosity, but there's also been a lot of good things on all sides.

Naturally, when they ousted all these personnel, I went to the Health and Hospitals Corporation, and I said to them, "You've got to have somebody running the hospital, because Norma Noriega takes the nurses out every Wednesday and she leaves the hospital unattended. I don't know how the city allows that." The few nurses that would remain to take care of the patients, I understand that when they went to the other hospital, they were put to work at night and treated very shabbily because they had remained to take care of those patients in the hospital. A lot of the community was up there feeding the people, bathing them, and doing things because the hospital was shorthanded. They were pulling out the nurses, supposedly to train them for the new hospital, but at the expense of the patients. I mean, this stuff is documented. When I went out and I called the community, they came in. The next day there was one ward that Noriega had closed because she felt that she didn't have enough nurses, even though Misericordia Hospital, which was the affiliation, had promised to send some of their nurses over to fill in. But she preferred closing the ward. The Health and Hospitals Corporation went along with it. I don't know what kind of pull she had. The community came in and they took over the ward. They knocked down the lock and they lived in that ward for about seventy-four days. People in the community brought food, and all kinds of things came out of it. It was a real brotherhood.

About two years ago, people that had worked at Fordham Hospital under the affiliation decided to give a Fordham Hospital reunion. But they only called the professionals. Some of the people in the community found out about it, like myself, and we went. It was the only reunion I can think of that—even though the hospital had died—people were still reuniting around the hospital. Even this woman was there, Norma Noriega, and even the administrator that we had at the time, the executive director, he was there. Some people talked to Noriega and some didn't. But it was a nice thing to see a lot of these people from before because a lot of the nurses wanted the hospital to remain. I think, in New York City, there's not anywhere a hospital like this one, where people really cared for each other, no matter where they were at. The doctors actually associated with the "low," the lower people, the lower echelon, and back and forth. Everybody loved each other. It was a real rare thing to see that hospital. It was a real fraternal kind of thing.

Woman in wheelchair: a patient at Lincoln Hospital, 1980
Photograph by Walter Rosenblum

Friends, Lincoln Hospital staff, 1980
Photograph by Walter Rosenblum

Mother and child, patients at Lincoln Hospital, 1980
Photograph by Walter Rosenblum

Father and son, patients at Lincoln Hospital, 1980
Photograph by Walter Rosenblum

We Need Jobs: Street Scene, 1980
Photograph by Walter Rosenblum

Bishop Ernest Crooms, Rapture Preparation Church, 1983
Photograph by Georgeen Comerford

Choir, Rapture Preparation Church, 1983
Photograph by Georgeen Comerford

Eae Mitchell, Togetherness Realty, 1982
Photograph by Georgeen Comerford

CHAPTER FIVE
CARMEN

Carmen Bermudez, National Association for Puerto Rican Affairs,
Community Organizer, 1918–2001
Interview: January 27, 1982

"This organization is my heart, and I'm going to continue to serve the community as long as I can."

I was born in Puerto Rico in 1918, came to the U.S. in 1940 to continue my education, but then I married. I lived in Manhattan for two years and then came to the Bronx. I bought this house in 1950, and I am still living in the same neighborhood, in Belmont. My heart is in this neighborhood. I started doing volunteer work helping people because at the time I moved here there weren't any Spanish people. We had Arabs, and Italian, and some Jewish. I used to help the people in my house. I had everything in my house, and I started doing volunteer work helping them with problems like housing and education. When my son went to school, I tried to help people with their problems. The neighborhood started to have blacks and Puerto Ricans moving in, and I was proud to do stuff because I was the first Spanish person here.

I raised my children here. Because we'd been helping and doing all that work, in 1960 we founded an organization, Upper Bronx Neighborhood Association for Puerto Ricans.[1] When Puerto Ricans came here, they mostly weren't speaking English. The organization was founded by Ramon Morales in New Jersey. I happened to meet him, and he said, "Well, in your neighborhood we have a few changes. It would be good to have an organization in your neighborhood." That's when I started. Then, you see, I was not only a volunteer. I was the founder of a federation and also a founder of the East Tremont Action Community.[2] Then we had different organizations helping people within the community.

In 1967, when the antipoverty programs came to this area, I founded and ran a summer program. We serve one hundred children from the neighborhood, especially in the summer, with fifty volunteers, six teachers, and about thirty neighborhood youths. We started fundraising, and we've been funded every year. Now, with the budget cuts, we don't know whether we can survive in the future. But since 1967 we've been in continuous service here and working with the Federation of Puerto Rican Volunteers on 186th Street.[3] Ada Quiñones, Rachel Flores's sister, was the secretary, and I used to be the chairman of that organization. I went to two or three training sessions, and then I started reading a book with the idea of helping people. We have to serve everybody because we are being funded by federal and also city funds, but most of the people that have moved here and need help are Spanish, not only Puerto Rican, but also from other countries.

So that's the way we started the first year—with the summer program. Then we had a year-round tutoring program that we run in P.S. 118. We have six teachers, six neighborhood youths in that program. And then the next year they started the manpower program. We were so proud that we were one of the five organizations being funded at that time. It was the team of Community Council[4] (Father Banome was the director), Upper Bronx NAPRA, West Bronx Villagers, Bronco, and United Bronx Parents.[5] We were the first five organizations being funded in this neighborhood. We didn't have a corporation; we were just funded from downtown.

Since that time we've been here helping people. I was so proud that we are the founder of this guest center. We founded a "Host a grandparent," and we serve hundreds of senior citizens on a volunteer basis. And we just got an out-of-school program for GED youths. But I myself have helped about five hundred youths that today are professionals. The director of the center came from our organization. He started working with me when he was fourteen. He went to school, and he worked part-time with us. And then in the summer he worked with us. He came from a poor family. And now he's got his master's degree, and he's the director of the center. We have about six teachers that started with me when they were fourteen years old in the youth corps. There are not only Puerto Rican; there are blacks too. We have about five assistant teachers that started here—were working with me here in the center. And we've got a secretary. We have a lot of professionals. In Lincoln Hospital they have an associate director, Angel Laport, who started with me. So the people who started with us then showed that they had an interest in helping with problems; we kept many of them.

So that's the way that we started. Now I'm sixty-four years old, and in one more year I plan to retire because my husband is going to retire. But I feel that if I retire I'm going to volunteer because when I start something I want to volunteer. I feel sorry about the neighborhood. When we lived here it was a nice place to live. There were working people. But now the problem is that we don't have any working people in the neighborhood, and we had to cut our services because we didn't have any children in the center. This was a nice neighborhood. My husband and I work shifts. I used to meet and work with my door open, and we didn't have any problems. But the neighborhood now is deserted. The neighborhood has more housing and more programs coming through the federal programs, but the state has cut back.

Only a few families stayed, about three families. There used to be a lot of professional people living here. I've been living here for about fifteen years. After they started moving out we had a lot of changes. The comptroller used to live in this neighborhood. We called him Dr. Pocachino [Mario Procaccino]. But Pocachino moved, and then the neighborhood started going down. We have a church, a nice congregation, a lot of funds, but when the working people started moving out from the neighborhood, we had to have fundraisers and other kinds of things in order to survive.

In the seventies we had a lot of drugs. I was involved in that. I was the representative advisor. I used to work with Rikers Island. We accepted about two thousand youths. Rikers sent me a list of youths that were out on bail, and I started helping them. I'm still doing that but on a volunteer basis. We want to conserve the neighborhood. We sit in the jails helping those youth to try and change their mind. We had a lot of drugs, stealing, and people moving away.

Father Banome is doing a lot of work trying to rehabilitate the buildings in this neighborhood. Here where we are we have a nice house. A doctor lives here; it's a very nice house. In front we have about six family houses, and across the street from here we have a big building, beautiful apartments. But there are a lot of people that are not working people, don't have jobs. And we have a problem at the day-care center because we are underenrolled. We're supposed to serve 168 children but now we don't have working people, and we don't have the families. But we are still trying. We have a tutoring program here, and I'm still trying to help the people to become useful. We serve two- to ten-year-old children at the day-care center. The preschool is from two to six years, and then the after-school is from seven to ten. Depending on their income they have to pay. We help with reading, math, and anything else. You see them doing their homework. The program is from nine to three, and then from three to six we start the tutoring classes.

Father Banome used to be chairman of the planning board, and I'm a member of the planning board. Father Banome is working hard on some building he has in Monterey. Can we take the neighborhood back in twenty years? We have other people in my neighborhood like Juan Santos. He works as a volunteer. He's the founder of West Farms Projects,[6] from Tremont to 179th Street. He's a very active member of the community. West Farms Project was founded about nine years ago. That's primarily a housing program. We have about eight buildings. We have guards who walk you to your house when you come home late at night, so they are safe. We started with plans for about fifteen houses, but with the budget cuts we've been cutting and cutting, and I don't know what will happen in June when we will have more budget cuts. If we are not funded at the end of June I will still continue serving the community but on a volunteer basis.

I feel that people should have to work hard to support their families. Of course there are some with problems who can't work, and welfare is for people who are sick or have other problems. That was President Roosevelt's idea. But I see other people who don't try to do anything for themselves and their children, who came here just to live on welfare, and their children will do the same from generation to generation. We have to do something about that. They try to live from the taxes that you and I pay, and I feel that they should get training and they should work. And I think youth from poor families who want to continue their education should get financial aid, and it's wrong to make cuts in that. I disagree with President Reagan about that. But I do feel that people on welfare should get training and then get decent work.

We have a foster grandparent group with people sixty and older who work four hours with children that have emotional problems. It's a program run through the hospital, and they work four hours with a stipend of two dollars an hour, and their travel is paid. There are 110 older people in the entire Bronx working in this program. It's the only program like this in the Bronx. We look for more people to join the program and work with these children. We have thirteen sites, and we want to cut costs at some of our sites in order to open other sites. The children in the program call the older people "grandparents."

I have three children of my own. My oldest son is sick; he's in Schuyler Hospital. My daughter is working in the community as the counselor in an after-school program. We sent her to Elizabeth Seton College in Yonkers because she wanted to be a nurse, and my husband wanted her to be a nurse. She was there one year, and then she dropped out. She was out for two years, but now she says she wants to start again and get a degree.

My son was going to Lehman College, and he was very intelligent, but then he got sick, and in the hospital they gave him some treatment, but then his leg got paralyzed. Father Banome was helping me complain to the hospital, but the doctor said there was nothing wrong with him, but he kept on complaining, and now his leg is still paralyzed. He didn't want to live, was suicidal, but now he's getting better. He's in Schuyler Hospital, and he's improving. He's just twenty-eight years old. He went to college for two semesters. He was taking economics courses because he's very good in economics. When he applied to the college he took a test, and he had the ninth highest average out of four thousand youths, and they gave him six advanced credits when he started college.

Now he wants to continue his education because when he goes to the hospital he sees people that have more problems than he does, and he's comparing, and this helps him; it's like therapy, and then he wants to help other people. The doctor says that what's wrong with his leg is he was born with a problem, something in his brain. But it's getting better, and he wants to live and help other people. So I hope my son and my daughter will be able to continue their education, and they grew up watching me, and they both want to help people in the community. I am proud of them.

This organization is my heart, and I'm going to continue to serve the community as long as I can.

CHAPTER SIX
SUSAN

Susan Boyd, Community Organizer, b. 1944
Interview: May 24, 1982

"We stopped traffic on the George Washington Bridge all the way back up to Bruckner, all the way up to the Whitestone for about an hour, and then we left."

I was born in Springfield, Massachusetts, on December 12, 1944, and I didn't discover the Bronx until I started grad school at Fordham University's Rose Hill campus. As an economically poor grad student I ended up renting an apartment in the South Bronx. I gradually began to get to know the families in my neighborhood and to get interested in what was going on in the South Bronx, and eventually I quit grad school to become a full-time community organizer. I ended up living and working in the South Bronx for ten years.

In the summer of 1969 I took a summer job working for the East Tremont Housing, which was located on Tremont Avenue right near La Fontaine and right across from Crotona Park.[1] I got the summer job through a guy named George Fuller, who was executive director of the Twin Parks building.[2] He worked for the city, and he told me about it, and I interviewed for it. And this agency was a delegate agency at the Tremont Community Corporation.[3] And they had had some problems. I don't know too much about the problems, but evidently the director just before me did some stuff that he shouldn't have done, and they were going to lose their funding if they didn't bring in a director that, you know, the city would go along with. So while it was supposed to just be a summer job, I stayed there for two or three years.

When I got there the community was still a pretty viable area. I would define the area as Fordham Road on the north, West Farms on the east, Webster Avenue on the west, and the other end of Crotona Park on the south. And at that time it encompassed the Arthur Avenue neighborhood, which was primarily Italian and white. The population was just about one-third Hispanic, one-third black, and one-third white at that time. There were very few abandoned buildings. Tremont Avenue was still a pretty viable shopping center. Crotona Park was pretty much in demise. I think the first summer I started, one of the things was to try to get that swimming pool, which hadn't been opened for a while. The whole playing area had been let go. The signs of deterioration were there, but it didn't seem hopeless, but over the course of ten years—roughly 1969 to 1979—it was simply lost. I think people will argue forever about the reasons for that.

When I first came in, the Community Planning Board was fairly well representative. Blacks and Hispanics were just getting on the board because of the antipoverty program. It was pretty much dominated by Italians and Jewish, I'd say, in terms of ethnic groups, and just beginning to get some black and Hispanic leadership. It's funny, because the area, whenever we went to the city or we did anything or we argued for anything, one of the strong points that we always made was that it was a third, a third, and a third. That was interesting, that it was one of the best-integrated neighborhoods in the area. But actually the third whites really lived mostly on Arthur Avenue, and one of the things that eventually almost brought Arthur Avenue down to its knees was when they were going to build Fordham Hospital, the new Fordham Hospital, and they destroyed about a five-square-block area of private homes. They relocated 450 families out of that area and of course never built the hospital, right beside St. Barnabas Hospital. I think you can go there still and see a blank, nothing there, unless they've started to build housing there now. I haven't been in a long time.

I used to live in the northwest area of the Italian area in the Dennis Lane co-ops for a while.[4] I lived in all the different parts of the neighborhood. I always lived in the neighborhood while I worked there, until the last two years. I decided that I wanted to check out Manhattan, and then I came back and bought the house here. But I started off on Marion Avenue and then Park Avenue and Crotona Avenue in the Dennis Lane.

At that time the Hispanic population was almost all Puerto Rican. I knew hardly anybody who wasn't. It wasn't until the last three or four years that the Dominicans came, and the Spanish Haitians, French Haitians, and even the black population was mostly what I guess you'd call American black, southern black, a big migration. There was a tremendous amount of rivalry for the antipoverty money between them.[5] Usually when I went into a building to organize a building, it was either all black or all Hispanic. So a street could be integrated, but buildings were usually pretty much black or pretty much Hispanic from what I noticed. And always one, two, or three whites, and if not elderly, extremely poor white people that were living around the Tremont nucleus area.

When I got there, Twin Parks was about to be built, and I got very involved with Twin Parks. I was in the Twin Parks Association, and I was an officer in that. The clergy was very strong in those days. There were a couple of Lutheran ministers and a Baptist minister and Father Mario Ziccarelli, who was the pastor of Our Lady of Mount Carmel over on Arthur Avenue. And there was another priest, Pat McCormick at Our Savior's Church. He was very involved with the community, but he never got too involved in the antipoverty program.

He saw a lot of problems right away, and he got out of it. He eventually married my roommate, and they live out in New Jersey now. Pat was in the Bronx for many, many years. For a while Crotona Park was sort of a barrio, and that's why Twin Parks was built. The concept behind Twin Parks was what they called "vest-pocket housing." They never did Phase II, though. Phase I was to go into an area where there were vacant lots of buildings that should be torn down, and they would build this housing. And Phase III was to rehabilitate the housing next to them. They only carried out one of those rehabilitation projects that I recall. I don't think they ever built the public housing that was supposed to go along with it. When I left, that was all on hold. I know that they were starting to come before the Community Planning Board with designs for the public housing that was supposed to go on 180th Street, but I don't know if they actually went into the ground.

So there was this whole neatly conceived program, but there was a lot of politics too, because before I came in, the community had already lost the battle of high-rise. They did not want high-rises. High-rises was definitely against the wishes of the community. In fact, one of the interesting things that I noted in my whole career: We were very good at predicting dire consequences. We were always right. We knew what the community needed, and we knew what we needed. The government always came in and told us to do it another way. We were forced into the positions of "either you don't get it at all, or you do it our way." And they were always wrong. They just created new slums. The big mistake they're making over on West Farms now was something I argued about until I was blue in the face, and that's that they redid almost every single building in West Farms, and every single one of them is subsidized, which means that they created a community of people on welfare—thousands and thousands and thousands—with no other economic mix. This neighborhood has a good economic mix now and may make it because of that, if it keeps its economic mix. But they took that away from a lot of neighborhoods by going in just crazy, crazy, and they wouldn't listen to anybody. If the funds were there, they'd take it. Twin Parks was an example of that.

They also, of course, made a tremendous amount of money, and we were supposed to get money from the sale of the equity on these buildings, and I don't really know whatever happened to all that money—hundreds and hundreds of thousands of dollars, a lot of shoddy workmanship. You know, the same typical UDC.[6] And UDC in those days could come in and do anything they wanted. They didn't have to go by local zoning laws. They could bypass all the local laws, and they pretty much pushed us around, and we didn't have much choice, and the fights were endless, and the squabbles were endless. And when they finished building, they left.

One of the things that was done when Twin Parks was begun was that they opened up a community office or what they called a relocation office. And the woman who was in charge of that was Ann Cunningham, and they kept track of every tenant who was taken out of the building. And so when new buildings were built, they had first choice if they met the income requirements. And that was handled to the best of everybody's ability. To the best of everybody's ability, the people that were supposed to get into these buildings got in them. But it was in the days before computers and stuff like that, because computers weren't readily used back then. Nowadays all that stuff would be put on computers, and you could keep better track. A lot of people fell by the wayside and probably didn't get in when they should have, and then a lot of politics, "my friend," "your friend," that kind of stuff. But that's kind of normal stuff. But what happens with a lot of these buildings, and what happened with Twin Parks, is that what they call a fair-market rental, anybody that could afford to pay that amount of rent in those buildings didn't want to live in the neighborhood. So you ended up with practically 100 percent subsidy throughout the buildings, and some of them are in pretty bad shape today as a result. If you are so poor that your rent is subsidized, you can't afford to take care of the place, so it's the whole cycle all over again. And what the community wanted was low-rise, which would have prevented a lot of the problems, because you just have a more manageable, controllable situation, and they didn't get that.

Some of the big successes were the senior citizen housing at the end of Arthur Avenue on Southern Boulevard. They're pretty successful to this day. That's what the Italian neighborhood wanted. That's what they needed the most. That's what they requested, so that's what they got. There was a lot of racial flare-up when those were being tenanted that I recall, as to who was really getting into them. I think they're probably 99 percent white if one were to go and look at them today. It wouldn't surprise me. There's hardly any black or Hispanic.

There were a couple of race riots. I remember one night there was a race riot on Crotona Avenue, which was at the very edge of the Arthur Avenue neighborhood. There is another church there, I think it's Thomas Aquinas. Some black kids wanted to go in and play in the gym, and the priest closed it. The tactical police force was up there and all that kind of stuff. So there were tensions. There were those kinds of tensions when Twin Parks was coming in.

You didn't get paid for being on the planning board. And those people varied. Some were professional like me in a sense, and some just had other jobs and were on the planning board. The planning boards, when the city government was restructured—ostensibly giving the planning boards much more power and having the planning board areas contiguous with a police area, trying to make them all contiguous lines with a hospital area and whatever—became very political. And the planning board when I left was becoming very abused. A lot of things that shouldn't have happened were beginning to happen. People were using their positions on the planning board to get their own housing projects through, were voting for each other ("You vote for me, I'll vote for you"), and a lot of control was lost. Kind of sad. It wasn't the way it was in the beginning. Housing money came in, and people began to understand how it worked, and how the financing worked, and where the money was. That's when the fighting really started, and what was once a cohesive neighborhood where we all would get together and party together and have a good time ended, as each person wanted a little piece. That's when I left because it wasn't worth being involved in anymore. It wasn't where it was at. And then, of course, when you work twelve to fourteen hours a day for ten years and often seven days a week and see it get worse and worse and worse . . . every single day another building would go or this would happen or that would happen. That's what I mean by burnout. After a while you really kind of burn out.

There were a lot of good things that happened. I started out with the Tremont Community Corporation, and I built up a reputation in housing, and this group called Phipps Houses, which is where Rae works now, they had groundbreaking probably around 1973. Howdy Phipps was very involved, and it was to shore up that area where people get off the El and go into the back part of the zoo. That had a lot to do with it. At that time, West Farms was a very viable little area. A lot of it went fast because of greed. People were fighting over housing, over "I'm going to do this block and you do that block." If you were in a community group and you were smart, you could make big, big money on the sale of the equity, because you could keep the developer from coming into your neighborhood, and you would make financial deals with him on the sale of the equity, and you'd get a playground or you'd get actual cash or you'd get your thing funded, or you'd get a church built. Oh, yes. So once the community learned how the financing worked, then they became quite aggressive as to what they were going to do to get a piece of that money, and that's when it became quite ugly—very, very, very ugly—I mean threats and beatings and all kinds of stuff. You could be talking big, big dollars—in the hundreds of thousands of dollars.

Tremont had power when they were all together, and that's what they blew. They lost their power when they started fighting each other. They blew power for money, and they really could have done a lot more if they had sat down and done it in a more rational way. But after a while it got to a point where you took your life into your hands to go to a planning board meeting. I mean almost literally, from what I understood in the very end. That's how they lost their power.

I think another thing that hurt the Bronx—which is kind of a hard thing to say and hurt us to a large extent—is that at that time Bob Abrams was the borough president of the Bronx,[7] personally a fabulous person, somebody I admire very much. But he was a reform Democrat, and he was the person we had to go to all the time, and we were a little naive in those days and didn't realize that a reform Democrat couldn't get a darn thing done. And we were always going to Bobby for stuff, and he'd be able to pull off a few things, but we didn't realize that where the real power lay was with Patrick Cunningham,[8] and that's who we should have been going to and laying our eggs in that basket. I really think that that's something I probably would do differently again even though I'd have to pull in some of my own ethical standards to have gotten involved with those guys. You wouldn't have had to do anything illegal or anything. You might just have to support somebody you thought was a schmuck. But we certainly would have gotten what we wanted a lot easier and a lot faster, and we didn't realize that back then. We were outside the establishment, and it was a big mistake. But I can only call it a mistake with hindsight, because we didn't know that until a long time later. But that was one of our crucial errors that we had made because I was too naive about politics at that time. We couldn't pull anything off. And when it really got to the nitty-gritty, we had trouble pulling stuff off because of that. I'm pretty much convinced of that now.

There was a commissioner of health in New York City, Dr. Howard Brown. He was quite well known because he came out of the closet when he was commissioner, and that kind of undid him. He was one of the first gays to come out of the closet. I don't know why he had to come out of the closet. He was pretty much obviously a gay man, but I guess in terms of a stereotype, a lovely man in many ways, a nice guy. He was a human being like anybody else, and he could play his politics too, but he was a nice guy. He ended up as the head of ambulatory medicine at Fordham Hospital. When he came into Fordham Hospital he was pretty much tuned into the community, and I think one of the first things he noticed was that all of a sudden there was this incredible amount of Albanians running all over Fordham, and it got to be a pretty serious problem at the hospital because the husbands would pull a gun on the doctor if the doctor started examining their wives, and stuff like that. The Albanians were wilder than the other groups. There were always shootings under the Third Avenue El, just unbelievable, and vendettas all the way from Yugoslavia and Albania and Italy, because they were refugees from three places—Albania, Yugoslavia, and Italy—and it wasn't until the late sixties that the federal government made good on one of its war relocation promises, which was to bring these Albanian refugees to the United States. And of course, where did they put them? In the most rural setting in the whole United States, in the Bronx, New York—in Fordham, Tremont. I think the government did this deliberately. And once one came, everybody would end up here. That was how Dr. Brown explained it to me.

He decided that something had to be done about this, plus a lot of other community health problems, so he got himself a grant with the federal government. This was all happening when the Health Services Administration was coming out and all the new laws about community participation and all kinds of stuff like this, all happening kind of at the same time. So he got himself a pilot grant, and he hired two people, a Puerto Rican woman, Blanche Sanchez, and a black guy named Butler. He hired them, and they went out into the community, and the first thing they tried to do was establish a community council, a health council. So they came to me because I was in an agency, and they came to Al Rivera and people like that, and they asked us if we would come to this meeting, and lo and behold, we'd all been invited to the same meeting, and here we were. And because of Dr. Brown, when the whole Health and Hospitals Corporation restructured, Tremont already had a knowledgeable lay group that had been working in health for almost two years. They had taught us everything. Blanche had taught us what was going on all over the Bronx, what the health-care issues were, what the problems were, and we ate it up. We had ourselves a new issue. Fordham Hospital had an issue. When I first came down to Fordham University as a student, my roommate had said to me, "There are two things I want to warn you about. If you get sick, never go to Fordham Hospital, and if you get hungry, never eat at White Castle."

Anyway, that's how I got into health, and when they started with the whole reorganization of the Health and Hospitals Corporation—because it used to be called Department of Hospitals and then they created a whole corporation, and then they created all the subcorporations of the hospitals and all this kind of stuff—we were there. And when it came time for the community boards of all the hospitals, we were all ready. We were the very first community board in New York City to be installed. But we gave up. We went back to Harlem when they gave us our certificates. We all refused to take them because they wouldn't let us structure our board the way we wanted it structured, and they wouldn't accept our by-laws the way we wanted our by-laws. We played our power, and we won. That was their mistake. They let us win that issue. Our by-laws said that if the doctors were on our board, then we had to be on the medical board. The Health and Hospitals Corporation was against that, and we refused to give in, and we won. And we were the only hospital community board that I know of that had community representation. This happened in the early seventies. I was still at Tremont Housing Clinic when Dr. Brown came.[9] We were going for almost three years before Fordham Hospital was closed in 1974 or '75.

Then this psychiatric group came along, Dr. Ed Hornik, and they wanted to open up the Tremont Crisis clinic and all that kind of stuff. Well, here was our group, and we became the board of the Tremont Crisis clinic, and we tried to integrate all the health services, and we got all these people involved, and we helped to design that program, and that program is still going. We had a good group: me and Al Rivera and Petra Laman and Brother Patrick and Bob Banome and Paul Matson and Dewey Sands. There was a core group of about twenty of us, including Harry Keifitz, who I always fought with all the time, but he was usually involved. There was Ada Quiñones, Edwin Martinez, a lot of people from the antipoverty program, a core group of about twenty people that were pretty much involved in everything, and we could get our forces together in a hurry if we had to. We were very well organized, and a couple of people from the city were very helpful to us, people that we could pretty much trust. Bob Abrams was very involved in all the stuff that we were involved in.

Anyway, in those years Fordham Hospital went from one of the dingiest places to one of the finest emergency-care places. You could ask any cop. If he was shot in the Bronx he wanted to go to Fordham Hospital because Fordham Hospital was one of the only municipal hospitals which had no interns and residents in the emergency room. They were all licensed physicians, board-eligible, every single one of them, and specialists in emergency care. It was one of the very first emergency-care areas that didn't use interns and residents. They only came down to cover. There was a permanent emergency room staff. Fordham Hospital made money. It made three million dollars a year for the city of New York.

The city of New York lied about everything about Fordham Hospital when they closed it. Everything they said about Fordham Hospital was a lie, and it was a lie to cover up their own mismanagement and their own justification for building hospitals where they weren't needed, to give Montefiore a new hospital in the North Central Bronx. Fordham Hospital was code-compliant to the old law. In other words, there were two laws on the state of New York books because it was like a grandfather clause. When they started coming in and building new hospitals and coming up with new techniques and everything, they began to say you had to have so many square feet for a patient, but they protected older hospitals by saying that they could be code-compliant with the old law. And Fordham Hospital was always accredited year after year, every year, where Bellevue and Coler[10] always had problems with their accreditation because they didn't even comply with the old law, but Fordham always did. And yet they were saying that we couldn't stay open because we couldn't be accredited, and yet we were. We always passed our accreditation, which came up every two years, and it was a tremendous service to the community. They could almost walk to it. You could get to Fordham Hospital very, very quickly. Removing that destroyed the community. A lot of businesses on Fordham Road went when the hospital left, and then you had to go another three miles north to get to a hospital, which for people that were in the lower part of the district, like West Farms, it was a six-dollar taxi ride and a double-fare bus sum. So it really caused a tremendous amount of hardship. Basically, what it does is people don't go to the hospital. That's basically what happens. And North Central Bronx would have trouble outreaching its facilities, whereas Fordham was beginning to outreach its facilities. We tried to get Barnabas Hospital to take the place of Fordham, but they just couldn't see it at this time. And they did have one major problem. They could not get their pediatrics approved. I think that if they had let us in there and on their board and started working on it, we would have done it at Fordham. But St. Barnabas has no pediatric care, so therefore it's really not a full-service hospital. It cannot serve that community without pediatric care. It can't do it. So that's one of its big problems aside from many others.

The city used the 1976 fiscal crisis as an opportunity to crack down on a lot of city services, one of which was hospitals. They wanted to close Fordham. They wanted to close the ones they're fighting over right now—Greenpoint—because they're opening up Woodhull.[11] That fight never did get finished. And then there was another one down in Harlem, which they eventually closed. But Fordham Hospital, because we had been involved for so many years, had gained a lot of expertise. We were able to put up a fabulous fight. We just put up a heck of a battle. We lived in Fordham Hospital for seventy-nine days, and we went down to Washington to see Secretary of the Treasury Simon because we had found that the city of New York had lied on its application for funds from the federal government. They had lied on the finances of the Health and Hospitals Corporation. We knew what we were talking about. We found out things like that Columbia Presbyterian Hospital was noncompliant (and it still is, and Columbia is in trouble now), non–code compliant to the old law. And they've been very stubborn. We got very much into, "If you're going to pick on us for the reason that we're old and decrepit, okay, but what about Columbia Presbyterian? They are non–code compliant." They had something like hundreds of beds that were in violation of the New York State health codes. And when we got into it, we found that one of the main reasons why they were still non–code compliant was that the state wouldn't allow them to go through with applications to build unless they used their endowment, and they weren't willing to use their endowment, and so they couldn't get money, and they would rather be non–code compliant. So there was a lot of hanky-panky going on, and we were the kind of people that could find all that out.

The other thing that people didn't really know about the Health and Hospitals Corporation law was that it had a provision that eventually all of the hospitals would be spun off as subsidiary corporations where they could become independent. And we asked to let Fordham Hospital be the model. "Spin us off. Let us become a subsidiary corporation." We went to Booz Allen, one of these big financial consulting agencies, and they helped us work out a plan. We had it all down on paper, and we knew exactly what we could do. We had five-year projections of our income. We were so well prepared that the people at the corporation were really afraid of us. As a matter of fact they tore down Fordham Hospital one week after we met with them. In a week it was gone. It was the fastest teardown of a building I've ever seen in the city of New York. It was done with a vengeance. It had been empty a week or two when they came in with the wrecking crews. They were so afraid, because we were right. It was the classic case of "you can't fight city hall." It really was the classic case. And we gave it everything. We gave it absolutely everything we had in our physical and mental beings. We couldn't pull it off because they were just determined to close it down to protect North Central Bronx Hospital.

The doctors were all on our side. The doctors lost a lot because our affiliation was Misericordia Hospital, and they ended up going down to Lincoln. I don't even know if they're affiliated with Lincoln anymore. They had terrible problems down there, their cars being vandalized, this kind of stuff and that kind of stuff. They were on our side in the sense that they didn't do anything to mess us up. There were some people in the hospital that did. There were administrators and staff in the hospital, in Fordham Hospital, who had a vested interest in North Central Bronx, and they did everything they could to mess us up. But the doctors, the interns, the residents, and those kinds of people were right out there with us all the time. The nurses were fabulous. They helped us open up those wards. The maintenance men turned on the water for us so we could shower. They hooked up the electricity and gas in the kitchen so we could cook. I mean half of what we were able to do was because the employees in the hospital helped us to do it.

There were patients in the hospital when we took over. We took over an empty wing. We were never near any patients. In other words, we never interfered. We took over the administrator's office symbolically, and then right next to the administrator's offices as you walked into the hospital there was a wing that had already closed down and was sealed off by an iron gate. That's what we took over. So we were occupying an empty part of the hospital. We never got involved with patient care until they started sending nurses and doctors up to North Central Bronx before it was open for training, and we began to realize that there were whole wards with patients and without nurses. So we went to the State Department of Health and complained that they were in violation. I mean, somebody could have died easily. And the State Department of Health agreed with us, and the hospital was cited and told to bring those nurses back and that they couldn't go up there and train until they made provision for the patients that were still there in the hospital. And then eventually we just lost. There wasn't anything more we could do, and so we left. In the meantime they had violated the law so many times it was ridiculous. You can't close down a public hospital without having a public hearing, and they had announced the closing of the hospital and had never had the public hearing. And that was one of the things we had harped about in the press. We had press there every single day for seventy-nine days. Every day we were on television, the news. The *Post* reporter just lived there. It was incredible how we were able to sustain that. It was absolutely unbelievable. We would stay up all night long trying to figure out what we would do next to keep their interest. It was amazing.

Lowell Bellin was the head of the Health and Hospitals Corporation at that point. He announced that he was going to have a hearing, and this was just sheer sham and hypocrisy. So we decided that the best thing to do was to boycott the hearing. So we called up everybody we knew in the community health network, and they all agreed that they would boycott the hearing, and we decided to hold a press conference out in front of Worth Street instead of going to the hearing. So we hired a bus and we got about thirty, forty people, and we all dressed up, and we all went down to Manhattan for the hearing. Bob Abrams was there and Louis Gigante was there. I think Stanley Simon was there.[12] A whole bunch of the politicians were there. And about nine or ten of the media showed up. Heather Bernard was there for Channel 4; the *New York Times* was there, the *Post*, the *News*. Channel 5 was there. It was a really great press conference. Everybody showed up. Mostly they were talking to Abrams. He was being interviewed a lot. The very last reporter was interviewing him—I think he was the guy from the *Times*—and I'm standing on the side talking to Bert Weinert, who was Abrams's assistant, and I started noticing the horses, the police horses being put up. I remember saying to Bert, "Boy, if that's for us, they're about an hour late." We were just ready to go home. We were ready to go home in a few minutes. And Bert and I were talking, and I said, "You know, Bert, Lowell Bellin's probably upstairs," because he was going to have a hearing. And by the way, only one person showed up at his hearing, and he closed the hearing around nine-thirty, so we were successful. We knew he was fuming. And I said, "Why don't we see if Bobby's got some time? Maybe Bellin will talk to us. This is a great opportunity. We're all at the same place at the same time." So Bert said, "Great idea," so I went up and asked Bobby, and Bobby said "Great idea, no problem."

Rae Flores was an employee of the Health and Hospitals Corporation, so we dispatched her upstairs to go and tell Bellin that that's what we wanted to do. She comes downstairs and says "fine." They were so afraid of us that the front door was padlocked, so we go around to the side door. Al Rivera and I had IDs. I had a Fordham Hospital ID with my picture on it. There's a portico there. You have to walk through a portico. And then there's the doors. We're in the portico and just about to go through the door, and Al starts to open this door, and this guy comes running out from the other door and grabs Al and hits him, and before you know it, we are completely surrounded and beaten up, and I mean literally beaten up. I was knocked unconscious. I remember Bobby Abrams getting hit, and I remember him saying, "Stop!" And the guy creamed him and knocked him against the wall. Gigante got hit. Brother Patrick got hit. They just were gunning for us, and they were really gunning for me and Al. Al had a concussion. I'd been occupying the hospital and so had Al. They were really gunning for us.

I woke up—I don't know how long I was out, maybe two or three minutes—and there was nobody there. I woke up and I was still in the portico, and I walked out to the sidewalk, and my friend Marietta Myers (she was an architect and a hospital planner, a fabulous person who really stuck by us all the way through on Fordham Hospital) comes running up to me, and I'm kind of in a daze, and she says, "Get out, get out." She was very upset. And I walk out onto the sidewalk and there's Al on the other side of these barriers—they're all up now—lying on his stomach with handcuffs behind his back in agony. And Al's my best buddy, you know, so I was really, really upset. So I charged through the barriers thinking I know subconsciously that the barriers are there to keep people from coming on the sidewalk because of the fight, not to keep the people who were in the fight from getting out. I crashed through the barriers and some cop yells at me that I can't do that. And I said something like, "Well, my friend is hurt," and all of a sudden I'm in a full nelson. Now all I see is a suit jacket. So I swing like this and like that and I'm trying to get out of this full nelson. I don't know what the heck is going on, and this guy comes over with a billy club, and I see the billy club coming down, and all of a sudden a cop grabbed me by the arm (and it left me black and blue for almost two weeks), threw handcuffs on me, and threw me into the car. Later he told me he'd arrested me to save me from being hit by the billy club by the other cop. It turned out it was the captain of the precinct who had grabbed me. That's why he was in a suit.

Al and I ended up arrested and in jail and everything. Five years later we won a suit. I won fifteen thousand dollars and Al won twenty thousand dollars for false arrest and all that kind of stuff. We had gone there for a press conference. Al was in his best suit. The irony about it was that up at Fordham Hospital we had tried to do everything we could for eighty days to get arrested, and the one time we went down to Manhattan to have this very respectable press conference and to be respectable ourselves, we ended up getting arrested. I remember after I was hit inside the portico and was still in a daze—before I got arrested—Heather Bernard coming up to me and saying, "Don't worry about it. I'm not going to ruin your story tonight by making this the most important part of it. I'm going to get your point across." I remember her saying that to me in my daze. Shortly after that the city won and moved all the patients out.

But there's story after story about living in Fordham Hospital for all those days, wonderful stories. Abrams was terrific in trying to get the new Fordham Hospital built. But the whole sad part about it was that we had succeeded in getting the go-ahead on Fordham Hospital just prior to all of that fiscal crisis happening. The plans had been drawn. We insisted that there be a black architect or a minority architect, and they agreed to it. It was the first hospital in New York State that was going to be built as a joint venture with a minority architect. We had gotten pretty good at what we knew how to do, and we knew that we couldn't have a minority architect do the whole thing. So we worked out the joint venture. We helped interview the minority architect.

The whole neighborhood was shot to heck, and a lot of people lost a lot because the new Fordham Hospital was never built. It had gone all the way to full design, had been almost completely designed. Everybody was so excited. There were pictures of the new hospital. It had gotten to that point. There were endless meetings where we talked about design and how this should be and how that should be, the doctors, the community, everybody. It was going to be a fabulous hospital because everybody was in tune to it. Fordham Hospital was a living experience. Fordham Hospital wasn't an institution.

We had a reunion a few years ago. Four hundred people showed up for this reunion. People that I didn't even know that had worked at Fordham Hospital maybe twenty or thirty years ago heard about this reunion and came to it. It was just absolutely amazing. The old Fordham Hospital was the dingiest, crummiest, but we had worked so hard. It was really funny. It was such a dichotomy, because all this time that we were trying to get the new Fordham Hospital built we'd go down to the planning board, and we'd go down to the city and say, "It's such a dingy, crummy place. How can you let this go on?" And then when they were trying to close it down, we said, "This is such a wonderful place." We could find arguments for both sides. People who worked at Fordham Hospital and patients at Fordham Hospital were passionate about the place. It's very hard to explain. We could fight with the doctors and go out and have a drink with them after or go out to dinner. We could fight at the medical board, and they'd come to the annual Tremont Health Council dance.[13] They'd all come, and we'd have a ball. It was a real family. Fordham Hospital was a wonderful place, a wonderful experience.

Our patients would go down there, our double amputees. Everybody would go down to Manhattan to the Health and Hospitals Corporation. And they gave Lowell Bellin such a hard time. It used to drive him crazy when we came down with our double amputees. They were fabulous people. They were our home-care patients. Fordham Hospital had one of the best home-care systems in the city, in all the city hospitals, a wonderful home-care department. And they wanted to cut that out one time, so we got all our home-care patients and brought them right down there. That just about killed them. We were always doing stuff like that. And we always had everybody's support—the doctors, the administrators—because it was the administrators who had to get all the home-care people together for us and provide the ambulances and transportation, and they did it. They always did it. They always found a way.

The residents of the community felt this was a neighborhood. When Dr. Holloman came up for the public hearings on Fordham Hospital, we filled up Roosevelt High School, standing room only, and that was the community. We filled up every single seat in that auditorium. But it was sometimes fickle. I think towards the end if more residents had gathered around and realized what was happening—if we had had more neighborhood power, what you would call grassroots or pavement-level—if they had come out in full force, I don't think the city could have stopped us.

We once did a parade with probably three to four hundred people, which is a pretty good amount of people for a neighborhood type of rally. Anthony Bouza was there.[14] We had an itinerary and we told the police. We were always very cooperative with the police. They were very good to us, and they wouldn't arrest us, even when we were trying to get arrested for the publicity, and that made us endlessly unhappy! So we decided to have this big parade and everything, and we were going down Webster Avenue. What the police didn't know was that the parade was going to end up stopping traffic on the Cross Bronx Expressway. We all knew it. The whole crowd knew it. Before they knew what was happening we were up on that ramp, all four hundred of us, and we caused a traffic jam that was absolutely unbelievable, and we drove those policemen bananas because they were under orders not to arrest us. We know they were, because the city didn't want that kind of publicity. We knew it. We caused a massive traffic jam. We went right up that ramp at Webster Avenue—kids, elderly, everybody—and we stopped traffic on the George Washington Bridge all the way back up to Bruckner, all the way up to the Whitestone, for about an hour and then we left. We waited for the newspaper report that afternoon. We told the police, "Get the papers here. Get the papers here, and we'll leave." We handed out leaflets to all the people. We had it all planned, too, about traffic accidents. If you were in a traffic accident on Webster Avenue, do you realize you would have to go seven miles to get medical care if they close Fordham Hospital? And we had statistics as to how many traffic accidents had come into Fordham Hospital in the last five years. We always had our act together. Peyser came in.[15] He helped us out a lot. He had a statistical survey done which was quite fascinating. This was one we hadn't thought of. He had the emergency room physicians go back about nine months. I think they did a thousand patients, went back a thousand patient records, and did an assessment of how many of those patients probably medically would not have lived if they had had to go another twenty minutes in an ambulance. It was amazing. It was something like 89 percent in their judgment would not have lived. I mean, that was the kind of detail that we were getting down to. We tried every argument we could think of to keep that hospital open, but we just couldn't do it.

PART THREE
THE STABILIZERS

Resistance to the Blight: One Apartment Building, One Church at a Time

I. Born in the Bowery in 1930, Father Robert Banome moved up to the Bronx in 1963 after seven years in East Harlem. His name surfaces in most of the community organizers' memories as he participated with them in volunteer and community boards to help with housing—often subsidized housing—with substance abuse and mental health issues, with classes for children and services for seniors. But balancing the story of his efforts to combat drugs and serve the community is the story of his fight to preserve St. Joseph's Church when the Catholic Church itself planned to demolish it, a fight that he won against all odds. Fordham Hospital was razed to the ground, but St. Joseph's still stands today.

II. Born in Baltimore in 1925, Eae Mitchell moved up to the Bronx from Harlem at a time when neighborhoods were going through the transition from European to black and Hispanic, when buildings that had been well kept—"lovely brass when I moved in"—were increasingly neglected, and decay was setting in. Rather than wait for landlords to act—and realizing that the landlords themselves were often overwhelmed as new tenants, instead of maintaining apartments, were vandalizing them—he formed a tenants' association and over time not only stabilized his own building but managed almost a dozen buildings after his landlord, Sidney Greenstein, Moe's brother, sponsored him for the necessary training and license.

III. Bishop Ernest Crooms, born in the South in 1925 and moving to the Bronx with his wife when he was twenty, found a building, thanks to Moe Greenstein, in which to house the apostolic Rapture Preparation Church. In a run-down neighborhood with abandoned buildings and rubble in the streets, the presence of that church building slowly improved the neighborhood as he and his parishioners fixed it up, restored the plumbing, mended what was broken, even put in storm windows. Welcoming many teenagers from broken homes, he was proud that after twenty years the children of those children were in the church and reaching marriage age. In similar language Mitchell told me that twenty-six children were born in his building, his second generation, and Carmen Bermudez told me of the many teens whom she trained as volunteers and who later earned degrees and were directors or managers in agencies or institutions, including Lincoln Hospital. In almost biblical terms, their influence carried from generation to generation.

St. Joseph's Church (BRACHS Archives)

CHAPTER SEVEN
FATHER BOB

Father Robert Banome, Priest, St. Joseph's Church,
Bathgate Avenue; 1930–1992
Interview: January 15, 1982

"I don't know much about economics. All I know is that the people who are the neediest are the ones who are suffering. I don't see these people who are millionaires as the ones who are suffering."

"The picture was torn, and we put it together . . . and that was a sign."

I explain my vocation by remembering what it says in the scriptures, that the Lord uses the weak things of the world to confound the strong and the foolish to confound the wise. That is how I can understand how he could even begin to use me as an instrument. What I mean by that: being a maverick. I am a maverick. I am not in the general mold of what people would consider a priest to be. Many people actually ask, "Are you a priest?" I don't dress like a priest. I don't talk like a priest. I guess I don't act like a priest.

I was born on Mott Street in Little Italy near the Bowery and lived in that area for twenty-six years. I was ordained at St. Joseph's Seminary in 1956 and said my first Mass at St. Patrick's old cathedral down on Mott Street. I learned Italian on the street as I learned Spanish on the street, and consequently both languages are pretty bad, but very useful. I spent seven years in East Harlem, which to me was a magnificent preparation for the difficulties that we encountered here in the South Bronx. When I came to this area in 1963 there was still a good number of middle-class Irish families, German families, and a good number of Hispanic families. I arrived here, and it was more or less a traditional type of ministry that priests were engaged in, providing services to the community and providing the sacraments. The church was very involved with the youth at that time through sports, social activities, and also politically. The Murphy Housing was named after a gentleman who had been a parishioner of this church.[1]

But already it was a time of transition. Families were struggling with the changes. It was hard to tell exactly what they wanted to do. Should they stay? Should they go?

Should they fight? They decided to go, and thereupon began the terrible deterioration of the neighborhood. They moved up north to St. Barnabas Parish, which would be south of Yonkers. They moved to north of Fordham Road, they moved to the Northwest Bronx, to the Northeast Bronx, and they moved to Yonkers. They saw that the area was just going down. There were fires starting, a great number of fires beginning, and people's language they didn't understand, people's language they didn't want to understand. They couldn't understand why people don't speak English. "They're in this country; they should speak English."

So there was this, and then you could see it in the church, in the little struggle. Are there more Spanish coming to Mass than there are English-speaking people coming to Mass? And who is going to use the hall, and who is going to get the attention, and who is going to decide what happens here? The very little things. I wasn't a pastor at the time, I was an assistant. Very distressed, very, very distressed by the whole thing, and completely outraged by the lack of charity and understanding that I found among so-called Christian people. That would always distress me because, you know, you read the scriptures and you say you believe the word of God, and at the same time your practice, your lifestyle belies that. I mean, you can be threatened by enemies, but not everybody that doesn't speak your language or dress the way you dress or eat the way you eat is an enemy, after all. No sense of understanding. It was an alienation, even on the part of the people who answered the door in the rectory. They made you feel unwelcome. That distressed me enormously. The priests tried very hard. In my time we attempted to learn Spanish so that we could work with the arrivals, the huge numbers of people arriving from Puerto Rico at that time. And I think that Cardinal Spellman was very foresighted in making the opportunity available to his priests and encouraging them, because our parishes were going to be inundated with these people who would need the solace and the comfort and the direction that our church could give them, should give them.

However, by 1970 I would say that this neighborhood was completely decimated, so much so that even the archdiocese was toying with the idea of tearing down St. Joseph's Church, this enormous church, because of a problem, a fiscal problem, that the church was having—and without much attempt, I believe, to really see whether or not that was necessary. This magnificent landmark, this church that had stood and actually towered over a good portion of this part of the Bronx, and then it was, I believe, the faith, the determination, and the conviction that I have that fought that decision and won.

I remember these consultants coming up to the Bronx. "I mean, what is here? This place can only go down. We're talking about Bathgate, Tremont. What can happen here? This can only go from bad to worse." And I said, "Yes, if you're talking about the next fifteen years. But if you're talking about the next fifty years, then not." That all will be coming down, there will be developments in housing.

This is the belly of the city. How could they allow this? Well, from that moment on, from 1970, you never saw such deterioration, such rapid deterioration. We had five hundred fires a month, going constantly. Whatever the reason for that was, it was the system; it was the welfare system. It was the greed of the landowners, those who owned these buildings and wanted to make a quick profit, who saw that a new element was coming in, a difficult element that they would have to deal with, skyrocketing prices, which made them want to get their insurance. And so people on drugs would be hired; they were professional arsonists who would be hired to do in a building, for a hundred dollars to set fire to a building. These were buildings in which people still lived. This was throughout the South Bronx. I remember the clergy, the ministers, the rabbis, the priests got together in the borough president's office. It was Abrams at the time, with Mario Merola,[2] the representatives of the federal government, the representatives of the Police Department, the representatives of the FBI, indicating that, let's accept the idea that this is an arson problem. They blamed the people in the South Bronx. Unbelievable. Would you believe that it was very hard for them to admit that it might be the rich, the landlords, and not the poor tenants? There was this Bouza, Chief Inspector Bouza. I remember him, and he thought that we were being very naïve about this arson. That was what they were saying.

But from that moment on, serious attention began to be given to the arson problem—not only here in the Bronx but throughout the city where insurance companies were paying out billions of dollars. They were saying that people were burning down their own apartments. So naïve. Yes, that is true for some people. I promise you, if I'm living in a garbage-y apartment, and if I burn it down the landlord may give the apartment to city housing, I'll burn my apartment down. That wasn't what was happening. The main cause was this profit motive on the part of many people making billions of dollars. The unfortunate decision was made to let things go. What do they call that? It wasn't Manifest Destiny, but planned shrinkage.[3] Let it go. You'll have to move out, everybody will go, and then we can begin to plan and develop that area. Tear down the buildings, let them burn themselves out, just clear the whole area and we'll have planned shrinkage, and then we'll be able to plan better for you. And the poor, of course, would have to shift for themselves. This is what happened during the time that I was here, and what I began to do was to determine that either I would leave my ministry if it didn't take a different tack or I would become involved in what was happening on the streets, involved in a process to bring change, to help people to realize that their involvement was extremely important. So I got involved.

Our hospitals were being closed. Fordham Hospital was closed. There wasn't a professional that lived within miles of the Bronx. I don't have any professional people living in my parish, no doctors, lawyers. Our people have office jobs, they have factory jobs, they are maintenance people, they are teachers' assistants, they help in the hospitals. The programs that we have developed in the Bronx, they are now in home attendant programs, working in homes, taking care of the disabled, and there are people who work in our community health center. They are people who work in St. Barnabas Hospital, they are people who are janitors in the buildings that are around. They are mostly black and Hispanic. Our senior citizen centers are mostly black. People who were here and have stayed here.

So then we got involved in the Community Planning Board, and we got involved in the political system, so that now I don't think there are many political leaders that I do not know or that I am not involved with or who are not involved with me or who are not aware of my presence and what we're doing here. In this time we started with a Head Start program, in this very office where we pay twenty dollars a month, and now we've grown to a multimillion-dollar service agency that gives the community mental health services, to children, to the elderly, to our committee of health centers. We are helping through our home attendant program 200 disabled or elderly people who are in their own homes. Our drug-free program, VIP,[4] of which I'm the director, dealing with 150 young adults who have been tortured and destroyed by substance abuse problems. That means 150 families. Through our housing we're bringing back revitalization to an area that was considered dead. Bathgate Corridor was horrible.[5] There was nothing there. This new housing will bring a great change and improve the quality of life for a good number of people. It's Section 8 housing, so they have to qualify according to the Section 8 housing government federal legislation. That means that you have to have a certain income to qualify for this housing, and if you do, the government subsidizes your rent. Supposing the apartment is estimated through the mortgage loans at five hundred dollars, you will have to pay one hundred twenty-five and the government will pay three hundred seventy-five. You pay one-quarter of your income for your housing, and there are people on welfare who would pay that rental. So that has been a great boon. The housing is really good. In the Hunts Point area, Father Gigante has over one thousand units of housing. We will have, hopefully, four or five hundred units that we will be involved in. At the same time we're involved in the city-owned buildings, those that are marginal, that are not abandoned. We have a lot of poor people living there. We're helping those tenants to maintain those buildings and to run those buildings if they don't become vacated and abandoned.

The fires have diminished. There's nothing left to burn down. Night and day, night and day, it was unbelievable, all the fires. And then the establishment began to restore jobs, housing, and health, the areas that we have concentrated in. And through the Bathgate Industrial Park[6] that Mayor Koch and the city have developed, with Ed Logue,[7] it will bring hundreds and hundreds of jobs to people in the community. That's right down the block. The corridor begins at the Cross Bronx, south to the Claremont Parkway from Webster Avenue to Third Avenue. It's an enormous stretch of land, like ninety-nine acres or something like that. These will be jobs for people living in the area, in the mid-Bronx. Already they are very conscious and aware of what's going on in our neighborhood. We have 174 apartments. Without publicity we have had two thousand people apply for those 174 apartments. When it just was put in the paper today we will get another three thousand people. So we will have five thousand people wanting to live here. The desire to continue to live here is very strong. Father Gigante's response has been overwhelming. He had had as many as five thousand people apply for some of the units that he has developed there.

But I have gone beyond housing. I felt that they had other needs, and I'm on the board of visitors of the Bronx Psychiatric Center, the board of trustees of St. Barnabas Hospital. I established the Community Men's College Center working with the substance abuse problems that we have. We even have now in residence twenty-five women, women who have had an experience with drug abuse, and we've located that residence on the property of St. Barnabas Hospital. We hope that will expand to fifty women. I believe really in love demonstrating itself in action and need. It is very hard for me to preach about the love of God, the concern of God, if I don't demonstrate that love and concern to the people by attending to their needs when they're hungry or when they're naked and when they're ill. I feel that the quality of life that we have attempted to develop—housing, jobs, health—that with this the church that has been here giving them that spiritual care is also fulfilling its true mission. We also have our schools for education, which we feel is very important, with children from first grade to eighth grade. There was a time when the fires and the dispersal of population made us think about closing our school, but it was the cardinal who insisted that we maintain it even though we only had four grades then. He subsidized us as they still subsidize our church enormously. The concern of the cardinal and the church is manifest vocally through the people that represent them on the local level. I mean I'm supposed to do the job, and I mean if I'm not doing my job he's responsible in a way. But if I'm doing a good job he should take the credit because he has me here able to do those things. He is the cardinal, other than the time when we had the problem with the church, and he was very concerned with it because there was nothing here to keep this enormous building. He's very happy that the priest and the sisters—we have our sisters working on the residence for women, we have our sisters working in the parish, in the school, in the drug program. We have Brother Patrick, who has been a magnificent, strong-armed, and zealous servant of the people of Tremont and Fordham, a fantastic advocate. They all live in the South Bronx. I have no convent because our convent became our Senior Citizen Center, but sisters live on the Concourse on 163rd Street. One person lives on Beach Avenue. So the sisters live within the area.

I would have left a long time ago if the opportunity of involving myself very actively in the community did not come about. I was very distressed. It was the most depressing thing. At the same time there's tremendous hope. I never felt depressed or sad. I see the misery, but I see the presence of my God, I see the presence of Christ walking through the streets. You try to alleviate this suffering. I mean, you can't be depressed by it. Life is all around you. You can be depressed on Park Avenue. People throw themselves out the window there, I hear. So I think that it is what you see your mission as. What is your mission? What is your goal? Who am I? What do I do? What am I meant to do? What does the Lord want me to do? That should be the first question. So I think that you determine that and live it every day. In twenty-five years of my priesthood I could never say I felt I had to quit. I have had a pain in my body, I have had debilitating kinds of things, but I have tremendous faith that the Lord is using the weak things of the world to confound the wise.

I do not wait for people to do things for me. I nudge them. I make them help me do things. I don't want them to do things for me. I want them to help me to do things. As my people tell me, "I don't want you to do things for me, I want you to help me to do things." And that's why, in regard to the politics, the mayor came one Sunday and I told him to speak to the people. Then I got a call from a local commentator, a news reporter, and he said to me that the pope said that you should not be involved in politics. I said to him that this is my mayor, these are my people, he has helped me to gain housing, health services, why should not I let him talk to my people? I'm not telling them to vote for him. I don't give a damn whether they did or they didn't. That's none of my problem, but it's like a distortion. I don't feel that I should be a political person. I should be training and preparing my people to assume the leadership and the roles that are essential in order to help them to accomplish changes to improve the quality of the life that they live. I should be doing that. I am a teacher. That's what my role is meant to be. You fight for what you believe, you make people listen to you. What are we going to do, fall down and die?

At first I was mistrusted, and even I believe that I was hated. They hated me. They saw me as supporting the Hispanics. They believed that I came off a banana boat, an Italian who was not a bit submissive, but arrogant, proud, opinionated, strong-willed, Taurian. I wasn't going to let anybody walk over me. And I saw them spit when I walked the street. And it took a long time for them to change. No matter what I put on I always looked Mafioso. No matter what I did. I could wear the most beautiful garments and vestments in the world, and I'd still look Mafioso. I'd look out of place. I didn't fit into the mold. Physically unattractive, Mafioso-type person who was proud, arrogant, and those other things, and I was not adapted to sit down on my behind when the pastor, who is a marvelous gentleman, didn't even really care about what was going on outside. That wasn't my idea, to sit on my behind. When I was in Harlem I was on the street all the time, all the time, walking those streets of East Harlem. I was never attacked because I must look very threatening to people, so, never. I was even in West Harlem. I was for several months in West Harlem in a parish that was 100 percent black, and I walked the streets, made Communion calls, visited. In the middle of the night I got calls and I walked, I had no car, and I walked those streets in Harlem and never felt fear. Now that I'm a little older and wiser I'm a little more cautious. I take nothing for granted. I take precautions. This is a dangerous neighborhood at night, very, very, really extremely dangerous. You can't see it. It's what you can't see.

People are desperate. These are becoming desperate times, and they're going to get worse. I wondered, I just glanced at Reagan's talk to these multimillionaires in which he's saying that churches should adopt ten families, and that would cut down on the welfare. I just feel, does that mean that that eliminates their responsibility? I don't understand that. Are they going to give what is necessary or do what is necessary to alleviate that? He's blaming the past for what is happening in the present, and I don't know whether that's true or not. I don't know much about economics. All I know is that the people who are the neediest are the ones who are suffering. I don't see these people who are millionaires as the ones who are suffering. Maybe that's what we are meant to do, make their life more comfortable, and we make the sacrifice so that their life can be more comfortable. I don't understand that type of thing, but that's what seems to be happening. And then he's telling me when I'm starving, he's telling me to tighten my belt. Well, I don't think that's a very sane, rational approach or acceptable to people who are out there. I think that we all—as an individual, as a Christian, I have a responsibility to someone who is in need. We all do, to help our brothers, and I don't think that any of us should have that responsibility taken away. I still feel that. I feel that we are responsible and I am my brother's keeper. I think in our way, you give me the tools and we'll feed them, we'll give them jobs, and we'll do what we have to.

It took me six or seven years to win their trust. First of all, the first time, is when I fought the system and helped to save this church. It was a battle which I did by myself, which indicated to them that there was a reason to trust me. I was strong, I was tough, but if I hadn't been we would all die. There would be no hope. And then, through these little programs of service I was on all the committees. I mean talking and yelling at every meeting. Fighting against a system that was making their lives more disastrous. And so it took time. Now I feel in a way that my work is finished, in a sense. I did what I had to do. That doesn't mean that there is not much more that has to be done. It doesn't mean that I would like to walk away. My term of office now is coming to an end. It is up to the cardinal to let me stay or not. I was here as an assistant seven years before I became a pastor, and my term is twelve years. I was appointed in 1970 so technically by 1982 . . . in fact, we've already gotten my evaluation papers to fill out, so I don't know. But I'm pleased, we've gotten housing, and our community mental health centers, jobs. . . . I'm very pleased. The church has about eight to nine hundred on Sundays and Masses in Spanish and in English. We have a very active youth program. Brother Patrick is involving himself very intensively with our youth. We've tried to help them go into college and to look for better opportunities. We've very proud of them, but we're only a small little area. It's an ugly area with the power plants and the Park Avenue Conrail, the New York Central and the Third Avenue El and Webster Avenue with all the car repair shops. It's ugly, ugly, ugly. The Cross Bronx.

Saving the church was almost a miracle. Literally every consultant from the archdiocese, the laypeople, the religious bishops and everything, all indicated through their surveys that the church had to be torn down. I hired an independent crew of Jewish technicians, and we did battle, and we won. And I remember the cardinal saying the first Mass, and he was praying and several times told me how hard he was praying. One day I was attending a meeting, and I said we had hope. I had a cane, I was crippled. But we determined that our hundredth anniversary day was going to be something special, and so we all went out looking for pictures. We sent out to the *Bronx Press Review* and anybody having any pictures that they would like to send. Our posters were all over the place. And we were making our brochure, and we didn't have a decent picture of the church. One day, as we were making our plans for the anniversary, a man came to the back door, a black man who said that he worked in Jersey, he was working on a demolition job in Patterson. He opened up this desk and he found these papers, these prints, and he saw St. Joseph's on them and he said, "I'm not Catholic, but I live on Tremont Avenue, and I thought that you might like to have this for your church." He knew nothing of our search for pictures of the church. The picture was torn and we put it together and into a frame, and that to me was another affirmation, was a sign really from almighty God that this church was meant to stand here long after I'm gone and after a whole lot of people are gone, that that church was meant to stand. That really was a miracle.

CHAPTER EIGHT
EAE

Eae James Mitchell, Togetherness Realty; 1925–1989
Interview: April 14, 1983

"People realize—be they black, be they white—that you must participate and become involved in your government, and this is the message of 1983 to all people."

I was born in Baltimore, Maryland, in 1925. It was difficult in those days, but I felt that there was more to me than going out and working in people's houses, cleaning and whatnot, and I began to find the ways and means of educating myself far beyond what my parents could afford. In doing this at the age of fourteen I twisted my mother's arm and my father's arm to sign papers that I was seventeen, and I went into the navy, and I served four years in the United States Navy. This was one of the best things for me, and I will tell that to any man, because I got the opportunity to learn discipline. Not only that, I saw quite a bit of a world that I knew nothing about, other states, foreign countries, and all.

Afterwards I came out of the service, and I decided that I wanted to really educate myself, and the government gave me that opportunity. I thought I wanted to teach, and then later I says, "Naw, I want to get into business administration," and I have a bachelor's degree in business administration from Boston University. Afterwards I worked for the Corps of Army Engineers for about three years.[1] Then I went to the *New York Times*, and I worked for them for thirteen years, and I headed up their List Department that took care of all their subscriptions. At the time I went in it there was 22 persons. When I left in 1969 there were 470 in the department that I headed. I left because I was afraid I was going to get terminated for my involvement in the community.

I was living in Harlem, and I began to not like Harlem because of the crime and the problems that were ensuing, and I decided that I would attempt to find a better neighborhood in which to live. At that time I had never seen the Bronx, but I had heard so much about it that I thought I'd check out the Bronx. I came to the Bronx, and I started looking around, and everywhere I went I was refused. I went to Parkchester.[2] At that time they weren't taking blacks or Puerto Ricans into Parkchester, and the reason they gave me was that my income—my bank balance—was insufficient to move in. At that time I had twenty-seven thousand dollars in Chemical Bank at 1629 Broadway. I called the bank and asked them, "What information did you give?" and then I sued for discrimination, and I won the case plus ten thousand dollars. I'd sued for twenty thousand. That opened up the Parkchester housing to Hispanics and blacks, I believe.

This was in 1969. I didn't win the case until 1972 when the case was settled, but I found this building here that was accepting blacks and Puerto Ricans. However, at that time when I moved in, there were only three black families and no Hispanic families at all. The rest of the families were Italian and Jewish, and of course as the blacks began to move in they became afraid. The whites were starting to move out slowly, to trickle out, those that could afford it, and as they did it appeared as though the Department of Sanitation and the Police Department were not addressing themselves to the community as they should have. I felt very badly about it myself, and I felt with my background and my knowledge I could rally people in the community to investigate and do something about stabilizing the community. And at that time Mrs. Mae Moton, a clerk in the grocery store, and Mrs. Mary McLauren, who owned a beauty shop, those two decided that together we would form some sort of a group and attempt to get volunteers to work with us to address ourselves to all the various problems within the community.

We laid out how much could we do, so we made boundary lines of 173rd Street on the east, to 175th Street or the Cross Bronx Expressway on the north, Southern Boulevard to the west, and Boone Avenue to the east, and that was south of 173rd on the south. These were the boundaries. We said we would look into the housing, sanitation, police, and whatever other problems that came about. At that time we had street-corner meetings. It grew to the extent that people felt something could be done, and we opened up the beauty shop every Thursday night, and we would bring in various agencies to address us and to respond to some of the things that we saw.

In the meantime I was living in this building, and I began to see that every weekend there was some problem with the boiler or the brass—lovely brass here when I moved in—wasn't being cleaned, the halls weren't kept clean. The superintendent that had been here had been terminated, and they brought some mop boy who slopped up and messed up, and I said, "Hey, this is not right," and then I says, "Hey, we have to do something," and I got about fifteen tenants to not strike, but to deduct three dollars from their rent with a note that I had made up telling the owners that we would continue to do this each month until our services were restored as in the past. At that time I was paying sixty-eight dollars a month in rent; the rent was very low. However, if he could maintain the building in those years for others, he was supposed to have maintained it for us, because as we came in we were paying eight and nine dollars more than the rent-controlled tenants that had been here for years and years. I have leases here where tenants were paying only thirty-seven dollars a month, and I have all those records from back in the years ever since the beginning. Some of them moved in when the building was built, and they never left because the rent was controlled.

However, we didn't realize that our landlord was having problems as well as other landlords. What was happening? The Department of Social Services found the neighborhoods that were opening up, and they shooed their people over to these buildings, and the majority of the people—be they black, white, or Hispanic—that are on welfare, they are irresponsible people. They have no sense of responsibility, or they are not educated to the point that they will help themselves. They've been in the habit of receiving so much that they feel it's the norm to go in and stand on a sink and break it down to put in a lightbulb rather than find a ladder or something of this nature. The ages ran from the twenties to the forties. When you find a community or a city where one generation after the other remains on welfare, this is a problem, and it's a problem that the government should look at very strongly, I feel. They are making it a way of life.

I work with a group at the HRA.[3] I involve myself with it greatly to bring about changes in the way that the government, the city is actually imprisoning these people. These people are imprisoned to the extent that they do more harm than good. They are afraid to vote, they are afraid to speak out because they feel they may get cut off. They have gone into—I will not use diplomacy—they lie, steal, and cheat just so that they can get some welfare check. If the government could really look into the situation they would see that many of these people do not need the help of the city. They—some—are faring better than most of the rest of us. They have Cadillacs and this and that, where we think before we buy a new car, and we may even ride the subways.

When we formed the Togetherness Tenants' League here,[4] we wanted to find out why the owner, the landlord—Mr. Sidney Greenstein—could not service this building. He had owned the building for twenty-three years. After I moved in I was here for about a year and a half before it started deteriorating—not only this building, but others that deteriorated to a much greater degree. We nipped it in the bud. We found that the working persons living in the building were maintaining it with their rents, and the landlord was fighting battle after battle in civil court with the recipients of SSI or welfare—who mainly I'll still say were not being subsidized properly for food and clothing, so they would take the rent money and do this and find excuses under the code enforcement to not pay him the rent, and sometimes this would go on for four or five months. He would then get them out, and they would go and play the same game somewhere else. But meantime it was destroying other people's buildings. Most landlords would, I feel, take care of their buildings a little better if they saw an income of 80 percent of their rents each month. However, in these communities, except for the rehabilitated buildings, most of them only see from 55 to 60 percent, and they have to fight for the balance.

In forming a tenant association we found that we could assist the owners in holding the building and stabilizing the building—as when there was a problem and he wasn't collecting rent, we formed a committee, and we went over and talked to the tenant, and we told the tenant either they would pay without the repair being done or we would go to court and support the owner so that he could get tenants in that would understand that we were giving him one year to get back his building on a financial plane. We would dictate practically just what he should do with the portion of the maintenance and whatever returns he received, but we would see that the building was brought back. This was one of the best things that was done. Why? We began to get more tenants that were working to rally around us, and then it put the recipients in line. But unfortunately it took a period of almost three years for this to come about, and at that time no other buildings were getting this support. They attempted, but they didn't have volunteer people such as I and Mr. McGee, Mrs. Lee, and a former tenant, Mr. Miller, who worked night and day trying to find ways and solutions so that we could stay in our community and in a home which we all thought was all right.

The change in population was a quick change. I'd say the migration began possibly in 1968–69 to make this a predominantly black and Hispanic community. By 1970 the turnover had been made—in just two years—and it was brought about through fear, and that fear brought in crime. Rather than people fighting and demanding protection of people—I don't know, I yet today don't understand the black and the Puerto Rican race. I mean I am black, a true black, I am not exactly a southerner—I was born in the mid-Atlantic states—but there is no respect or very little respect. If you've seen the graffiti, the things here in these communities that are going on—and I work with the 42nd Precinct Council attempting to do something in this area about it—but it's not only here, it's all over the country. The things that I was taught when I was a child, to respect, these things are no more. Parents curse and go to bed with their children, and children now are no longer children. When the girl or boy is twelve or thirteen their future is sealed up. We had a case here. We had an eleven-year-old boy and a fifteen-year-old girl having sex under one of my stairwells, and then when it was brought to the attention of their parents, we were the wrong, the dirty guys. We threw them out—the families—because we said we didn't want these types of families in here. However, this is a unilateral thing.

To continue on about building up or working, what I attempted to do as an individual here in this community, I would seek out all sorts of agencies and information so that I could bring it back to the people in the community, educate them in that this should not be the way of life. In Togetherness Housing it may not have come voluntarily because we have forced upon tenants things to show them that if this edifice is to stay here for years to come, they will have to participate in doing something to keep it. Their dollars have serviced them well, but they would not have unless they voluntarily committed themselves to being a part of and taking care of what they have. We set up committees of tenants—not outsiders—to see that these policies are brought forth. Then they are placed before the tenant body with options. You accept it, we all live by it. You do not accept it, then we all may suffer by it. This is going to help housing here in the South Bronx greatly when you let people know that we will not allow you to destroy.

At one time people in this community used to say, "I pay my rent, I'll do what I want." This is not it today. You pay your rent to lease an apartment that belongs to someone else that has invested many, many dollars, and if you do not wish to abide, then you find your own home, and you will see the difference. And I think most people now are beginning to realize this because the government and private persons and so on are not going to continue investing in something that's going to be destroyed by others, so I think many persons now that used to tear apart are not. One of the major problems again is that someone will have to—and I hope some day we will get some legislators that will put a vast study on our welfare system and do something about it—because it is the recipient now, today, that is yet attempting to destroy.

I had a building at Walton Avenue—I did not own it; I managed it under a receivership from the courts—and they just walked out with seventy-five thousand dollars' worth of unpaid rent, and neither the courts nor Social Service did anything about it. They are yet not doing. We have in our buildings persons that we attempt to educate: "The government is paying and you give us the rent." When they don't, we did get a policy where they would pay the rent direct, but because of the federal government's rules and regulations it's only for a period of three months and then go back to get the money into their own pockets.

When I was working at the *New York Times* I had whatever staff I needed to assist me for any reasons, so I had three clerks and a secretary, and my secretary was doing nothing but community work. She was making flyers, keeping records, keeping tally lists of this, and I would go out—actually I was stealing time from my company—I would go out on conferences, which I would have to for my job, but rather than be in the conference I would come into the community for a Fire Department meeting or a police meeting or some meeting concerning my community, so when I looked at it I said, "I've never in my life been fired from a job," and when I looked at my savings I says, "Okay, I think I have sufficient to carry me on maybe through my work in the community, and I can do something here." So I left my job to work for the community.

They had the Morrisania Community Corporation,[5] which was supposed to have done the job that I was attempting to do as a government-funded agency, and knowing the director I spoke to him and told him I just had to get back into the community and was there anything? I didn't care if it was only one hundred fifty or two hundred dollars a week, but I would like to work with community people, and luckily I was given the job of the housing specialist for Morrisania because of what I had done. We formed here in the building at 1705 Bryant Avenue—it's one of my responsibilities—we forced the New York City Housing even to allow us to select and screen the tenants. That was one of the first in the history of New York where community people had the orientation, the screening, and accepted the applications, and placed people into the Turnkey that is—what is it?—thirty-five families over there. That was a site that was built in a memorial to one young man that killed another young man over dope in front of the Boys' Club, and at that time I was so angry, and I wanted to enlighten the community on what was happening to their children, as we are beginning to do again. We formed a coalition of about seven groups sponsored by the Concerned Citizens,[6] and we had a raffle and we raised three thousand five hundred dollars because we gave two prizes, five hundred and one thousand dollars, to get the sort of things we needed to demonstrate to the community the plight. We had every politician, and we demanded every store in this area to close one hour in memorial to the dastardly manner that one mother's son was killing another mother's son over something. It was over drugs, and the politicians at that time felt "well, we'd better quiet these people down, we'd better do something."

So they brought in the Tactical Police Force. They not only did that, they brought in the Fire Department, and Mrs. Genevieve Brooks, who is yet working hard and harder than I. She started this fight against the insurance companies paying off owners that were burning down their buildings and putting people out of homes. But there are so many things in the history of this particular community that if it were not for persons such as I that still feel there is much more to be done, this community would have been razed years ago. This particular building now, which is Togetherness Housing, I thought I would give up. But the owner, Sidney Greenstein, after a while when he saw what we were doing, he asked me if I would like to manage this building for him, and I told him yes, but I had to have an income. He told me I would have to go to a special school, but he was a broker and he could sponsor me, so I went to the New York School, and I got my license to manage this building. Unfortunately it was chaotic. I had my license only three days, and he had brought other landlords in, and they gave me seven buildings to manage for them only two days after I graduated with my license. I manage three of them today.

Then the city of New York had advertised—not broadly, but through my going around to the various seminars and whatnot—that they were going to attempt another method in saving housing, and they would, if buildings would qualify, the tenants would be able to purchase the building. And if the tenants would purchase the building they would loan them up to one million dollars to rehabilitate. I investigated that situation, and I felt this is something good for us, because these buildings were old, and they were sick and becoming cancerous, and something had to be done to give them new life, and after investigating and working with the owner we felt that we could apply, and we did. When we applied, of course, we had then gotten all tenants to pledge that they would aid in my getting ninety thousand dollars together to purchase the building from the owner. He wanted one hundred twenty thousand dollars, but we told him either come down or we would report every violation, and then, of course, he did, because the building wasn't worth one hundred twenty thousand dollars maybe not even ninety thousand, because everything around us had started burning down, and the area was becoming abandoned.

All was well until a month prior to going for the closing when we found out that the tenants who had made commitments were not going to keep them, so I had to come up with sixty-eight thousand dollars. Between my sister, mother, and what I had I came up with sixty, and Chemical Bank had faith enough in me personally to loan me the eight. We closed. After closing we went through chaotic conditions because the city had given us a list of recommended minority contractors—a new law came into effect. Minority contractors were complaining that they weren't getting enough work out of the city because they did not have the big bucks to put up the bonds, so they reduced the bonds to fifty thousand dollars. The recommended company persuaded me and the board of directors that they could do the job effectively, and they sent in a Hispanic who came in, and this office is one of the gifts from him for me accepting him. He renovated this office with paneling and a stucco ceiling and a chandelier and so forth. In the beginning I was subletting just that front office from a lady who had the apartment, but the lady wasn't the cleanest person and she had a dog or two, and the tenants would come in and react to the bad smells, so I bought her out of here. It was funny.

Then after we got into it we found the rehabilitation couldn't be done. Renovating—even moderate rehab while tenants were in occupancy—was a very difficult situation. We were fighting back and forth with the city about their contractors, the slipshod way that the contractors were doing, inspectors that we proved were doing something other than what they were supposed to. I handled all monies coming from the government based upon approval of certain jobs. The city inspector would approve the work, but I would not, and the checks would be sent to me, and I would withhold them, and then I was a criminal for withholding money from various contractors when I wasn't satisfied or the board wasn't satisfied with their performance. This made a big stink in the city of New York. There were allegations that I had personally misappropriated funds, and at that time I was disturbed. I just took all the records. I didn't do an audit or an accounting; I just showed them. "There's no way I can handle your monies other than through checks. Here is the checkbooks, the cancelled checks, do what you wish."

They let it sit for one year and didn't

do anything and let me struggle here the best I could. At that time I was managing nineteen buildings, and I did not suffer financially other than I managed this building from 1977 to 1982 before I even got a management fee or any fee whatsoever. And the audit showed—the audit was done in 1979—that Togetherness Realty management invested eighty-one thousand dollars into this project. This is money over and above the rents collected or what the city invested. In turn when I saw this—and the audit cost me seven thousand dollars—we assumed that after the audit was sent to the city, they would restore this building. This building is in-rem,[7] owned by the city of New York, supposedly. However they alleged that they will not do anything for this building until I get out. They asked me to give up my presidency of the board. They will pay me off. They negotiated. I think the attorney said that they will give me seventy thousand dollars, and I told them no.

It was a political thing. I carried a lot of weight here against the politicians, and a group formed that wanted to do what they are doing now. They wanted to bring in a training program which the federal government had offered them one hundred forty-seven thousand dollars to train managers for these buildings. I and my group resigned because of the processes that were going to go about. We felt that there were enough educated people in these communities here that had attended high school that should be able to avail themselves of these courses and these particular jobs. But most of these buildings are being managed now by outsiders—Long Island, Chicago—people who have no interest other than collecting the rents, paying the super, and they never see the building, maybe every six months. All right. I was very much against it, and I influenced my group why I was against it—and my group which had two votes, we would not vote for it, and they lost the money. But it was the city who had come here and asked me to become involved in this group.

No legislators would put their hands on me, but I showed them I would fight. I have fought to the extent that the city has not put their hands on this building since 1977. They have not collected one dollar of rent. I do not pay taxes, but I have taxes in escrow, and I have sued the city of New York for $2 million. They have negotiated, they want an out-of-court settlement, and I feel—I strongly feel and the board does too—we will not allow the city to take it over. All we are asking for is the deed to the building restored, $44,000 in unpaid taxes that was not our fault, primarily because if you cut me off from funds and I had to use my rents to maintain the building, then you are obligated to take care of the problem which you created. They feel that it's an embarrassing situation. They don't want it to go to court because when it does, I do think the media is going to cover such a story as this, and I have been trying for going on a year to really put it down on paper well because I know the media is going to want to know the story, and they don't want to hear my side, they want to hear the legal ramifications. But there is a story of community interest, human interest here, because these people fought to save their own.

The whole community is now being

rebuilt. If we did not stand ground to hold this building here—Togetherness—there would be nothing in this neighborhood for people today, and we strongly feel this, and we are finding that there are others. I think this is why the Association of Neighborhood Houses has honored me,[8] and I've had many honors for some of the work that I've attempted to do.

This building stands out in the neighborhood, but three years ago it stood out more. It was like a mecca. But now that the federal government and private money is coming in to build, of course we are sinking back, but we promise ourselves never to let this building go down. We have great plans and are still modernizing more. The only problem was this is an eighty-eight-unit development and when the city cut off our funds we only had forty-one apartments occupied because various people could not stand what was going on—some because the services had gone down, some who refused to pay rent and that we had found ways of getting them out. But thanks to whoever it is above that looks over people gave me that fortitude and twelve other persons the fortitude to stick it out, and now we have only two vacancies in the whole building. Our rent roll came up in four years from five thousand, six hundred twenty dollars a month to seventeen thousand, eight hundred and forty dollars a month. This well maintains this building.

Again, I must say the city has attempted to apologize for two years because for two years I have not paid for a drop of oil in this building. The city supplies me oil, and they haven't asked for one dime. But I feel that this is a payoff of monies that they owe me personally, so I do now take five thousand a month from the rent roll legally. We calculated that. I submit to the board and the board approves that this is my money. It's a long way to go. I won't be paid off because it started back in 1975 when I stopped taking the management commissions. The ninety-five thousand dollars that I put in personally I have a note from this board. Of course I'll be dead and gone long before it's paid off, but my heirs will be able to collect that money. Now, the city stated in negotiating that they would pay me off 60 percent of it immediately if I wanted it, but they would not give us the deed, and I am holding out. I don't need the money. I am not rich and I never intend to be. However, because of my community involvement I made this money, so I feel that I would like to see these persons who had faith in me and people that supported me to have this restored to them as their own, because when the city comes in they do not take care of buildings like an individual does.

We did fight, or I did fight, to get people into putting the high-intensity lighting into the area. It looked like nighttime here, pitch black. We fought and we got it. We have repaved the streets from one end to the other through fighting for it as a group. Now, there is a bridge that's very dangerous on the other side of 174th Street. They said they weren't going to do anything about it, but we got one and a quarter million dollars, approval, and commitment to do it.

I feel that there will be a change here in these communities very soon because of what happened up in Chicago. People realize—be they black, be they white—that you must participate and become involved in your government, and this is the message of 1983 to all people. I feel that you must become involved, and that if Washington [Harold Washington, mayor of Chicago]—I don't care if he was white or black—does his job effectively, then he should remain the mayor, and all these rabble-rousers or racists—maybe not necessarily racist, people are just afraid. People were afraid of me at one time. They said, "Mr. Mitchell is for himself. He buys a new car every year." But I have books here since 1969 when I started the business. Every financial record yet remains. I will never destroy these because if anyone after I am dead and gone happens to accuse me, the record will stand. Too many people who do great work have their hands in the till. I don't live high. I pay rent every month. I pay my own electric bill. I draw a check for managing the building through TRM, and TRM, which is my private company, pays me a salary of four hundred twenty-five dollars a week. That's all I get. The other money stays in the corporation, and it does things to benefit the corporation. And not only that, 5 percent of the income of Togetherness Realty Management goes into a separate account that's used for programs—summer programs—within the community. You very rarely find a landlord or a management company that's doing that today. I was attempting with another company to get Sidney Greenstein to do it, to take 1 or 2 percent and put it into community involvement, because I felt that if you take an interest in the community, the community will take an interest in you. And that's what happened here. I was utterly surprised. The people of the community threw a party for me costing three thousand dollars when I was fifty years old, and I never in my life saw anyone honored like that, so I said, "Hey, I can never let these people down."

It was intended that the tenants would own this building, that it would be a tenant low-cost co-op after the rehabilitation. When the funds were cut off, there were about ten tenants that had invested in it that wanted to withdraw their monies, so I paid them off personally and I hold the notes, so in essence the city and I own the building. I'm still trying to gear it so that it will be a co-op, but I'm afraid to open Pandora's box. When buildings are in-rem you can go into a program which is called the Interim Lease, and the tenants then lease that building from the city of New York for a period of not less than one nor more than three years for a dollar a year. They would have to live under the guidance or manage the building themselves. The city would coordinate what was going on with the funds after that. Then the city would sell each unit to the tenant for two hundred fifty dollars. This is the route that I would like to take, but I am afraid to because of the financial situation that's going on with me personally and then the commitments that the city has committed themselves to the corporation. There is a bona fide corporation here, Togetherness Housing Development Fund. Because of tax problems and other problems we re-formed and called it Togetherness, Hope, and Deliverance as an interim so that we could do business because we had problems because of construction monies owed and whatnot with Togetherness Housing Development Fund Corp. So rather than let this group go, I said, "Well, we'll keep the same letters," and we came up with THDF—Togetherness, Hope, and Deliverance Fund—and we are operating under this now, but we had it written in the minutes that Togetherness, Hope, and Deliverance was formed only for the purposes of collecting monies for Togetherness Housing Development so we could continue to do business.

Now, if the suit is ever settled, it's my hope and desire that the city will—and I am sure this is coming about soon—give us the deed to the building. Once that is done, then we will—I don't know how, because there is vast monies owed to the city for some of the rehabilitation that they did invest money into; I don't know how it will work out—but I am sure that this will be a tenant cooperative before the end.

I operate four buildings under the city of New York on interim lease. One building I owned and I lost it to the city; however, the tenants felt that they would care to keep me on as management. But this building—I guess you would say it's laissez faire—I just run it, there is no question I do, as though I have to answer to someone. I do because a board of directors who are all tenants except one—they receive a monthly statement from me each month showing the income and the disbursements and the tenant rent roll, and they do meet to comment on it—so I am sort of answerable to them. The majority of them don't even pay too much attention to the information. They very rarely question anything, and they feel that, "As long as you are doing it, we know you are doing it well," and they don't bother. They just bring about changes in policies. The others are three private owners that I operate for, and I had two offerings yesterday, but I had a heart attack a couple of years ago, and since then I've decided to calm myself down because you just can't go night and day, and how much money can one make? And I don't trust anyone else to handle the funds here. Mrs. Allen, of course, she's been with me for nine years. She started off working for fifty dollars a week and now she makes four hundred a week. And we often talk about it, and she says, "Ha! I don't want to work." She didn't want to work, she had a husband who was taking care of her well, but after he passed he left her a little, and I say it's not going to last forever. She lives in the building so pays no carfare or anything.

Togetherness started as a tenant league in 1969, and then it was taken over legally by the tenants on July 18, 1974, but we had formed prior to that for working with the owners of the building. It was only supposed to be buildings 1003 and 1005, but the other owner of 1007 and 1009 and the tenants said, "Aha, how can you do this and leave us to fall down?" So they became involved, and this is why it took us much longer to get these persons in 1007 and 1009 on the same plane that the others were. Actually the 1007 and 1009 is really what created most of our problems in construction because the people weren't disciplined, they didn't have the seven-month educational program that was given to these people in 1003 and 1005 as to what to expect in construction while living here. I wrote several times and brought in the city a number of times to show them why it wasn't feasible after we'd started.

We have a good balance now with approximately 12 percent tenants subsidized through SSI or Social Security. We are beginning to set a policy to shy away from the welfare recipient because we yet find that these people will not attempt to comply to many of the rules and regulations, especially in paying their rent between the first and eighth of the month. We can set a policy because if this were a cooperative sponsored under the city of New York, all we would have to have is 10 percent welfare. With the contract that was drawn up with the city of New York, we must accept 10 percent of welfare recipients, 15 percent senior citizens. We do not mind the senior citizens; we have no problems from them. Workingmen, no problems, but our major problems are stemming from the welfare recipients.

The renting is done by the tenants. I have set up a committee made up not only of members of the board but made up of volunteer tenants, and I give them for each vacancy, they are allocated fifty dollars to do their investigation. They must go to the building in the community where that person is living and without any embarrassment attempt to find out what sort of tenant we are bringing in, because we feel that we have gotten the premises to the place where we want them, and we would like to see the tenants all working together in unity. Most of the persons are moving from other buildings within the Bronx. Very rarely do we accept a tenant from out of state just moving in or a tenant from Manhattan. We feel that we would like to accommodate those that live here and have lived in the Bronx and do not want to relocate to other areas, because the Bronx is a beautiful place if people really would look at it, and this particular building is really a mecca. We have the subway here and nearby schools, although the schools are nothing.

I have thirty-two children here, and of the thirty-two children twenty-six of them were born here in this building. I have had this, which makes us feel proud. We have had children of seven parents who are now tenants in the building, showing the inheritance phase that can go on, that this building can remain within the same family structures, and this is what our hope and desire is. We are now attempting to groom the youth. I am myself sponsoring a young lady and a young man for management so that I hope within a year or two not to retire but to get out of management. I am tired, and my doctors advise me, "Why don't you take it easy?" And Mrs. Allen, my assistant, doesn't want to take on the responsibility, so rather than bring in an outsider I prefer to use someone in the house, and I have two persons now that allege that they would like to try it out, and they are pursuing such a course of study.

If families who grew up in other areas of the Bronx come into this particular area and they see it's being rebuilt, they feel much more secure than they did in the other areas. The Hispanics and the blacks that are on the poverty level have lived with these sorts of conditions for a number of years and taken their chances. There was a time when a Caucasian or a black that dressed well and wasn't used to this community was afraid to walk here, but in this particular area I'll say we have very little crime. If you will look at this particular block—and I have gained the respect of everyone around in what I am promoting—parents bring their children to me to sort of let them know, "No, you can't do this, you shouldn't." This is spreading out more because now we have eighteen tenant associations under my direction or under Togetherness, and I receive no remuneration, no pay for this at all, but it is an educational phase. The outsider that comes in and looks at the area may feel depressed and wonder, "How could these people live like this?" But if you look all around the Bronx where the poverty people live, it is far worse. Take Wilkins Avenue, on which I have a project going as the president of the 42nd Precinct. I've dedicated myself to cleaning that area up. There's dope, numbers, policy joints, this sort of thing. But until the government or someone comes in and educates them—this is the main problem in poverty areas, there is poor or no education of these people in social behavior and other aspects of the quality of life. This is the way I feel. Others may have other opinions. I've never cried, "I don't have soup to eat." There is soup out here to eat if you reach out. It just happens the government has these people imprisoned to the tune that they don't know where to go, but they are awakening more and more every day, and I feel that communities like this—this I am sure—there is another building over on Arthur Avenue run by Hispanics just as well as this building. I've spoken with them several times—they don't need my assistance, I don't need theirs. There will be more of these because now there is a leadership of unsung heroes coming about.

This leadership of unsung heroes which I am dedicating myself to—to build a memorial to—a few of them have died and they have done something. They are dead and nobody has placed a plaque or a little statue. Well, one of the things if the city ever pays up, I'll place in my will that the Mitchell Mall, which is this up here and it's being rehabilitated now, will be dedicated to community leaders that have passed on so that some day in history someone will know that there was an Eae Mitchell or a Sarah Harris or an Arthur Smalls that did something far beyond what they had to do—because none of us get paid. I feel sometimes very elated that I've been able to help someone, but during the meantime I realize that if I had not done this maybe I would have been one of these that can't lift their feet off the clay, so they are helping me as well. It's being done from the inside out, which is the right way, rather than people coming in from the outside. Now that the corporations and perhaps the city too, but more private monies are beginning to see the Bronx as a place to invest again, to build or to bring businesses, are they consulting with the communities or are they just coming in as investors? I see that they are going to come in if they can get the space cheaply. There are problems. The private developer is not coming in speculating as he did, but he is getting his foot into the door through closed corporations or housing sponsors who are not yet involving the communities as they should.

I have a situation here where they are going to make an industrial park because they allege there's no further monies to rehabilitate housing. Right here. The boundary lines run from 175th to Southern Boulevard to 174th and Longfellow.[9] They is all city-owned property now. They are getting abandoned and in-rem and whatnot. There is a group that has the sponsorship for this area and all its plans, and against my objections they submitted plans to make this an industrial park. They cannot build new homes. There are certain new code enforcements that say they can't on account of the noise pollution, the high decibels here from the Cross Bronx Expressway. However in razing these existing buildings—it will take approximately a year or a year and a half—while they are razing them, during the interim before the industrial park, these will not become anything but a city dump. We have that problem here already. This street is abandoned. Of course I heard they would close it up for me June first. At nighttime, trucks, meat trucks, whatever, come through and they dump because of the high cost of legal dumping. This is going to happen, so I've been attempting to fight that before any demolition is done that there will be funds available to green and to fence off not with a chicken wire but stable fencing, and that my parking lot—I have a parking lot that I own that I rent to tenants and community people at a nominal fee—would pay or subsidize some security personnel to identify anyone.

I have it in writing that they would hold off, but I was at the meeting of the community board, a public hearing on Tuesday night, and Ed Logue, who is the South Bronx Overall Economic guy,[10] stated that they have one hundred ten thousand dollars for demolition, and they are going to proceed. This is going to begin another heart attack for me because I am going to start a war. I am not going to allow them to proceed when I have it in writing that they would not begin demolition because I have families here. It's bad enough to walk by some of the rubble and whatnot as it is. What is this going to be when they tear it down, all this vast open land, and kids will go in and begin to play, and there will be rats and whatnot? I don't think that I could allow myself—being a community leader—to let these people suffer these indignities, so I am going to start studying the plan again and try to find a route to begin to fight that plan. And I'm thinking again of Mr. Washington up in Chicago. He mobilized, he educated. And what I am going to have to do is to find ways and means of getting the people interested enough to know what it's going to mean to them for the next five or six years. Bathgate is coming along well now—it's an industrial park—but it took them seven years to get that park going. Luckily there's no one that had to walk through or by it as much as here. So I feel that if the people look into the future, not look at the present, and this is the way I do—I may not be here next year, I may not be here in seven years—but I feel that in these communities the quality of life again is at stake. So this is another thing where I will be involved and hope others will become involved to save their community, because if agencies or sponsors come out and make plans and they don't bring in the community until it's too late, I feel that's unfair.

It's very unfair, and when they publicize—believe it or not there was a public hearing being held and notice was given to me only the day before—and this is done in many community boards, and there is going to have to be a change. In the better neighborhoods, if they are going to put in a sewer, the people are well notified in advance and those that are interested in what does that mean to me, today, tomorrow, and the day after tomorrow, they are out there to contest, protest, or put their blessings on it, and I feel that this is what has to happen in these types of communities, poorer communities, to make them better. The people must become involved. This is another problem. The majority of the people that are moving into areas such as this—this building or any of the other rehabilitated buildings—are looking for better places to live, and when they go there they see what they are compared to what they lived in. But after they move in they close their door, and that's the end until the building falls down. And this attitude has to be changed, and how or who or what to do to change this I don't know. I would like to find a solution because I feel that the government isn't going to continue throwing money into the poor areas if the people don't take care of them. There are premises such as at Boston Road and Wilkins Avenue up there where buildings were rehabilitated in 1970, and in a period of six months they were abandoned. But that was Mayor Lindsay. He took welfare recipients out of the Concourse Plaza Hotel and threw them all in there. These people had no sense of responsibility whatsoever, and they moved in and they began taking the refrigerator because it was new, and, "Oh, we can sell this, we don't need this large one," and they would buy a secondhand used one and other things of this nature.

I'm sure there is going to be a change, and I am pleased in a way that I'll be a part of history because perhaps some day—forty years from now or fifty—people won't believe that these things happened and that there were people who did not care and there were people that *did* care and helped to maintain and make the Bronx the great thing that I feel it's going to be again, because we have everything here—and I mean it.

The neighborhood now has no merchants per se. We have a bodega here, a bodega there. The majority of what we have—and we are attempting to find a way to fight it—are policy operators, numbers operators, about sixteen of them here right in one little area, and the police don't put their hands on them. If the people didn't want them and didn't play the numbers, then you wouldn't have them. As soon as they can find a store they open up, and this keeps out the legitimate merchant because he wouldn't want to have a nice little store next to a policy joint because they are sort of unsavory and anything can happen. But prior to this when there were merchants here, the majority of them lived out of the neighborhood and this was one of my fights. I forced many of them to join in a merchants' association and contribute something to the community, more than as though we were collecting for a church: "If you are going to do something, here is a dollar." No, I had them to the tune that they were paying two hundred dollars a year and they had to meet once a month and try to fight some of the evils that were besetting this neighborhood. They were getting guns on their own, and instead of getting the police to set up vehicles to stop the holdups and whatnot they were out saying, "I'll take care of it myself." I says, "No, we are not going to have those cowboy-and-Indian days." But when the neighborhood died, most of them left. Very few are yet here. I think Sonny's Check Cashing is one of the old businesses here. Most of the businesses here now are just fly-by-night type or someone taking whatever they can out of the community.

Mrs. McLauren, who has the Salon of Beauty did live in the community and contributed great, not only financially, but she was heading up my education committee, and she did a tremendous job that was undone after she left. Our group really broke down because of the neighborhood's beginning to die. They couldn't stand it, and we lost members. Now there are only eighteen members to my Concerned Citizens of East 174th, but we had a member at the Lorraine Hansberry School who got the school district board to approve that the school doors would not open once during the day until the time they were let out. And Mrs. Allen, my goddaughter, attended there at the time. It was one of the better schools. Now, somehow or other, they've stopped that, and they let them in and out, and of course there's been two rapes in the school, there's drugs being sold to ten-, eleven-, and twelve-year-old children. But we now finally got sixteen mothers who have volunteered, and they are now patrolling the outside perimeters and in the hallways of the school. That came through due to our group. I don't have the people to do what I'd like, but we are trying to negotiate with the principal and District 12. We are going to wait until after the election to go back to that same program because most of the kids that were there and attended that school during—I think we started in 1969 through 1975—were well disciplined. I have asked Mrs. McLauren if she yet has records so we could demonstrate the difference between then and now. And I feel that that's one of the things they are going to have to do with some of the schools, because the kids are wild today. They need lunch programs in school or parents can fix the lunch. That's better than for them to eat out in the streets.

Religious leaders are often self-interest groups, but without the religious leaders, especially the Catholic religious leaders, this neighborhood would not have moved. Father Smith, who has St. John Chrysostom—I don't know his interest and I do not really want to know—but he was elected chairman of the board because religious leaders have great influence on various politicians and circles. This has helped. Father Gigante was very powerful in building SEBCO.[11]

Over here in the 180s by West Farms, that is being done by St. Thomas Aquinas. Now here this is basically being done by St. John Chrysostom. Father Smith heads the Mid-Bronx Development as the chairman.[12] This is why in most groups now that want to go ahead they look for a church, except for the Hispanics. I have a church across the street, Hispanic, very, very good attendance, but they do not become involved. I've invited them through letters saying, "You have your church here." But very few of the membership live here in this area. They bus them in. And another thing I've done is to communicate in Spanish with my Spanish friends to make sure that it's fully understood what's going on.

Looking ahead, looking at what these industrial parks will do, basically I don't feel they are going to help this area. The majority of the young men and women that are being educated today are being educated in other areas than working in factories, so it means that we are going to have transients working here. A transient may spend a dollar to get a pack of cigarettes, but the majority of the money is going to be taken out of the community, and it's not going to benefit this community at all. It may benefit the city to encourage them to invest more or receive more remuneration than they have in tax dollars, because what builds up a community is the tax base. If they are subsidizing this particular building or that building, everything is going out and nothing is coming in. Perhaps industrial parks is to bring in revenue that perhaps an area that might die in ten years can be saved with the dollars and the strength that perhaps—if the industrial parks become involved, form a coalition, and demand that certain agencies address themselves to the sewers, the lighting, the street, and so forth—but what will it do for persons such as the persons living here? I don't think it will benefit them at all, and I don't think it will bring back housing as quickly. I think it will bring in perhaps more businesses, but. . . .

And then, as our children grow and learn that this is not the way of life to live in these low-lying areas, they are going to migrate to better areas, and this is going to forever lead us to nothing but poverty-type people.

Mrs. Genevieve Brooks and her group, they are bringing in this Charlotte Gardens.[13] This is homes that are going to sell from fifty-three to sixty thousand dollars. I understand there are only ninety of them, and whether they are bona fide applicants or just people trying to get information, they have 450 people that are interested. I say good, if we can get more of these. Why? Because they say that only poor people live here. There are people here that make twenty-three and twenty-four thousand dollars, because if you have a sixty- or seventy-thousand-dollar home you are going to have to have that sort of an income. These people may bring about a change because if you are a homeowner you take more interest in your community, and you may become involved and fight. So this is why I was hoping and desirous of having residential housing rather than an industrial park that is going to be owned by Mr. Jones and Mr. Smith that lives in Long Island or Westchester, who hires from another area qualified factory workers who may not live right within the area (although I've been assured that a certain percentage of the persons working in these industrial parks will be recruited from the areas surrounding them). What benefit does the community derive from all of this?

So in the future I feel that as people are getting more educated and realize what's going on, it may change the tide in ten years. I do feel that in ten years if I am still around you will see a difference in any community that's being rehabilitated, a great difference, because some—I won't say a great percentage—but many of the people now that are getting into the rehabilitated housing are appreciating it and are taking care of it, again, because of the structures of management. I hope to involve myself in these some day so as to have a central screening component so that persons that are irresponsible cannot tear up and run from building to building without going through a special screening process. This is a way for our neighborhoods to grow, but you do have those destructive types that will always attempt to tear down. It's innate. We've talked about it, and it costs a lot of money, but we said, "Why not? Why don't we set up a central management screening so that if Mrs. Jones wishes to move in, we would have her already checked out?" With computers it's beautiful, just run a study on her. If you want her she will have to know this, but when she knows that she is being screened she is going to take care, she will become involved, and she will give some voluntary service. And I think this is what people in the poverty areas should do: find a way through whatever they like to involve themselves in one aspect of community life and build up for the future, for their children.

I think this is what it's all about. We must build for the future. I have had my day. I know what it is, and I don't think there is much more that I could do with the span of life that is expected, but I feel as though somebody must pick up where the other one leaves off. It's happening, but I don't think it's happening great enough. I live here, I work here, I am in fear sometimes—this is not the best community to live in—but what is the best community unless you live in one of those enclosed sort of things? I've grown used to it, and I feel as though I would like to continue in this vein, helping people that cannot help themselves. And I suppose this is my story as far as it goes.

CHAPTER NINE
THE BISHOP

Bishop Ernest Crooms, Rapture Preparation Church, b. 1925
Interview: March 3, 1983

"I called him and told him I wanted the building, and he said, 'It's yours.'"

I was born in North Carolina in the year of 1925. My father died when I was five years old. My mother died when I was five months old. And I went from adopted parents to adopted parents. My other adopted parents died in 1968, leaving me a house and some land in North Carolina. I married at the age of eighteen, and my wife was fifteen. We have eleven children alive, one dead, and twenty-four grandchildren.

I moved to New York in 1945 because my wife's mother lived here. So she come to her mother and I come with her. I had tried to volunteer during World War II, but I was born with a nervous condition, and I was told that it couldn't be healed. My head moves and also my eyes. For this reason I was not accepted in the armed forces.

My wife's family was originally from North Carolina, but her mother lived here in the Bronx and she worked here, so we moved to the Bronx, and I lived in the Bronx for thirty-nine years. We moved first to 158th Street and Union Avenue. It was like a new world coming from the South. I never seen a big city. It was like a new world. A thing, you just have to wait and let it grow on you. But things have changed now. When I first come to New York a newspaper was two cents. A subway ride was a nickel. And we had trolley cars, not buses. New York was New York then. It wasn't looking over your shoulder like it is now. All of my children were born here. I have seven sons and four daughters. I have four daughters with me in the church and one son. The rest are not ready to accept it yet.

It never entered my mind to be a minister. This came later. Around the year of 1958. I went to school through tenth grade, and I left school to work. I was brought up as a child in the church. But you go if you want to. If you don't, you don't. But due to the fact that we was trained to go to church, I started sending my children to church. So my little boy asks me one day, "Daddy, why do you always send us to church and you don't go?" So that give me something to think about. So later on I decided to go to church. And in going, the message of the minister or preacher really did something to me. And it made me start thinking in a different direction than I was thinking.

At that time I was going to a little small Pentecostal church. On the day of Pentecost, this is the day that the Holy Ghost was first on earth. They come down on the day of Pentecost. So the people that believe in this are called Pentecostal people. We believe that the Holy Ghost did come and we believe in receiving the Holy Ghost. But what we are into now is a little further than Pentecostal, because all Pentecostal people do not believe to the extent that we believe. We believe in the Apostolic teaching, in other words, the Apostles' teachings. And because we believe that, we are also called Apostles. And then I went to a seminary, but I don't remember the year, and I did not go that long because the course that I wanted, it was not available.

I started pastoring around 1962 or 1963. I started a little storefront church on Prospect Avenue. I don't remember the year, but I stayed there a couple of years, and we outgrew it because it was very small and would only house about fifty persons. We left there, it was on 1376 Prospect Avenue, and we moved around the corner on Boston Road to 1374. There we stayed about twelve years, and we accumulated quite a following, people from that area and from the surrounding areas. What would happen: if a member of a family that lived near was in the church, then maybe some other member of their family that lived a distance would hear about it and through them would come to the church. So we do have parishioners coming from Long Island, from Jamaica, and also from Brooklyn. I think that is about the furthest.

In 1979 we met Moe Greenstein. What happened was that my wife and I was on Fordham Road shopping one day. We were looking for a place to worship because the place we had, it could not satisfy any longer. Buildings being hard to find and also, if we get a place too far away we would lose the parishioners, so we needed a place nearby. I had spoken to my wife, if I could only find a building that we could put together, if it just had the walls, I'd be glad to get in and do the rest. So one day coming from Fordham Road shopping back to our home on Boston Road, we passed this building that was 2015 Crotona Avenue. My wife noticed that this building was boarded up from the bank, and the bank does a wonderful job of closing up the doors. So we got out and looked around. I did not see any signs. We loved the building from the first. It had a two-car garage and it sits on a fifty-by-one-hundred-foot plot. It has a wrought-iron fence all around it. The trees were beautiful in the summertime. It was beautiful. We wanted the building and had very little money because we have mostly parishioners on fixed incomes with children. But we really wanted the building. I come back by on Saturday. This was a Friday when we saw it. I come back Saturday, and there was no signs of life there. At that time I had a truck. I did a little trucking for myself. And I had a stop near the church here, and on Monday it dawned on me that I should come by the church. And when I come by the church Mr. Greenstein had been here on Saturday after I left and put a sign up. And we called him, and I told him I wanted the building. And he said, "It's yours." I'd never met him, he did not discuss money right then, but he said the building was mine if I wanted it. I don't know what month this was, but it was before Christmas because I know I was going away to the South for Christmas, and I wanted to give him a deposit, at least two hundred dollars. He said, "You don't have to worry. The building is yours." I had never met him. Later on, when I come back from the South and we did get together, he put a sign up on both doors. We have a door on the side and a door on the front. And he wrote on the signs: "Future Home of the Rapture Preparation Church of Christ." With no money exchanged. We believe that this was an act of God.

This man was so dear to us, he was like a member of the family. This man, he went out of his way. Real estate people don't do things like this man did. He went out of the way to help us, and later on around April the final details were worked out, and we went to the closing, and the Lord again worked a miracle for us because we needed a certain amount of dollars. I don't remember just how much, but we did have the down payment. We had gotten together the down payment, around four or five thousand dollars, and we was told that we needed

Rapture Preparation Church, 1983 (Georgeen Comerford)

five hundred dollars in cash to take care of the necessary things at the closing. We did not really have the money, and we needed insurance. So I got in touch with a broker, and this broker found out that there was insurance on the building already. He said, "We could just snatch it from you. Why not?" but instead he fixed it so that he turned the insurance from the other company over to us so that we did not have to get any insurance. We went to the closing with the five hundred dollars.

When we got to the closing I had a lawyer that I had known down through the years, Harry Reichenbaum, a Jewish man that lives in Long Island. And the Lord touched his heart, and he did not charge us a dime. He said that he could not charge us for the closing. And the charge would have probably been around seven hundred or seven hundred fifty dollars. At the closing not only did we come home with the five hundred that we carried, we did not have to use any of it, but somehow in the closing monies that the building was supposed to be paid, bills, they somehow turned the money over to us so that we could pay them. We come home with about sixteen hundred dollars to start work on the renovation of the building. When it came time for the dedication service, Mr. Greenstein was here with his wife and with friends, we had members from the bank, and we was highly honored.

The newspapers were there, but at this time the *Daily News* was on strike so they could not get it in the *Daily News*, but small papers did carry the story and we did get some clippings from it. But since that time Mr. Greenstein has never let us go. He has always been there when we needed him, and he's a great friend. And even at the closing I had trouble with the carpenter, and he did not finish the work, and we had the closing, and we did not get the front door fixed. Mr. Greenstein came down first thing on Sunday morning and painted the door. And I think he had to make a trip home and then come back to do that. He saw that the door was painted, and he worked like a member of the church. And he come down and he lettered our bus for us. This is a hobby of his. He is a great artist. He did not charge us a dime. He has been a great friend. And this is what we have to offer today, and we have on this floor one apartment in the back with about five rooms. We had in the front about three rooms, and we have taken all the partitions down, and now we have a place here that will seat up to two hundred, give or take a few.

And we have a broadcasting room, equipment and whatnot. The Lord has done a marvelous job. And this was done mostly through faith because monies we did not have and building we needed. And not only did we get a building, but we count it a great blessing because upstairs we have eight huge rooms that we live on the premises with the parsonage over the church. And in days and times like we are living now when people have no respect for the church, with vandalism and whatnot, we are right here and so far by the grace of God we was only vandalized once. And we think that was someone that maybe come to the church and knew their way around.

When we first got the building it had been gutted. Vandals had taken out all the pipes. The radiators were disconnected. Probably someone was coming back to take them. Some windows were broken, the walls was cracked, the ceiling was coming down. And when the bank man came the place looked so bad—this was in our favor, I suppose they felt that if they did not make a move with the building it would not profit them anything and they would have to tear it down—and they let us have the building for twenty-five thousand dollars. And that was a gift. The building is worth one hundred thousand dollars now.

We got the mortgage with Mr. Greenstein's help. Mr. Greenstein was very instrumental in helping us. We went over to the Dollar Savings Bank. He had the know-how; we did not have it. And he applied for a loan which he did not think we was going to get. The bank sent us a nice letter saying that they could not do it on account of the abandoned buildings around, the vacant lots and so forth. They gave us a letter, and in turn Mr. Greenstein got in touch with something called the Institution Security,[1] and they let us have a loan. But in the meantime the bank was holding the mortgage, but they asked us not to relax with the mortgage, that once we got in we should try and secure a mortgage, which we did, and we was able to get through Mr. Greenstein. And they come in, and they look around. What happened, the bank executives come to our dedication service and saw what we had done, and we made a big dinner, and we fed people downstairs and the executives upstairs. They saw what we was doing and our sincerity, and they did not wait until they went back to the bank, but they held a meeting that day in the corner of the room by themselves and okayed the loan and told me that we would get it, and we did get the loan. And all the people from the bank was very nice. And I keep saying that Mr. Greenstein has been a great friend. He still is. We often call. If he don't call me I'll call him.

It was a miracle because why would he take up so much time with me, being a businessman? Naturally he's out there to sell property. He's out there to make money. But he spent a lot of time on me that he did not get any money for. And he would not let me give him anything. He picked me up in his car to take me to the closing, which was in Hempstead, Long Island. And when I went to pay him he said, "Don't insult me." He would not take a dime from me. When he come down to look at the books he would not take a dime. Never for any of the work that he has done for us has he charged us five cents. Everything was a gift. All of this was, in spite of what Mr. Greenstein did, we did give God the glory, because we feel that the Lord worked through Mr. Greenstein, also through the lawyer and different ones that did so much for us.

We have a lot of teenagers in our church, young people coming from broken homes. I am like a father to a lot of children because they come from broken homes. Some of the young ones are married, and they don't know about life. I am constantly encouraging them, and this is why we worked to get a bus so we can take them places, we can show them things that they would not ordinarily see. We take them to North Carolina, and I take the young people here all the way to Tallahassee, Florida, not only the young but also the adults for fifty dollars round-trip, and this includes their lodging. Fifty dollars!

First, we had an old school bus, and at that time gas was cheap, and if we didn't have any problems with the bus we could go and come pretty well. With fifty dollars each, and with the amount of people we had, there was about eight or nine hundred dollars, and we could take them for about one hundred and change each way. We had to spend a little bit for motels, and something for the drivers. The only thing was we had two blowouts. Other than that we went and returned with no major problems. If we had run into major trouble, it could have been serious. Since that first time we ran an ad in the *Times* asking that someone would donate a bus for tax purposes, because we were in a position to give them tax exemption. We weren't successful with that, but later on we found a bus, a nice bus, a diesel, which was what we wanted, because if diesels are in good condition you can go cheaper and faster. We found a diesel for five thousand, five hundred dollars. We had no money, but we raised the money and paid off the diesel.

Since that time we sold that bus and got a little later model, still an old bus, 1961, what you call a 4106. First we had a 4104, now we have a 4106 from 1961, more than twenty years old, but it looks good. We have another church in North Carolina, and we take the young people and the parishioners to meet other people, and we are able to do it cheap. Now we can take them all the way to North Carolina and back for thirty-five dollars per person. Now, where can you travel for thirty-five dollars? Not even one way. We take them and bring them for thirty-five. The motels will cost them approximately thirty or thirty-eight dollars. We put four persons to a room, and for two days this will cost each person around seventeen dollars and change. So this is the way we try to do things. We try to work out the cheapest way because we deal with a lot of poor people.

For some of them that came to the Bronx from the West Indies, they have never seen the South. Some New York children are fortunate in that their parents have migrated from the South, so they are able to go down and have family. But some have never been out of the Bronx, and this gives them a chance to get out. We take lunch on the bus, and they sing, and this is something to keep them interested and keep them in church. And if we could get more ministers and people to do this, we would have less purse snatching and more people praying. And if more people would pray, we would have a better South Bronx. We have thirty young people in the choir now, we have Hispanics and some French. They come from one of the islands, I don't know which one, and they speak Spanish and French and English.

This neighborhood is black and Hispanic, but most of the black community moved up here from the South. Some moved up before me, some later. In the South they are very religious, and when they come to the North, some of them stay with religion, and some of them leave it. Our church doesn't have any drug programs. The young people mostly take part in church activities in the different auxiliaries like choir and ushering. They do like to sing, and many of them are very talented. Some of them play instruments like guitar, organ, piano, and drums. They have programs, and sometimes they invite other churches to come. There is always something to keep them occupied, and this keeps their minds in a spiritual state. As long as we keep their minds spiritual, they have less time to think about other things. We don't win them all. Every so often we might lose one, but I have children here with me now that have children, and their children are about ready to marry, and they started out with me as teenagers. That's how long they stay with me. I have always loved working with children. My wife and I both came from small families. I was the only son, although with one half-brother. We didn't want a large family, just a boy and a girl, but we ended up with four girls and seven boys. The more children there were, the more I loved it. So we also welcomed all these children in the church from broken homes.

Some of them have gone on to college, Stony Brook and other colleges and universities. Some of them go at night and are working their way through. There is a lot of unemployment in this area, but we have been blessed. We have only about three that are not employed, and I got a call just today for one of the young men to call about a job. They don't all have good jobs, but it is a job. When I say not a good job, some of them have like guard duty jobs that don't pay an awful lot, but at least there is something to come home with. We learn to be thankful for whatever we have, and we wait, and we trust the Lord that he will do better things for them, but at least we have some employment.

I have had the title of "bishop" for about five or six years. You start out as a minister for maybe three years, then, if you are proven in the sight of the elders and the bishops that you can qualify, they ordain you as an elder. And not everyone who is an elder wants to offer himself as bishop. But they felt that I qualified for it, and the organization that I was working with assigned this to me. I am over New York and the New England states. In fact, we have one church in Connecticut and one in Brooklyn. I myself personally established three churches: this one, one in Long Island, and the one in North Carolina that was just beginning to get started. Also I have another minister in Mount Vernon—I didn't establish his church, but he worked with us—so I have four churches under my direct supervision. I do a lot of traveling, so I don't have much time to be with the other ministers. I have broadcasts to do, and a lot of people want to meet in our district. I'm also meeting a lot of new people in a place called Statesville, North Carolina. These people don't have a pastor right now, and they are listening to my broadcasts. I have a station in Norfolk, Virginia, and one on Chesapeake Bay, and I am supposed to go down there and meet with them and see what I can do to get a church started.

This is the bishop's job, to travel

around and to establish churches. Sometimes this office is abused, of course; not everyone that is called a bishop really does the work of a bishop. But this is really what a bishop should be, to go different places and start new churches. I am blessed that we have ministers here in my church that can take on the services in my absence. They are so efficient that if I were to leave overnight I would not even have to point out what should be done. If they know I am going to be gone, I don't have to leave any outline; they know just how to do it. With the broadcasts, we tape services here every Friday night if possible, but no later than Sunday afternoon, and then mail them out on Thursdays.

We still have very little money. One person once who did not want their name mentioned donated us one thousand dollars, and this is the most that we ever got, except that people have donated their time, like the lawyer and Mr. Greenstein, but other than that we don't get anything. We wish we could because there are a lot of things that we would like to do. I wanted to get a house and fix it up for old folks, for senior citizens, so that each one would have their own room and one big kitchen or maybe a kitchen on each floor so they could help themselves and do their cooking and share a sitting room but have their own rooms. We wanted to do this, but we are not able now. We have about eight senior citizens in our church, some within walking distance that can walk, some that come by bus.

The neighborhood now is mostly Hispanic, and many of the youth, black and Hispanic, are not properly educated. This makes a great difference, but I have no problems. I did have a problem once when we first moved into the neighborhood. Someone threw a bottle and hit one of my sons, and it could have ignited into something big. A group had congregated, and I went down to the corner, and I walked over to the young man who had thrown the bottle, and I talked to him, and then it was all over. Thank God. It could have gotten into something big. So we don't have any problems, but you have to know how to deal with people, to talk, to be nice. I get along with everyone, and I have no problems. Thank God.

From the time we came to the neighborhood we got a lot of comments about what we did to fix up the building. We are always active, always fixing up something, and people can see this. Someone put in storm windows for the upstairs. It cost about one thousand dollars, and people watching what was being done here started asking where we got the windows, and pretty soon other people starting putting storm windows in their buildings. They could see we are not here to tear down but to build. We keep up our part of the neighborhood, and this makes others want to pitch in. Very few of our parishioners live in the neighborhood. They come from some distance, often by public transportation. But we do have to be careful and keep watch. My daughter had her car stolen and never got it back. And we had a visiting church come some weeks ago, and when they went out to go home, their car had no battery. It was gone out of the car. And one brother lost his hubcaps right in the daytime. For one thing, very few people will say anything if they see anything, because people are afraid they would be retaliated on.

Looking ahead, the church is growing, and we may need a larger place. And we would like to get into different programs for children to give our children something to do. We would like to get into typing, sewing, free lunch programs. We want to be more involved in the neighborhood. Many people have the wrong opinion about churches, especially if it's an Apostolic church.[2] Stories are told about us that are not right, that we feel we're just a people off to ourselves and whatnot. But it's not like that. We love people very much, and we want to do things for people. We would like to show them the way of the Lord. If we can get more people in the church, more people serving the Lord, we will have more people that could look where they are going and don't have to look over their back. We'll have a better neighborhood. We will have less people on drugs. We will have less people selling drugs because a Christian parent will do all that they can to keep their children from selling or being involved in drugs. It won't be a dollar sign in front of our eyes. Where now a lot of people that might note that members of their family are involved in drugs, the dollar sign keeps them from saying anything, but if they really get involved in the Lord's work, then they will see the danger, and they will come to put their trust in God, and not in the things that really demolish the neighborhood. I hope this will happen. This is my work and my life.

PART FOUR
MOVERS AND SHAKERS

Building the Bronx, One Factory, School, Museum, and Social Institution at a Time

I. Irma Fleck, born in 1920, living in the Bronx from age three, came from a middle-class professional family. Her father was a doctor, but as a Jew couldn't practice in Poland and left for America along with many others. Her future husband, also a doctor, escaped first from Germany and then Italy, one step ahead of the Nazis, and was one of many refugees taken in by the Flecks, whose home was open to many who needed shelter when they first arrived. Irma's public service began when she reached out to less fortunate families, inviting children and parents—many of them black—to share in her garden and her yard. When the government was funding high-rise public housing that lacked a community center or any place for youth activities, she worked to provide that neighborhood center. Later, she said, "I wanted to tackle the whole borough," and she went to then borough president Herman Badillo to get his backing to develop what became the Bronx Council on the Arts. Later still, she was the force behind the Bronx Museum. No one told her what was needed. She looked, saw lacunae, and filled them. She described herself as "the spearhead" and "the idea person."

II. Mike Nuñez, born in Harlem in 1930, moved to the Bronx when he was ten. His father, a welder who never went to college, insisted that both his sons get a college degree. Mike's brother, Luis, went into politics. Mike tried politics, like Stanley Friedman was active in a political club, but then tried a succession of roles in business and community work before deciding on economic development.[1] While recognizing the good done by social programs, he concluded that they just permitted "holding ground," not changing things for the better, and to achieve real change you needed economic development through investment. "First you stabilize, and then you stimulate," he told me. His first business, recommended to him by Moe Greenstein, was Ace Spray Finishing Corporation, and once Mike and his Bronx Venture had invested in it—a mix of government and bank monies—Ace grew from a small business with eighteen employees and a budget of six hundred thousand dollars to seventy employees and a budget of $2.3 million. "When I started out," he told me, "people thought I was a madman." Not mad—Mike dreamed big, as did Irma, on behalf of the entire Bronx.

III. Ramon Velez, born in Puerto Rico in 1933, came to the Bronx as an adult. While in high school, he joined clubs, founded clubs, and ran clubs, organizing student protests as he later organized Puerto Rican protests in the United States against discrimination and civil rights abuses. Before the influx of antipoverty government money into the Bronx he worked with volunteers, small storefront businesses that loaned their facilities for meetings at night. He helped start the National Association for Puerto Rican Affairs (NAPRA). He took credit for the creation of Hostos Community College, Lincoln Hospital, and the South Bronx High School. On the sidelines of mainstream political office—although he was at one time on the city council and also a district leader—he affirmed that "politics is the ultimate power," and ran, mostly unsuccessfully, for higher offices. Wanting as broad a mandate as possible, he headed up the Multi-Services association located at Hunts Point that dealt with the range of social services—housing, education, health, and welfare. Always a controversial figure, no one questioned his activism on behalf of the Bronx or of his fellow Puerto Ricans.

CHAPTER TEN
IRMA

Irma Fleck, Program Developer, 1920–2004
Interview: July 19, 1983

"Beauty is nothing if it's not shared."

I started my life in the Bronx at the age of three and that means—it just occurred to me—that I have been here for sixty years. But it's splendid. My parents came here from Poland. My father was a physician. He had studied at the University of Vienna, and because he was Jewish, it would not have been possible for him to practice in Poland, and as a non-Austrian citizen, he couldn't practice there. So he had no choice. My mother said, "Come to America. That's the place of opportunity." And they came.

They first spent about two months in Manhattan—just a transition period—and then they got a place on 169th Street and Washington Avenue where there is now the Claremont Village.[1] We lived in that apartment for about a year or two. My father started the practice of medicine then, and it was not easy. It was quite difficult, as a matter of fact. He didn't have patients right away, but he didn't want his neighbors to know that, so he would take his bag with his instruments and all that and walk around the block.

My parents spoke very little English when they came, but soon enough people came to see him, and then when he had the possibility he purchased a home and a practice from a physician named Dr. Magida, who was moving away. That was many, many years ago, and that was the house on 1206 Washington Avenue, where we lived for over thirty years. It was more than just a house and a home. It was also a medical office, and there was a waiting room with patients, and there were people streaming in and out of my home continuously. All sorts of things happened there. Organizations were founded. I started one while I was living there.

This was in the late 1920s, shortly before the crash in 1929. The area was what I would call low-middle income at the time. The house had been built by the owner of the brewery that was on Fulton Avenue and, I think, 169th Street, where the Bronx

Hospital [Bronx Lebanon Hospital] is now, Eichler Brewery. He built the house. In the beginning, like most of the Bronx, there were Irish, Italian, Jewish, German families in the neighborhood, and then slowly, as the migration began from the South, there were blacks moving in. Slowly after that, after World War II, the Hispanics started migrating from Puerto Rico, and the neighborhood changed. Most of the blacks who moved here before the war lived in the basements of many of the buildings because they were the supers. It was difficult to find jobs at the time, and there was still a lot of prejudice.

What happened after the war was interesting. Shortly after the war there was a shortage of housing—quite a bad shortage—and so the Italians and the Jews and the Irish who lived there learned to get along with the black people who were moving in and with the Hispanic people who were moving in, and it was a very good communal feeling. Suddenly they discovered that there really isn't very much difference under the skin, and people lived together for, I would say, about four or five years until housing improved, people found better jobs, and they were able to move out, which they would have done at any rate. But the time in which they were forced to live together became an interesting learning period for many of the people, and for me, too, of course. We all learned. Many of my father's patients were of the minorities, and we had close relations with them.

When I went to school as a child, the school was still mostly European and white. It was the old P.S. 2, about one hundred years old. It was said that it was a hospital during the Civil War. They still had privies outside where we had to go when we had to go, and I remember them very clearly. That was my first touch of the primitive. But it didn't hurt me. The teachers were superb. I can remember the names of my teachers in that school, and I can't remember the names of the teachers in high school or in college. Strange. Maybe I was more impressionable, or perhaps because I spent—we would spend six whole months together in the same classroom. Those teachers made a strong impression on me.

Most of the children knew English, but I didn't. I was in kindergarten and still did not speak English. I went to first grade, and I remember sitting there like a dummy, and I think the teacher thought I was rather stupid, but I just didn't know the language, and they were not prepared for non–English speaking children at that time. But I learned it pretty quickly, as most children do, but I think I was the only child at that time who didn't speak. My mother's tongue was German, and that was the language that my family spoke at home. And I also quickly unlearned German as I learned English.

My mother had to learn English because she had to deal with the patients. They had a wonderful arrangement. After we moved into this big private house at 1206 Washington Avenue, it was a haven for many, many people. Our relatives who had to flee from the Holocaust in Europe all came here to us. My father did everything possible to rescue as many of the relatives as possible, and of course there was no place you could put them up so we didn't double up, we tripled up. You had to make room for people who had to be rescued, so the house was really a haven and a home. They would stay with us a couple of months, and then they'd find an apartment in the neighborhood, which was still low-rent, and they would find jobs or whatever and settle. But that period, that interim period until they found a place, would take about three or four months. In the meantime, there was a home for them with us.

Life for me is divided into before the war and after the war, and the war for me is World War Two. Before the war there was a depression, a very bad one, nothing like we have known in recent times, and the community surrounding Washington Avenue was poor, but somehow or other they always found the two dollars to come to the doctor or three dollars if he had to go to their house. However, there were also times when he was called to the house—and, by the way, when you got a phone call to see a patient you went that very same day because there were no miracle drugs. You had to be there on time; you had to be there at the first instance of symptoms. And we had dreaded diseases—scarlet fever, diphtheria, and all the children's diseases, and there were no cures at that time, no serums, nothing of that sort, and so everything was an emergency. Medical practice has changed on account of the wonder drugs now.

So time was of the essence, and I remember that my brother and I were the first telephone exchange—because at that time there wasn't one—and the phone had to be answered every time it rang. My parents liked to go to the movies, and when they would go to the local movie—there was no television, of course, and that had to be the entertainment—they would leave the seat number with the usher, and if a call came in we answered it. I was about twelve at the time, and my brother fifteen, and yet we had the sense of knowing how to answer the phone. That was the first thing we had to learn, and if there was an emergency, we would call that movie theater, and more often than not my father could never see a film all the way through, because he had to go immediately to make that house call. We did the same thing when we went to the Castle Hill Bathing Park.[2] At Castle Hill there were many other doctors as well, and they had a system of numbers—each doctor got a number—so when a call came in at the central boxes they would hang the number up, and if you saw your number you went to the phone and called your office and left the beach. That was medical-practice life in those days, and it was essential, and doctors had strong feelings for their patients. Very often when my father would go to see a patient with a sick child, and knew that that child had to have some medication, and could see by the surrounding poverty that there was no money for the medicine, not only did he not take the three dollars for the house call but put his hand in his pocket and took out three dollars to pay for the medicines. But that's the way it had to be. I think I got my first sense of public service from being there and seeing that.

I had two brothers, and it was very important in my parents' mind that they go to college because they would have to support a family, and it was not that important for me to go. And besides, I was not a brilliant student, and I never thought I really had the makings of being a college student, so I didn't make a fuss about it, and my two brothers were sent with the money that was available—remember that this was still the Depression—and I was sent to take a medical assistance course so that I could work with my father, which I did for a number of years.

This was a period of time when we were rescuing people. One of the people who was rescued just about in the nick of time became my husband, and maybe that's why my life is divided—before Henry and after Henry. We were married in 1940. I was at that time working for my father. I was a medical assistant, and I was an X-ray technician, a lab technician, and most doctors had all that equipment in their office because there were no really good labs to send work out to, so they had to do it in-house. My husband came to work with my father. He was a physician too. He had just graduated from the University of Bologna, Italy. He had left Berlin one step ahead of the Nazis, and Bologna one step ahead of the Nazis, and came to us here. He worked with my father, and we had many arguments together, and we fell in love, and we married in 1940. Shortly thereafter, my husband was drafted.[3] I don't know if he was drafted or he enlisted, though as a physician he would have had to enlist.

I had my little daughter while my husband was overseas, and then I decided that it was time to pick up on my schooling. I took courses at Hunter College. Later on, I took courses at Columbia University, but with a family at that time it wasn't easy to go back to school fulltime. I discovered while I was taking these courses—they were courses like physiology, math, things like that—that I really was a very good student. I was an A student, as a matter of fact. Finally, when my children were old enough—I had two, when my husband came back from the war we had our son—when they were both old enough I went back to college. I studied sociology, and I also learned that women too were important, and there was a place for us, and that education was very important. But how I learned that came about from my work in the community.

My work with the community dates back to that house on Washington Avenue. After the war many of the refugees came to live in the area because it was inexpensive, and they lived across the street from us. They had seen so much of the misery of life, because many of them or their family members had been either in Auschwitz or one of the other camps, that they had a great feeling for life. They had children right away, and there were many baby carriages with children, and they would sit out in front of their house on the sidewalk, and I had this big yard and a lovely garden that I had created, and I couldn't see that. Beauty is nothing if it's not shared, so I invited them to come in and sit around my little tub pool, a goldfish pond that I had made there, and enjoy the flowers, which they did. That was in the back of the house. On the side of the house we had a basket hoop for basketball, and a Ping-Pong table, and a fireplace. And a young man who came to work for me doing windows and such—a young black fellow—had a baseball team, and they had just gotten uniforms, and they had no place to put them. He asked me if they could use the basement, and I said of course they could store their stuff in the basement. And they were intrigued too by the Ping-Pong table, and in short order it became a playground. We never had to worry when we left the house on weekends that anything would happen, because we had our own security system, and nothing was ever touched. So in the backyard there were the women with their little children, and on the side there was a whole team of young people playing basketball or Ping-Pong or whatever, as they wanted, and again there was a joy in seeing all of this utilized because my children were very small at the time, and they couldn't, and I don't like waste. And they enjoyed it.

At that time I began to feel that there were things that could be done for the neighborhood. I had been working with my father a long time, and I got to know the people as individuals and knew their problems, and I felt that certain things had to happen, like better housing. This was right after the war. The neighborhood was mixed and low income, and everyone was getting along well; there were no problems. Everyone knew everyone else, and it was cordial, warm, friendly. Nevertheless, parts of the community needed new housing. It was all old housing to begin with. They were walk-ups, and it was time to replace them, I guess, and the federal government started doing projects, and I was interested in this. I started working with the people at Forest House who were involved with projects.[4] The director of Forest House—Forest Neighborhood House—at that time was George Gregory, a handsome young black, and through him I learned a great deal about the black community and what their interests were, what their desires were, their sensitivities, their feelings. It wasn't just from him alone, but I think he gave me the more formal education that I needed, and I was part of a committee at the time that included some very remarkable people, and I learned a great deal about community work.

The leadership of the community were the minister of the church and the director of the community center, and these were people who were very well educated and who were remarkably articulate and could speak for the black community.

I started the Claremont Neighborhood Center.[5] There was the intention by the government to build the Claremont Village, and I knew that there wasn't any place for the young people to be, and to add so many families—I don't remember the number of families—coming to live there without including a community center would have been disastrous. They made other mistakes too—they built it too high also—but in those days, they had to learn. So I went to the Housing Authority and said, "You know, we have to build a community center there." And they said they would only build the center when they'd have a sponsoring body, and an organization that would run it. I said, "Okay, you'll have your organization." So I pulled together a number of people from the community, we set up a board, and we became a corporation. And that was it.

Claremont Park was a small park in the area, further down, around Claremont Parkway and Webster Avenue. But it was too far down. And there was Crotona Park as well, but there was really no place for anyone to go that was close enough to Claremont Village where the families would move in. And the parks are only good three or four months anyway, not the rest of the year. And in the whole year there wasn't any community center in the area, and that was essential. These were mostly young families with young children, and they needed some place for the young people to be. This was the beginning of the era of the juvenile delinquents. They have advanced now, they are no longer juvenile delinquents, and with all the drugs they are much worse than delinquents, but at the time it was the juvenile delinquent problem that we had, and so there was a great need for a community center. With a number of good people I set up a board of directors and a good organization. Of course, it took eight years until they actually built it, until the center was there, but it's there now. When I look inside once in a while I realize that the gym is the way it is because that's the way we designed it. They let us work with them on design and on what we wanted and where we wanted it, and Bill Hopkins and I—he was the cop in the area—worked on that end of it.

At any rate, after nine years with Claremont Neighborhood Center I felt that I'd really done everything I could in terms of organization, administration, getting the place opened, and all that. I would have liked to be the executive director, but I didn't qualify because I didn't have the education. I didn't have that piece of paper. At that point I said to myself, well, this is as far as I will ever be able to go without that diploma, and that's the time when I said, "That's it. I am closing everything up, and I am going back to school."

And I did. I went to Queens College.[6] I went through the ACE Program—that's the Adult and Community Education Program—which was a joy. I spent two years going to school, and I loved every minute of it. It was wonderful. They gave me enough credits, and I saved about a year, and with the time that I saved I invested it into getting my master's. I went to NYU. I went to the Center for Human Relations. I got my master's there.

When I got out—when I finished college—I decided that I wanted to go back into community work. This time I wanted to tackle the whole borough, and so I met with Herman Badillo, who was at that time the borough president. I didn't just meet with him. I had him come to dinner with his wife, and I gave him the best dinner he ever had at that time, and I told him that I wanted to set up an arts organization in the Bronx, a boroughwide arts organization. I was always very keen on the arts. I loved it. I had an aunt who would take me every Saturday to a museum, and to concerts and all that, which was great, and that's where I got the first taste of it. And I felt that the Bronx needed something to give it more class.

This was in the late 1950s. There

was a Bronx Council on the Arts that had been established by Rev. William Kalaidjian,[7] but it was more of a local group that served mainly to put on some theater in—I think it was Walton High School—in the north-northwest Bronx. And for quite a few years they weren't doing anything, so the organization was rather moribund, and I felt that the Bronx needed something that was more vibrant and reached out to more people and really served the community. When I started I had absolutely zero funding. I told Herman Badillo what I wanted, and he said, "Go ahead, I'll help you." And so we got together on picking a board of directors, and we got help from the Bronx Community College—they gave us some drawer space—and got started. There was no money at the time, but there was a lot of good talent.

Jim Colston, who was then the president of Bronx Community College,[8] felt that there should not be two arts groups, and he suggested a merger. We were calling ourselves the Bronx Committee on the Arts because we knew there was a Bronx Council on the Arts, and so we took on the name of Bronx Council on the Arts and also got one hundred fifty dollars from their treasury. We took a few of their board members also, and so we became the Bronx Council on the Arts.[9] I worked first as president—I had founded it.

Slowly we got a little money. I had written a proposal to the New York State Council on the Arts for what I thought was for a tremendous amount of money. In the proposal I put in all the things that I felt had to be done in the Bronx with the ways to do them. The budget was one hundred fifty thousand dollars, which at that time was extraordinary. I never thought we'd get it, but we did get a piece of it. We got a piece for a summer program of performing arts, and with that we were able to fund a group called the Chuck Davis Dance Company.[10] They were nowhere at the time. Chuck Davis was doing some fine dancing and teaching, but really had no company, and we funded them, and from that summer on they did touring in the Bronx, and that's how they got their start.

We also got some money from the city. The idea was to ferret out where the money was. I got ten thousand from the city department—it was then P.R.C.A., Parks, Recreation, and Cultural Affairs—and that was divided up with the Bronx Opera Company, which was not yet called the Bronx Opera Company until I suggested that they call themselves that.[11] I think they were quartered at NYU, and they were calling themselves the Heights Opera Company. That was when NYU was on the University Heights campus. I said to them, "We are interested in supporting Bronx groups." So they said, "Okay, we'll call ourselves the Bronx Opera Company," and they got the first grant, which I think was two thousand five hundred, which was a lot of money at that time.

We were able to open a storefront office and slowly, slowly, we were able to raise money. At first we were working with volunteers and I was a volunteer, but after I got the master's in human relations and I was working at Bronx Community College as a program developer—that was my first professional job with a degree—we realized that the council needed full-time staff, and I said, "Well, I'm here, you can hire me, and I'll work." I was willing to work for any amount of money because I knew that I could raise the money. I'd have to raise the money for my own salary. What I didn't like was that when I got members of the board together to discuss budget and salary lines—and at that time I knew that we had to have a secretary, and we'd have to have the money for the secretary who was not willing to work for peanuts like I was—they set her salary at something like eight thousand dollars. And when it came to setting my salary—and remember I had after all this time gotten my degree and done all of the work and raised the money—these three men on the board (and I say three men for a reason) who set the secretary's salary at eight thousand set mine at something like nine thousand, five hundred. That may not be the exact amount, but it doesn't matter.

I was shocked. That was my first experience with sex bigotry. And for that I had to sweep the floors too. I had to do literally everything. No way was I going to take that. I didn't mind working for nothing, but I wasn't going to allow these men to put a price tag on what I do. So that was my first experience of discrimination. I exploded, and they got the message. And in any case there wasn't any money to pay me even at nine thousand, but when I wrote the proposal I wrote the budget, and I put the amount for me—or for any executive director—at what I thought was reasonable at the time, and that was sixteen thousand. It wasn't extraordinary, but it was reasonable for the job that was called for, so when you got the money and it was for that amount, there was no question. I felt I knew what was right, and no way were they going to put me at a salary that was close to being a secretary. I meant, was that what I went to college for?

I ran the Arts Council for nine years. When I left it, there was a quarter of a million dollars of sure money coming in. I had in that time created—with the help of many other people, of course—the Bronx Museum of the Arts.[12] When I say "I created," I mean that I was the spearhead for most of the things that happened. I was the idea person. I was the one who got the money and got it pushed through. Lots of other people were involved, but I question whether if I wasn't there whether certain things would have happened. Maybe that's egotistical, but I know the role I played, and I know that that's what I did for the council, and that's what I did for the museum. And because I worked with the Department of Cultural Affairs, working out budgets, or rather "lines," as they call them (lines in the city budget that were permanent, they were never there before), every year they would get the money. Once the museum was on a permanent line, they would get the money every year just as the Metropolitan did. That took quite a lot of work. I did the same thing with the State Council on the Arts.

There was a group of us. There were the five councils in the city: there was the Brooklyn Arts and Cultural Association. Charlene Victor is still working there. There was Staten Island, and Manhattan, and Queens, and Brooklyn. Charlene and I were known as the bookends; we squeezed everything between us. There are a lot of stories I could tell about how the Bronx Museum came about and our working with the Metropolitan, how we got our first loan exhibition from the Met. Many things were done in that era that are now paying off.

The State Council on the Arts started at pretty much the same time we did, around 1967.[13] They also had no money until John Rockefeller came. John Hightower, who is now with the South Street Seaport, knew him quite well, and he tells the story that they were sitting somewhere, and out of the blue Rockefeller said he was going to give something like $18 million to the State Council on the Arts. That was the first real money they ever got. At that point when we heard there was going to be money, our five council people went down en masse and asked for a piece of the action, because we were doing a job in each of our boroughs, and we insisted that New York City is not just Manhattan. That was the message we had over and over again, and that's how we bludgeoned the Cultural Affairs Department into giving us regular funds, and how we got the State Council on the Arts. That was the heyday of the councils, really. That was when everything started, and recognition of the cultural life, and it was a wonderful time. I enjoyed it very much, but at the end of nine years I felt I'd had it, and I had reached a level of funding that I felt was good. I was tired, and this was the time to leave and let somebody else come in and take it to another plateau. This was about seven years ago, around 1976. I felt I was ready for retirement.

But after two months I was climbing the walls. Retirement isn't for me. I had thought I would be able to spend more time at my hobbies. My hobbies are plants, and I was going to take some courses, and I was going to do this and that. But a hobby is just that, and you can't make it into a full-time occupation. Some people can, but I was not able to, because I was always involved with people, and this removed me from people. Anyway, my next idea just came to me. This was the time when the South Bronx was really degenerating. That's the only word that comes to me. It was really being burned down. It was a very bad situation, and I got the idea—and I probably wasn't the only one who got the idea—of the greening of the South Bronx, taking certain acres and making them into green, either meadowland or vegetable gardens, because it was useless, it was all barren land, rubble strewn, and I wanted to work on that. This was my green thumb coming up again.

First, the idea had to be worked out. What do you do with rubble-strewn land? How do you grow anything on that? And it occurred to me that all the negative factors—of which there were plenty in the South Bronx—could be made into positive factors. There were three things that there was plenty of: one is the vacant land, two is garbage—a tremendous amount of it because we have the Hunts Point market there—and three was the manpower, a lot of unemployed. I figured if we could get the three things together and make it positive, perhaps we could do something. And being an old gardener, I knew about compost. I thought if we could take the vegetables from the market and compost them with leaves from suburbia—of which they had too many and they had no place to incinerate them—we could make a soil which would be good enough to put on the vacant lots, and you'd turn them over to the people in the community as gardens that people would take care of.

The first thing I did, of course, was to go to the Hunts Point market and see what they had there. I was amazed at what they threw out—pure green vegetables. Every time they bagged something, if it was cabbage, the outer leaves came off. If it was carrots they had to cut the tops. Whatever it was went into this big, enormous vat with which you could have made a soup to feed an army. And if we could just get that and use it, it would be great, so then I got in touch with the contractor who hauled the vegetables away, and he said yes, he'd be glad to go with us. Then we had to find a place where to dump it. All of this of course took three years. Also getting money took three years. I was able to raise quite a lot of money. I should say that we named the organization Bronx Frontier Development Corporation,[14] because we thought it was like a new frontier in the South Bronx, and we could help the developers. The redevelopment process is still going on. A number of good gardens were established and maintained by the people in the community, and we achieved a good bit of success. After five years I left that too.

I had a partner who had been a policeman in the area and had a feeling for all this just as I had, and he stayed and took over after I left. I had already raised a tremendous amount of money for them, and I saw that what we were doing, what we had dreamed about, was indeed possible. Whether he continues in that vein is something I can't say, but I do know that he worked out an arrangement with the zoo, and they get all the zoodoos, and they now package the compost with the zoo dung, and they call it the ZooDoo, and they are selling it.[15] When I left there were about fifteen gardens that had been done, but I also had written up a program for wildflower meadows, and they got money for that just as I was leaving. I don't know exactly where the wildflower meadows are or will be, or whether they will function well. In the gardens we had community labor but also plenty of manpower from the CETA program, which was really very good.[16] In spite of its detractors it was good. And we had many young people to whom we gave a good start, and good training in various fields, and that helped Frontier and it helped them.

When I left Bronx Frontier I decided that I would work on my own as a consultant, that I had gained a great deal of knowledge and information, and I knew the community. I knew fundraising, public relations, and I was going to work as a consultant because it meant I could control my time. I called it Ideas Unlimited. That's what I'm doing now.

CHAPTER ELEVEN
MIKE

Michael Nuñez, Bronx Venture, Economic Developer, 1930–2004
Interview: March 4, 1983

"The important thing is that something has to be done, and we are doing it."

I was born in East Harlem, in fact on 99th Street and Third Avenue. I came up to the Bronx when I must have been around ten years old, and I've been more or less here ever since. So in reality I grew up in the Bronx and was educated in the schools here. My father is Peruvian. He comes from the town of Callao in Peru, which is a seacoast town near Lima, and my mother is Puerto Rican. They met here in New York during the 1920s and got married, and had me and my brother. They are still living here. They own a condominium in Parkchester, and they have retired there.

My brother, Luis Nuñez, is in Washington where he heads the National Puerto Rican Coalition. Prior to that, he was a presidential appointee heading the United States Commission on Civil Rights for several years, first in the Nixon administration, then the Carter, and then the Reagan administration.

We lived first on Tinton Avenue and 158th Street, and then from there we moved over to Beck Street right off Longwood—Longwood and Intervale, right next to P.S. 39, an elementary school that's now abandoned. I went to Morris High School in the Bronx, and from there I went to City College over on Convent Avenue and 138th Street.

Moving to the Bronx represented a step up for us. There was a bevy of trees. The Bronx when I first came up here was a strikingly different place than what it is now—I mean the South Bronx. I remember people pulling up to the local movies in chauffeur-driven cars with fur coats and whatnot—going to a movie—and for us who were just coming up from East Harlem, that was amazing. I still remember that to this day. That was the Prospect Theatre,[1] which now is a Spanish theater, and that whole area now is burned out. But I lived through those times, and I saw the slippage as it just burned down and this mass exodus of businesses, so I watched it—not that it just happened, but over fifteen or twenty years—and I've just been working in the Bronx trying to turn that around and bring it back to what it had been and maybe even better.

It's funny the way it happens. It happened slowly. People move like in dribs and drabs, and all of a sudden there is a mass exodus. Before you know it you are in this flood of movement. You are not conscious until, all of a sudden, you are being drowned in it. It's that type of thing. And then everyone gets worried, and everybody starts trying a program, and politicians make it a platform, and that type of thing. It's not something that the people living here, the residents here, were aware that it was going to happen. Maybe there was a dumping. The South Bronx became a dumping ground for the social service agencies. We had a concentration of welfare clients in the South Bronx, which caused a movement of the middle class and upper middle class, and before you knew it everything else started to go with it: the fires, the burglaries, the crime. Everything started to go because with too much concentration of any one particular group the need was so great that you are aggravating a situation to the point where something is going to give or something is going to explode. And it did.

I don't want to say that I have the last word in the analysis of how an area goes down, but there were certain things. As roads became better traveled, as more cars were being sold, suburbs became very fashionable and everybody started to move out. They wanted property, they wanted more trees, they wanted a better environment for their children, et cetera, et cetera. Of course, that goaded the exodus, and as the buildings began to be vacated they were beginning now to be filled by these agencies that were putting in their clients. Of course, that's a very simplified explanation of what happened, but that's one of the theories that's being expounded.

We first moved to the Bronx in the 1940s. When the war ended I was already in the Bronx. I remember I was on a fire escape in 1945 when it ended. I remember V-E Day and then V-J Day, the European theater, and then the Japanese. I was too young to fight in that war. My war was the Korean War. When World War II began I was still living in East Harlem. I was about eleven years old, and then right around 1941 we moved up to the Bronx, at the beginning of the war. I remember the day, that Sunday in December, December 7, I was on 113th Street. My father at that time owned a candy store on 113th Street right off Park Avenue, and I was on Park Avenue with one of the local merchants who was a friend of mine. He was very interested in radios, and this announcement came through: "Pearl Harbor has been attacked." I was very young, and he says, "Did you hear that, Mike?"

I said, "What?"

He says, "Oh, they just attacked Pearl Harbor. That probably means there's going to be a war"

I says, "Ohhh." Then I went around to my father's store and there was a lot of excitement there, and lo and behold, that was December 7 for me.

When I was very young, all we spoke was Spanish. Then when I went into elementary school it was sort of a shock because it took me such a long time to catch up. I always felt like the world was very mysterious and very scary—as I think back now to when I was very young and how I used to look at myself in those elementary years, how everything looked so vast and so beyond me. Now that I think back I would say the language had a lot to do with it because I had to go through dropping one language and picking up another one, and there wasn't any great emphasis on that. It just happened, but there was a lot of pain, a lot of insecurity, a lot of fear. Most of all I remember how afraid I was of talking, of being confronted, of being asked something. When you are very young, that sort of puts you always on the defensive.

Then I remember in junior high school when the war was on it was the days of ration stamps and things of that nature, and they asked all the Spanish-surname students to go and act as interpreters, and I went to act as an interpreter in Spanish, and I found myself having difficulty in interpreting from Spanish to English, and I says, "Geez, what happened? I thought I used to know this language." It was sort of a revelation, and I smile now at that little thing. And I think now what is happening in our educational system where the great emphasis is on English as a second language and all these other types of programs; they didn't have that when I was there. I am a case in point. I remember those very young, insecure, scary years because of language and how important that was. There really was no one coaching me or paying any special attention to me. If you said anything in Spanish or you thought in Spanish they'd pounce on you, so you were always afraid to forge ahead. "How come you don't speak English? What are you, some kind of dummy?" and so forth. During those periods in those days—I remember I was in P.S. 57 downtown—we used to have some very tough teachers. Today they just don't make them like that—they are all too easy. But in those days they would think nothing of clobbering you with a ruler or throwing an eraser at you across the room or calling you names, so you were always very, very insecure.

I remember being surrounded by Spanish students, but really not that many. The majority of the class was very English-speaking. I remember the Jewish segment of our population there, and they were also on the move out. As a very young child I remember thinking that they have a difficult religion and all that, but they always used to be excelling in class, and I used to admire them, like, wow, this is like a super-breed or something, and I was always very impressed with the whole Jewish mystique as a child, the emphasis on education. They would always be getting high marks—80s, 90s—honor students, and I would say, "Well now, look at this." The two groups that have influenced me—besides my own, of course—have been the Jewish group and the black group. Through my whole life growing up these are always where I've found myself. These were always the two groups. Obviously, the Jews were moving out, and the blacks were coming in, and we were coming in right behind them, and I would meet them in school. In fact, in the war in

Korea, I remember my officers being—at that time I think they were just beginning to get rid of the Jim Crow in the service during the Korean thing—a lot of my officers were black. And again in City College it was mostly Jewish and black. Right through my whole life these are the two groups that I really feel more comfortable with right now because I am so used to them, because as a child that's really where I've grown up. I don't know too many Irishmen—in fact, hardly any at all or any of the other groups. My world has been sort of insulated because I've kept my interests here, and my whole life, my whole livelihood, is right here in the South Bronx.

During the war years I knew there was a war going on because you'd see it, and there was a lot of activity with defense work. My father sold his business, and he went to work in a defense plant. He was a welder. Being of the old school, of the old working-class stock, my father wanted me and my brother to work right away, but my mother goaded us to go to college. My brother and I, we sort of gave them both what they wanted because we worked right through college. We were always working during the day, and I went to college in the night time.

But I was very young. I was in my twenties when I became more interested in communities and politics. Of course at eighteen I was already in college so I was already becoming aware of a lot of things, of discussions, current events, and whatnot. But I actually became active when I came out of the service. When I was maybe twenty-three or twenty-four I began to join civic groups and then from there one thing led to another. For a period of time I was very active in politics. In fact I headed a political club in the Bronx, the Robert F. Wagner Association.[2] At the time Mayor Wagner was sort of the insurgent, and usually you get into politics through insurgent movements, and then you become a regular, you become staid in the community. But at that time I was very active and I headed a political club, and I was attending meetings, making speeches, sometimes even managing campaign candidates and things of that nature. Then I sort of ebbed out of that, and I got into business. While in the service I had learned the workings of IBM equipment, and when I got out I worked as an IBM data processing operator. I worked for companies that used IBM equipment—they weren't called computers or data processing—the machines I used to work on are now rather archaic and historic pieces. There were big boards that we used to wire to get the machine to give out reports and whatnot. I used to wire boards—it was sort of like a plate of spaghetti, that thing—and they all used to think I was brilliant, but it was just after a while you get the knack of it. I worked for American News Company. I worked for London Records for a while. I worked in that field for about ten or eleven years.

Having left that, then I came into community work during the Great Society programs, and that lasted until around 1965, '66, '67, maybe 1968, and then I got into economic development, which was also very much involved with community, and I've been in that ever since. The legislation for the Great

Society programs came in 1964. Kennedy started talking about it, and then Johnson carried them through, and in 1964, in fact in the very first Great Society Program that came into the Bronx that October, I was part of it, in the very first one going back to 1964. I was doing everything there. It was an orientation center, the first one. What it did was to give people in the area an insight into the different service-type agencies that were there—either city, state, or federal, or whatever there was—for whatever they needed, maybe housing or enforcement codes with buildings. Some of them may have had education problems to handle.

I remember my first job. I was doing everything—it was a very small staff—and I'd had a little bit of schooling, so I'd do everything from write press releases to organize block associations, represent our agency with different governmental levels of structure that they had or what have you. And I would put proposals together. It was social work at a buckshot type of level; I was doing everything. And yet, really, what were we doing? And that's where I began to think out, as the programs became bigger and more massive, with a concentration, let's say, in narcotics, concentration in housing, and I says, "What are we doing? We are not really changing anything. We're just holding ground as much as possible and then mostly losing." So that's when I went into economic development, in 1967, and then in 1968 I went two years to work in Harlem—to learn the economic development game, what investments, what profit-oriented proposals, how they would work—and we had to go see, and so on and so forth. Then when I came back to the Bronx I came in as a deputy director of the Multi-Services Center—the Hunts Point Multi-Services Center—worked one year, and all I did there was preach economic development, and then we branched off a special corporation where we just devoted ourselves to economic development.

In my particular endeavor—because economic development has many meanings—what we in the South Bronx and we specifically in Bronx Venture think of as economic development, to a large extent it means trying to stabilize a community such as the South Bronx, which is very blighted and deteriorated, and to also try to stimulate business, industry, commerce so that there is an economic anchor in an area like this instead of mass exodus of capital, jobs, industry, commerce. You stabilize, and then you stimulate as much as possible until more investments are coming in. Now our particular formula for doing that—and that's a big mouthful—is that as part of the legislation in 1967, which is the Economic Development Act, part of the antipoverty programs of which Javits and Kennedy were the engineers, the architects of that particular part, is that the federal government was giving community-based economic development groups monies for both administering an office and also for investing. So that's the type of money, and they were coming in as grants, and grants meaning that you did not have to pay it back. In other words they were gifts—but they were gifts with the motive or the goal of enhancing or bringing in more money into an area like ours. It wasn't just like a grant where you sort of administer service-type of programs and no actual money comes back; you give the service, it's done, the money is spent, and that's it. This particular type of grant for economic development was geared to—the profit motive was very much involved. I am not knocking service programs or anything—we do need that, and we'll always need that until our problems are finally erased one way or the other—but this other aspect or this other phase of developing a community, which is the economic development part, is very essential in our society because we are a capitalistic society, and we have to play the game of our society in every level that we can. Being a capitalistic society means that we must pay attention to business, profit and industry, et cetera, and if we don't have that part of the system in our programs then we are just going through the motions and not really paying attention to what we are all about.

Federal money had to be matched—the term was "leveraged." That was a key word during the early part of economic development, meaning that you have to match it with institutional type of money, and "institutional type of money" means bank money. For instance, if I had a package, a venture where I was to buy a plant and the plant cost eight hundred thousand, if I had four hundred thousand of grant money I would have to seek, I would have to borrow, I would have to leverage the rest of the money. So if I walk into a bank with four hundred thousand dollars and I need another four hundred thousand—here is the plan of the plant and all that—that's just fine. Now for an area such as ours the banks were not interested in reinvesting or loaning us money, so this was one way of opening up those redline gates that they had put up for an area such as ours. As soon as an area starts slipping, everything begins to work against it, and you will have the blight, the deterioration, the crime, and everything else, because banks, investors, money goes away, because nobody wants to invest there. Who wants to go into an area where you put money and it's going to burn on you, they are going to burglarize and so on and so forth? So, okay, so something drastic had to be done, and the whole justification for our type of economic development activity was that—that we can again stimulate, stabilize an area via bringing capital back in, enticing capital to come back with a lot of other amenities.

When I started Bronx Venture my whole raison d'être was that I had been in community work since 1964, and I am part of a very vast network in the Bronx that emanates from the Multi-Services Center. The center has its own building, a very large building, and they have a medical center also that they run and several other subsidiaries. I've been very much a part of that so I have never really been alone. It isn't just me alone, and I have just been given, really, the honor to run the economic development part for this whole network.

The money used to come directly from the federal government. The original program—the Community Development Corporations Programs, or the Title VII Programs, which are the economic development programs out of the Great Society or antipoverty programs—the money did not stop anywhere. They didn't want to put it through local politics so if community boards would turn around and if they were to be established by community-run corporations, they couldn't be involved with the local government. This was a thought that whoever devised the original program put together very knowledgeably, because it would probably become a big pork barrel if it would have to go through the various levels. It was coming straight from the federal government.

In getting monies and leveraging or matching monies that we originally got from the federal government, the banks play a very interesting role here. The bank really doesn't have that much to risk in a program such as ours. For instance, in the case of the eight-hundred-thousand-dollar package or venture, that factory we wanted to buy, when I walked in with four hundred thousand and the banks matched it with four hundred thousand, their four hundred thousand was insured by the federal government through SBA (Small Business Administration) programs to the tune of 90 percent of that four hundred thousand, so their loan was cosigned by the federal government, so it wasn't that much of a risk to them, only 10 percent, and that 10 percent is usually paid up front. With the very first money you make you pay the bank immediately, so that 10 percent is there, and with the rest they are on Easy Street. So the programs were hand in hand with the system assuring the banks that they are not taking that much of a risk. The risk was really with the community, because no matter what happened, we'd always have to pay that loan.

By and large in our system, which is a capitalistic system in our society—a very mercantile society where profit is the whole thing, and we hear talk of rugged individualism and how you don't need the government and all that—I have to laugh and smile at those statements. Why? Because by and large as we look at the history of America most businesses are tied hook, line, and sinker to the government.

Quite possibly in the latter part of our history—because at one time we didn't have to pay taxes—but as soon as you pay taxes you have an invisible partner, which is Uncle Sam, and he is taking a chunk of the money, of the profits that you are making. Now, if that is so, and that partner is receiving monies—your hard-earned money—he has to contribute something too. So don't feel—and the communities haven't yet learned this lesson—don't feel you are taking anything away from the federal government because it's your silent partner that you are dealing with. Big industry, big commerce, big business knows this. They have lobbyists, they have a battery of lawyers. All they do is to try to change the law to benefit their industries, to benefit their companies. All these types of little programs the community came up with since the Economic Development Act, the big corporations have had their game going for a very long time. I speak about the oil industry, the railroads, auto industries, steel, right on down, and when they run into a jam and they get in trouble, they run to the man with the whiskers,

Uncle Sam. And we as community people found that out, and ever since then we say we are going into business.

"How dare you? You have no money."

"Well, I am going to get a partner."

"Who's your partner?"

"The federal government."

"Oh, you can't do that."

"Well, you've been doing just that for the longest time, so cut it out." We are just learning our game now.

Banks have been the major investors. I've been after some insurance companies, but there I haven't had the success, none at all. We are just beginning. We are not limited to the banks—we could do it with private investors as well—but so far it's been with the banks. In one instance there's been one private investor, and that's the extent of it, but I am not limited. Wherever we can find funds and whatever negotiation, whatever deal we can cut, we will go there.

When I first started I was looked on as a sort of a madman. Nobody had even heard of this kind of thing. I would go to the banks and ask, "If you hear of anybody that's selling a business or something, tell us because I have access to federal money and I can do something." So we put the word out, and also there was a certain amount of advertising in the papers—some of the commercial and industry papers—that we were looking, that we were interested in buying.

Our very first venture came about through a broker who brought it to us, Moe Greenstein. He said he knew someone that was interested in talking. When I went over there it was an owner who was looking for a partner. He didn't want to sell his business, he just wanted a partner, and in fact he wanted someone that came from the area, a Spanish-speaking partner, that type of thing. The business was Ace.[3] The proprietor was Jewish, and he said, "All my workers and everything around here is Spanish and Spanish-speaking, and I'd like to have a Spanish partner, and I don't want to be—you know—completely alone here." So I was brought to his attention, we met, and then I started talking about selling the whole business, telling him, "You don't have to leave, you can still run it. We will own it, but we'll give you all the incentives so that you will be working just as hard and then some." So we gave him percentages on sales and things of that nature, plus salary and all that. So he agreed, and we bought our first business, and then we've been on the road ever since.

Ace is a spray finishing, it's a paint factory, paint items from different corporations. Some of their clients are Martin Marietta. Sometimes they do hatches for submarines, doors for ships, cooling systems for tanks, and then they do the whole electronics industry, all the different chassis, all the different consoles and whatnot. They do these things by the thousands. When we first bought it, Ace was a ten-thousand-square-foot plant, it had maybe around eighteen employees, and their sales were maybe six hundred thousand dollars a year. Last year, when we closed, sales were 2.3 million dollars, we had maybe around seventy employees, and it's now an over forty-thousand-square-foot plant.

In some ways it was an advantage that

in the Bronx there were empty buildings and lots of space available to expand into. When we first started in our economic development program it was very easy to pick plant sites, land, and all that kind of thing. It's becoming very difficult now. Industries are starting to come back, a lot of expansion is going on—we are a case in point—and we feel the turnaround is here, we are in the process of it now. Maybe it's only in the beginning stages, but there is a lot in store and we feel it all around us. There's a very positive climate now in the Bronx. We are all anticipating and awaiting the designation of that enterprise zone, and different types of federal, state, and city levels of government are all focusing on the South Bronx and the Bronx per se. So it seems that the turnaround is here, and there is a lot of proof to that in that it's hard to find industrial space now.

We started in 1973 during the worst times. The 1960s and early 1970s were the worst. We were never sure this would work, but that doesn't enter into it. The important thing is that something has to be done and we are doing it. We can't just stand by and let it happen. Let's do something, so this was one of the somethings. It's not the only way, but it was one of the ways. The tragedy is that I wish what we've done here could be emulated all over the Bronx, maybe one hundred fold. We do now work for the whole Bronx, but we concentrate on the South Bronx because that's where our bases more or less are, constituency and whatnot, but wherever a deal takes us we'll go, so long as it benefits the Bronx.

About 90 percent of the employees in our businesses are resident in the Bronx. We've created jobs, and a lot of our employees had been on welfare or out of work. We are not the only answer to the blight and the deterioration. Service programs still have to go on, and construction of housing has to go with it, and schooling has to keep up to par, and the hospital and medical aspect of our community still has to be very much in line, and all the different facets of what makes a community have to be keeping pace with what is happening. There was a gap, there was a void in the economic development part, and we are trying to fill it. And that's where it's at.

To use a Reagan term, it's the domino effect, the trickle-down-type situation. Banks will become more courageous in their investments in an area like the South Bronx if I come in and prove to them that I took care of a four-hundred-thousand-dollar loan, or a million-dollar loan, which we are doing now—we are up to a million dollars. It's here, it's happening, it's living proof that it can happen, so right now all the banks are beginning to look at the South Bronx with, "Hey, this may be. . . . I don't have to go to Brazil any more, or to Argentina, or Mexico, and lose millions. I could take a gamble. . . ." The banks could have done it right here instead of going over there, but of course they were enamored of big interest rates and whatnot, so they were willing to take a gigantic risk, and here they are now, five hundred billion dollars in the hole—not only American banks but some foreign banks.

So we watch that, and we look at that, and, as I say when I get up and give a talk, I mention it, and I say, "I hope you've learned a lesson. Take care of your own backyard. And there's money to be made here. I am not coming begging." Really, what I am doing is following the pattern of big business. With us, the banks are not taking too much of a risk, so it behooves them to make the loans. As I said before, when I first started, everybody thought I was a crazy man. In the last several years they call me up all the time. "Mike, you got any new deals?" They are chasing me because they caught on, and they say, "This is very nice." Their lobbyists in Washington took care of them very well, which is the game that we have to know. I dream where I have a lobby down there that just looks out for the South Bronx. And that's what it's all about.

We have a metal fabricating plant. That was a big one. That's the biggest one. We put together a three-million-dollar package on that. We owe a lot of money on it. It's a brand-new business. It's maybe seven months old or something like that, but we have great hopes for it, and I think it will definitely put us in line for defense work for the military, which we see as we look out there that big appropriations have been made, such large and vast that I doubt whether in my lifetime we are going to go through all those allocations, because then they get bigger and bigger, and sometimes I look out and I say there aren't enough American companies to satisfy the kinds of monies that are being allocated. I have a funny thought that maybe there will probably be—right now they can't by law—but eventually I think they are going to be funneling that out to the foreign countries to do what they have to do in terms of getting money over there, and all the games that are played, but . . . okay.

But in the meantime that's where a concentration of a lot of money is—a lot of contracts and all that type of thing—so I have no qualms about being part of that. In fact, we've already begun simple things like cots and beds and that type of thing, metal things, nothing vast, nothing too heavy.

At Bronx Venture, the main office, we have no knowledge of any of these businesses. We are investors. We invest for a community corporation, a community development corporation, we call it. What we do is get the money, own, get the management in place, and then monitor to make sure that it's okay. Why are we doing that? We are the anchor. That company isn't going to go away as long as we are the anchor. It isn't like a company that comes to the South Bronx, buys, and then settles. That's why I use the word "anchor." We are not going anyplace. We have a commitment. Our board is community people. The flight will never happen again in the Bronx if they follow the pattern. They don't have that leeway unless something happens to our board, to all our community people, and they want to go off to—I don't know—Timbuktu or what have you. But by and large, I am just thinking of what happened in Puerto Rico, Operation Bootstrap, that all these large corporations there went seeking the advantage of tax abatements and free flow of monies for operations and everything else for periods of ten years, fifteen years, and after those ten or fifteen years they leave and they go off someplace else. So now you have a lot of people out of work, and you have empty buildings off in Puerto Rico, and we see them and we say, "Well." Not that we are wising up. It just so happens that in our formula the anchor is there. What is the anchor? The community people run and own those businesses, run to the extent where we monitor, but that is it. I am not in that plan, but I want to see financial statements periodically, every other week or every month, quarterlies and everything else.

When we buy a business or a company we look at their financial statements something like three to five years back. I want to look at their projections, and I want to know how feasible and how realistic they are, and if I don't know I will hire consultants, and if I have to get them out of Booz Allen or McKinsey & Co. I will, and I says, "You tell me. It doesn't look good to me. What do you think?"

Right now with Häagen-Dazs we are just merely exploring. We are talking with them about a trade-off. We have access to some land and buildings that they want for an expansion, so we are trading off that for possibly some franchises that they can give us in the Bronx. I don't know if that's going to come through. It's mostly retail, it's a different type of operation than we've done before. Most of our situations have been in manufacturing, industrial. But Häagen-Dazs is an interesting situation because it's a very prestigious business, and there is a certain mystique about that company and that ice cream. It's usually in a very classy neighborhood, so it attracts me that I'd like to have a few Häagen-Dazs's in the Bronx and people saying, "Oh, the Bronx must be coming up. Häagen-Dazs is there." It's like all of a sudden everybody started to drink Moët champagne or something, and you'd say, "My, what a classy area that must be." Things of that nature. I don't know if anything is going to come of it, but we are trying, and if it doesn't, we are still going to try and help them in any way possible to find them something comparable, something as good, so that they can feel comfortable, and they know that we are behind them, and we need them. It's an attractive company for us.

To change our image has to be played day by day, and we have to be as relentless as the media has been in the last fifteen or twenty years. They've done a thorough job on us, are still doing it. We have to be really strong and forthright and take them on and go to as many media shows as possible and try to show everyone the other side of the coin, and continue working as we are working, and wherever there is change try to highlight it and magnify it as much as possible so that everybody sees it. It breaks my heart to see these delegations of people from Europe and Asia—be they from Poland or Germany or France or China or Japan—busloads of people coming in and just shooting over Charlotte Street with their little cameras to show the rest of the world this is America. And it's a shame.

The other shame is that the real commitment of the powers that be isn't really there. They talk about it, and they throw a million here and two million there, or a hundred million, but that's not the name of the game. The game is billions, not millions, and as soon as we talk about it and commit ourselves—really commit ourselves on all levels—then fine. The most drastic tragedy of all was that Charlotte Street thing where everybody came, the pope, two presidents—Carter and Reagan. During the Carter administration, the federal government was willing to put up the money, and it got shot down in the board of estimate with all the people on there, the borough presidents. "No, why should it go to the Bronx?" That's the danger of local politics. It gets ground down to the ground. And it should have happened like what happened to us earlier, direct federal funding. Then it wouldn't have been blocked. But the tragedy of America and the tragedy of New York City is that they get bogged down in local politics. Charlotte Street by now should have been erased, and that's the tragedy.

There are some efforts there now, but they are doing it kind of quietly because Charlotte is too symbolic. I remember Carol Bellamy saying that we are not interested in symbols and all that.[4] Well, we have a symbol whether we like it or not, and it's a bad one, and we'd just better work on it. And it is being worked on very slowly. I hear that the land has been leveled now and there's plans for small housing, two- or three-story town-type housing, hopefully. It was a very foolish thing for them not to realize that it's not only a local and national but it's an international symbol. I mean everybody in the world knows about it, practically, who is in the know, and that's a shame. But they'll always talk about America and say, "You got your Charlotte Streets."

We're trying to change a community and trying to change the people because we primarily work with the Puerto Rican population. That doesn't mean that we are restricting it because that's insane—you have to work with everybody—but our constituency more or less is the Puerto Rican, and we've been at it, as I say, since 1964, primarily coming through the service-type programs, and then branching off to, say, economic development is the other part of this. But the aim is change for the better of a community that was on the slide or the skids, and we feel that we have more a sense of direction now than we had at the beginning, because at the beginning we were sort of feeling our way around. Now I feel there is more purpose, we can look at certain goals.

For instance, in my particular operation, I want to reach a level of ten million dollars. My next step is one hundred million dollars. With one hundred million dollars then I can be looking at the billion-dollar mark. I have a lot of respect, a lot of power that I can then talk to the insurance companies and then talk to the banks, and when I talk to the government I can talk to them like one of the big giants, which is a whole different thing. And if I say I want a lobbying office in Washington, in Albany, and in city hall, and I will have a paid staff just making legislation to better our community or better our industries or our corporations, then we will have it. And that's hard-nosed goals and ends.

CHAPTER TWELVE
RAY

Ramon Velez, Developer, Hunts Point Multi-Service Center, 1933–2008
Interview: March 21, 1983

"Death is the only thing that can stop me."

I was born in Puerto Rico—to be exact, in Hormigueros—fifty years ago. I am about to become fifty in a few days. I am an Aries. I was raised in the country in a small town, in my time maybe of six thousand inhabitants. I was a country boy on the farm. I was the third out of seven. It was the eve of the Second World War. I was born in 1933 and the war started in 1939. It was tough times. I went to school in my hometown, but then I went to high school in what was called the other town—behold the difference—Mayaguez, which was at the time the third-largest city in Puerto Rico. I dropped out of high school in 1950 and I joined the army—the American army—and I went to Korea and spent ten months at the battlefront. In 1952 I went back to Puerto Rico and reenlisted in the army. I went to Panama, spent three years in Panama, married for the first time in Panama, and my first child was born in Panama. My second child was born in Puerto Rico. I then got out of the army in 1955 and went to school and graduated right away. Then I went to college—Inter-American University in Puerto Rico—and graduated from college in 1960.

While in college as well as in high school I was very active in terms of organizations. Whether it was the 4-H Club, the Holy Name Society or the Future Farmers of America or the P.A.O., I was the founder of them all in my hometown, and I became active in politics in college as well. I was the head of different movements in the student body. While I was in Korea I was also a student of the problems that Korean people had to face, especially in the economy. I did the same in Japan and also in Panama.

From there it follows to the city—New York City—we came to see what is in New York, and I saw how it was in the Hispanic barrios, and it was the first time in my life that I found the type of discrimination and abuse that my people were victims of. I remember one evening passing by a street where there was a group of Puerto Ricans playing dice, and all of a sudden two patrol cars came in with their cops and they started to pick them up, to arrest them. And that stuck in my head. In my college records the essay written by me that was always done by every college student for graduation, and they were asking about the goals, and you will see my goals. My goal was to become a lawyer and to come back to New York. And why to New York? Because I wanted to be the lawyer for the poor and defend them against such abuse.

I was a person that was always for the underdog. I was fighting Trujillo in Santo Domingo, or Batista in Cuba, or Somoza, or fighting international causes, and I was the head of chapters for all those causes in Puerto Rico. When I left, I was a high school teacher. I left Puerto Rico to an extent disenchanted because I was an idealistic person and felt that the type of democracy that I had been fighting for in Korea was not the one I perceived. I went to study law in Salamanca, Spain. Salamanca is the oldest university in the world. While in Salamanca I had financial problems. I was married with two children, and I didn't have any additional income, and my G.I. Bill benefits had been exhausted already, so I decided to return and continue my education at a further date, make some savings first.

I was going home to Puerto Rico to continue my teaching profession. I came by New York just to say hello to my brother who was here, but for one reason or another, a couple of days after I came to New York I applied for a job with the city, and I was accepted as an investigator for the Department of Welfare. Then I worked for the department for two years as an investigator dealing with welfare clients primarily in the Hunts Point section of the Bronx. Now after two years I had some savings and I wanted to return to school, but first I decided to go to New Jersey to visit my fellow countrymen there. They asked me, they almost pushed me to help them to organize the annual Puerto Rican Day Parade. I organized it in the town of Passaic, and it was the most-attended parade ever been in the State of New Jersey. I was able to bring together Puerto Ricans from forty-four communities in the state. Then I helped in Pennsylvania.

By then it was 1963. While I was doing that I started to visit the farms in the south of New Jersey. I should never have done it. If I intended to continue my education I should have stayed away, but I saw the conditions, and I saw the abuses, and I organized the National Association for Puerto Rican Affairs, the first civil rights movement within the Puerto Rican community nationally organized. I started to organize Puerto Ricans throughout the country—whether in Chicago, California, Connecticut, Pennsylvania, New Jersey, New York—and I started to organize the neighborhoods in New York City, because that's where the concentration was, and I started to become more militant.

I was not living on anything at this particular time. I was between jobs and salaries—transitioning between Puerto Rico and New York—and when I decided to stay in New York the government of Puerto Rico—the Commonwealth of Puerto Rico—gave me a job as a community organizer, and from that position I was able to gain access to knowledge within the city. I went to Hunter College to take a course on community organization, then I went to the New School for Social Research to take courses in public policy. I started to organize in Brooklyn—in the Red Hook section, in Park Slope, in Williamsburg, in East New York in Brownsville, in the Fort Greene section; on the Lower East Side, in Chelsea, then on the Upper West Side of Manhattan, in El Barrio in Harlem; in the Bronx, the easternmost section, in Highbridge, in the Mott Haven section and in the Hunts Point section. And there we started to organize ourselves. At the time there were no antipoverty agencies in any community, so we started to develop housing clinics and consumer action groups and employment sections. We would share resources, work together. For example, we would buy a job for one individual and then expect that the individual would return the money to provide another job for another one. Then we started to establish storefront operations free. Anyone who had storefront—whether it was a record shop or a grocery store—we would establish there with volunteers at night. We started to collect clothing from the laundries, and we started to help those that were in need, especially welfare recipients.

The leadership all worked together. You had George Rodriguez on the West Side. You had Domingo Ramos in Hunts Point. You had Sandy Mercado on the Lower East Side, and Irma Santaella, and Jesus Gonzales. In every neighborhood I had a group of people, and we started to organize. We organized hometown groups, voters' clubs, we got involved in the voter registration drive for the first time, using the firehouses. We started to organize the cadets, we started to use boys' clubs, and we had a women's division. We had everything possible. We had three merchants' associations. We had everything organized and coordinated. These were like a committee.

The churches helped, especially St. Bridget on the Lower East Side—Protestant churches, Pentecostal churches also. We started to collect food and clothing and shelter for addicts through Mama Leo's church.[1] We helped them, so we were involved in social action. We had an office on 138th Street that was run by an old man that had a record shop, and that man went bankrupt because he used his money to help the people in the area. Our main office was on 116th and Third Avenue in Manhattan. I was involved with that. Oliver Soto and Franklin Pasa, they lived in the barrio in the beginning at the time that I was also a member of the board of directors. We were involved in the active development in Brooklyn, and we were involved across the board in every neighborhood and in every action. I also became—after the Commonwealth of Puerto Rico in 1964—I became the director of the Department of Human Relations of a local radio station, WHOM, which is now WEAT.[2] Through that station I was able to expose my ideas and to help people more directly.

Then, in 1964, I came to the Bronx, and I became the executive director of the first antipoverty agency that had been established. That was the South Bronx Neighborhood Orientation Center.[3] Today they are still in existence at 582

Southern Boulevard. As a matter of fact, my wife is the director of the agency, a small agency. But I became the director in 1964, and I became involved deeply in the political action situation, and I became controversial. Once you try to jump from social action into political action, and you are from the upcoming group—especially being a Puerto Rican—you become not only controversial, but if you are one of the top, they will try to shoot you down. And that happened to any group, doesn't have to be Puerto Rican. It happened to the Chinese, it happened to the Irish, it happened to anyone that is going up.

So I became controversial. My group had stopped the construction of the Hunts Point Market in 1964 because they fired the blacks and the Puerto Ricans.[4] We were always effective in developing a coalition with the Negro Labor Council and ASPIRA,[5] in order to bring minorities at the Co-op City project when they were beginning. We were able at least to make a dent and to force them to accept minorities in Co-op City that they didn't want to accept at the time. We were able to make a dent also in the educational system at the time and to have the first Puerto Rican commissioner—that was Luis Quiero Chiesa—and the second one, which was Luis Nuñez, Mike Nuñez's brother, and through them we were able to establish the Hostos Community College. That was an idea that we developed, and we were able to bring it to the board. We fought for the community, and they proposed it at the board level, and through that action Hostos was established in 1968. The first president was Nasry Michelen, a former director of Lincoln Hospital.

During that period of time—in the 1960s—because of the situation at Lincoln Hospital, which was a butcher house, I became a member of the board, and I started to make demands. Many of my people, including myself, we have been arrested, and we were going to jail for the first time as a result of taking action at Lincoln. I was a member of the board for twenty years. In fact, I just stepped out as a member. I was the chairman of the board of directors, and during my administration the new Lincoln came to fruition. We had to put on a lot of pressure and a lot of political maneuvering in order to gain access, but finally in 1966—I was Nelson Rockefeller's Hispanic coordinator[6]—and Nelson Rockefeller, and many others through our contacts, we finally got him to bypass the city bureaucracy and get the money and build Lincoln in the South Bronx and also to get the first office of the Department of Labor that was at 3756 Southern Boulevard and just recently closed.

In the meantime, in 1966, with the change of administration from Wagner to Lindsay, my office—the first antipoverty agency—was closed down as a result of the politics of the time, and the new CPCs—Community Progress Centers—came to power. They brought in a lot of very controversial issues because they were meant to deny Puerto Rican leadership the opportunity to develop themselves and to participate with equity and equality in the process. This prompted me to organize in two districts, and I am very proud of it, and I won. I won the elections in the Bronx, in Manhattan, and in Brooklyn. And then I was confronted by the city. They enforced a regulation by which people that had not participated in the electoral process only because of race had the right to receive a percentage of the seats, but it was established only in the Puerto Rican areas. It was not established in any other areas, which then I considered to be discriminatory, and I was offended because they were not considering Puerto Rican blacks as blacks. They were considering Puerto Ricans as Puerto Ricans rather than by race, and they were not being fair to the Puerto Rican community as it was written. In that period I then lost my job and I went through hell, but I kept my forehead up, looking and fighting, and then one day I was offered and accepted a job with the Community Development Agency of the city of New York, CDA. I was their program evaluator for a few months. This was in early 1967. I went to work for the city, but then I was being offered a position with the state of New York—a very good one, as a matter of fact. But then I presented my resignation, and I decided to come back to the South Bronx. I remember well that I resigned because I wanted to come back to where the action was. And here I am.

And I started with a grant of fifty thousand dollars and a concept, an idea, at 735 Prospect Avenue in the Bronx, and I got a group from Washington called Urban America, and I got a good group of consultants headed by Ted Simons, a professor of architecture at the Oakland University in Berkeley [University of California, Berkley], with Diane Lacy, Mike Baker, Tin Pei (the son of I. M. Pei), and a few others, and with them we started discussion, and we started to fight the city of New York. You cannot take on city hall. The first time I ever went to city hall I had to physically break the door and got arrested. The second time I got twenty-five people arrested, but the third time the same policeman who had stopped us had to say, "Honorable Ramon Velez, will you please walk in?"

The first time I went because I considered that the city was conducting discriminatory practices against Puerto Ricans. The police had injured a Puerto Rican policeman and injured a Puerto Rican Pentecostal, Gregorio Cruz. We had to demonstrate, but they were found not guilty, which was considered at the time to be a racist attitude on the part of the establishment, and then we had two Puerto Ricans killed by policemen up at 86th Street, Rodriguez and Soler. During those days there was fear and turmoil in the Puerto Rican community. I felt personally that the policies of the city of New York were detrimental to the development of the Puerto Rican community at the time, and I felt that it was my responsibility to say "present" and to fight those policies. And I started to organize community action, so when I came into Multi-Services on the 15th of September of 1967—that was my first day of work—the first thing I did was to call a community convention, and I had about twenty-five other people to participate. We organized thirty-three workshops that one week later were converted into community committees. We established a board of directors.

I asked the community to help me to develop a system by which they were going to receive services and not orientation because I was tired of sending people from one office to another office. We had to provide services all in the same group. I said, "We cannot ask you to come and then send you, make you pay another fare, to another agency and then another agency." They helped me, and during the past fifteen years, close to sixteen years, I have been at the helm of Multi-Services. We developed all types of programs. We developed the first community health center controlled by the community without the help of any medical institution or any established group, including the city of New York Department of Health, bypassing all the bureaucrats with the help of HEW [U.S. Department of Health, Education, and Welfare].

We developed the first community-controlled mental health unit also, which is still in operation, and we developed the parent and child center that provides help to parents that cannot understand issues of life like raising their children, getting together, budgeting, shopping, diseases. So we train the parents, and we train their children at the same time. While we have another day-care center where we take care of children—one family takes care of the children while the other family works. That way we take families out of the welfare rolls.

At the same time we work in housing. We formed a housing corporation that is responsible for the development of ten thousand units of housing in the South Bronx. That was the South Bronx Community Housing Corporation, which is now also under my direction, under my leadership.[7] We got federal money, foundation money, sometimes city money. At the beginning it came directly to us. Now it comes through the city. At the beginning it was bypassing all the city structures because I was fighting the city. The city was not in agreement that some programs existed, and I had to go to Washington and prove that such programs did exist, and that way we were able to bypass them. We went directly to HUD [the U.S. Department of Housing and Urban Development] and to HEW, and we were going directly to the White House. We were acting under an executive order by the president of the United States. And also we had a regional council and a city council. We worked hard. In the meantime, in 1970—I may have made a mistake or not, I don't know—Multi-Services had $12 million in operating budget. We were about to begin a new income center running from up here to provide services to the welfare population, and I decided that the action, even though it was here, it needed to be in the House of Congress or in New York City, and I started to run for political office. I was defeated, and with my defeat I also brought down with me a lot of programs. When you run for public office, your life is scrutinized, and there is no way. . . . I was running for congressman of the United States from the 21st Congressional District. There was no incumbent at the time. Herman Badillo was the borough president, and he was running for lieutenant governor. When I announced, there was no one running, but then Herman decided to come back and be a candidate. I was already a candidate, and I decided to stay in the race. He decided that the best way to defeat me was through investigations, and he started to ask for investigations and investigations and investigations. He attacked me viciously in many ways.

This divided the Puerto Rican community. We had five candidates running, like Father Gigante, Peter Vallone in Queens, myself, another gentleman, and Herman, and I was able to get a lot of votes from Cruz. That year I was one of the grand marshals of the Puerto Rican Parade. That was good for me at the time. But I lost after the elections—due to the investigations that Badillo had requested—$4 million in grants that never came back, and I lost also the access to different programs, and he kept a cloud over my head for several months. This was a result of my comptroller being a Badillo ally without my knowledge, and the books of the agency—since I was not in the agency, I was running for political office, I was away from the agency—the books had been taken away, destroyed, and in their place blank books had been placed, so when I returned I found that we had the city Investigation Department, and we had the feds at the same time, and I was unable to give them an answer. So, since I would not give them an answer, and they were not talking to each other, they decided that the best way was to say, "Here it is."

So it took me three months to personally reconstruct the books, and then I presented them, but nobody will ever print in the papers the result of an investigation. They would print the investigation. So the results came on page 60 in the *New York Times*, and nobody else said anything about it. The harm had been done at the time, and the goal that Mr. Badillo had set had been accomplished—which was to tarnish my administration—even though he himself after the campaign had come to my office when I offered to resign because of the investigation. I offered to the federal government to resign in return for the programs to be restored. He came to my office and pled with me not to resign, and the statement that he made was, "While in Congress I feel that you are the best administrator." And we kept working together, and I worked with everybody, and I instituted new ideas and new programs.

In 1972 I was the head of the Voter's Crusade throughout the city,[8] and we registered 350,000 Puerto Ricans that almost made Herman Badillo the mayor of the city of New York. I was his coordinator in the Bronx. In 1973 I ran for the city council, and I won in a district where I was not supposed to win. I became the district leader as well in the area, and I kept my job as president, and then I went into a leave of absence from my job, and I went into the city council. In two years in the city council I was a member of the Finance Committee, something that any other councilman would take twelve years to accomplish. I was a member of the Health Committee, the Education Committee, Environment, and Transportation.

During my tenure as city councilman my biggest achievement has been in the field of education. I was able to get monies to rehabilitate an old school and convert that school into the South Bronx High School, the first high school in the South Bronx.[9] I ran for public office based on the needs of our student population to get access to schools, because they were being transported to the north, and they were rioting in the north, and the white population was not accepting the Puerto Rican population. So we built the South Bronx High School that is today a symbol, and not only a symbol, it is supposed to be one of the best in the entire system. The first principal of that school is today the head of all the high schools of the city of New York. He was promoted at the South Bronx High School. And another local person went to be the chief aide of the commissioner.

Close to 99 percent of the students in the South Bronx High School are Puerto Ricans, and most of them have been going to college. There are a lot of bilingual programs in the whole district. In all these areas, bilingual programs have been very effective, which is important. So, by having organized or helped to organize the Hostos College with its bilingual programs,[10] being able to get the Lincoln Hospital—a new hospital—the South Bronx High School, then I was able to get the city administration to rebuild the infrastructure of the South Bronx, so when you walk you can see that the sewers, the curbs, the sidewalks, and the streets have been paved, and it was the result of Bob Abrams when he was the borough president and myself. We went into the fight, and we won the fight.

My other fight was to rebuild the infrastructure of the housing projects. The first one was the Webster Avenue, and I did it. If it had not been for the Webster project when I ran for public office, there was a black candidate against me and I won by a big margin, and when the people have that faith in you, you better deliver for them. And I did deliver, and I helped them as much as I could in jobs, entertainment, transport, whatever. I tried to do my best. In 1976 I then again decided to go into public office. Problems I had with Herman again, and I ran for Congress. This time, in 1976, I was elected. I had been elected in 1972 as a member of the National Democratic Convention. My slate in 1976—out of thirteen people, twelve were elected—and I was elected with only one hundred votes less than Herman Badillo. So, taking that into consideration, I decided that the people out there were looking for leadership and were looking to me, because I felt that there was a vacuum and that Herman was running for higher office and was not paying attention to the local problems. That resulted in the abandonment of the South Bronx and the lack of services and unemployment for the people of the South Bronx. So I ran, and again Mr. Badillo and his group decided that the best way to defeat me was through innuendos in a media campaign. At a time when I had been effective in getting some twelve to fourteen million dollars in a summer lunch program, he decided to attack the summer lunch program along with Congresswoman Holtzman and a few others, and in order to get to me he got to the program and destroyed the program. He could not destroy me because I was more effective than anything else, but he was able to stop the three programs that I had been able to get—one in Brooklyn, one in Manhattan, and one in the Bronx. That summer I was able to get twelve thousand jobs for the kids, and he attacked me also on the fact that I was giving too many jobs. My reply was, "Who else is doing anything for that? You do it, you get it."

Then they started to attack me in terms of the Puerto Rican Day Parade. I was the head and the organizer for the cultural events, and he was able to buy off one of the officers, and started to attack me and started to have investigations. At the same time he started to attack me on many fronts, and Channel 5 television decided that—they came here to this office at five o'clock on July 2, 1976—and they threatened me. They told me, "You get out from this race, or we'll destroy you." I said, "Destroy me." Mr. Pinsky—that was the person who came—I had another witness with me—he told me that it was a pity because I was doing a good job, but they had no other choice but to support the other individual, and that I had to get out of the race. So I say, "I will not get out." So they decided to present what they call a negative exposé, and every day for twenty minutes for three months on Channel 5 on the news—they negated me the opportunity to participate and to answer questions—and they brought in several witnesses that were part of the political club of my opposition, and they started to spread rumors and innuendos, and as it was the media, they were effective. It was so effective that I lost the campaign fifteen to five. I was able to get five thousand votes, so that it's sure that without the campaign I would have been able to get at least ten to five. They took out at least five thousand votes from my side, and I was defeated. I was again defeated, but I said, I am not defeated, here I am, I am working. And I kept working. The next day I was here in my office and I kept working. Then Herman abandoned the congressional seat and became the deputy mayor to get even with me one way or the other.

He became the deputy mayor, and I ran again. I was the Democratic nominee, and when I got the nomination I was threatened. I was closed in a room, and I was told, "If you don't give up your nomination we will close your programs tomorrow, and we will try to put you in jail, and your employees will lose their jobs." I had to accept, and I had to make a deal by which I was able to choose the candidate of the Democratic Party in return for me running as an independent, and I chose Louis Nine to be the candidate, and I ran as independent. I lost to Robert García, who was at least a decent person, and with whom I worked very closely. Herman went to city hall, continued his campaign, and in six months he dismantled almost all the organizations that I was able to put together, more than eighty-five million dollars in programs and jobs were destroyed, even though I asked him not to do it, and I was willing to give it to him. He stopped money coming to the South Bronx especially in economic development and housing, and I decided to wait. I was the target of more than 150 investigations. As a result of that my file in the FBI alone has over one thousand pages. In my files you can see that every regulatory agency, anything that had to do with funding investigated me, even the army of the United States. They investigated me for allegations that were made by Mr. Badillo that were fabricated by him through his own organizations. He was a member of the Judiciary Committee of the Congress, and as a member there he had access to the IRS. The IRS then went after me with their elite group, and they spent, according to their own figures, $1.5 million. To this day they have never, never called me to testify, and they had to return any book, anything that they took from me. My organization here never suffered, but the organizations that I put together in other areas like the Hunts Point Community Corporation, like the Puerto Rican Community Development project, like the Puerto Rican Day Parade, like the South Bronx Model Cities, they did suffer, and they did suffer primarily because I was not physically any more at the head. I was not responsible, and these groups were vulnerable because the people at the head were vulnerable—I mean weak—and they could not confront them the way I could confront them, and we lost. As a community we lost in that trouble maybe ten thousand units of housing, we lost at least twenty million dollars in economic development, and we lost eighty-five million dollars in jobs, and the welfare closed. It was like a mini-revolution.

I kept my position here. They investigated me for years, and finally they gave me a letter saying that I had the best administration and that my books—my accounting books, my time records, and all my process—was the best, and in closing, the comptroller of the city of New York, the Human Resources Administration, HEW, and HUD all made good statements about my administration, and here I am. I feel that I was effective in promoting changes in reference specifically to the Puerto Rican community in terms of power. Through my tenure, through the voter registration drive of the 1970s, we were able to elect to political office 51 percent of the Democratic Party, and through my political organization we elected people like Israel Ruiz, José Serrano, Louis Nine in the beginning. Then Hector Diaz and myself, and we helped Herman, and we elected José Rivera this year and Castaneira Colón. And we have helped others as well, the borough presidents, mayors, governors, and the president of the United States.

So it is my philosophy that in order to be effective a person cannot close ears and eyes to everything that goes on around, that politics is the ultimate power, and that if you want to express yourself effectively and promote changes, you have to be proud of every system that exists, that the United States has the most effective and beautiful democratic system in the world, but that the people that compose that system, they have their own personal ideas, and sometimes they have used their power to discriminate. But looking at Nixon—who is out of office—we know that the system works, and in looking at the South Bronx—when I came here it was a sin to be a member of a political party—and we were able to do that. So I feel, as a former educator, that education is a key factor in developing our youth. As a member of this community I believe that economic power is necessary in order to achieve progress, and as a member of this society I believe that political power is a need for all ethnic groups or religious institutions to accomplish what they want to accomplish for themselves. The Irish have the Catholic Church, the Italians have a beautiful organization, the blacks have the civil rights movement, the Puerto Ricans, we have our ethnic background to unite us, the culture and the folklore of our country. And those are the ways that we use to develop our people, to make them interested in what is happening around themselves, and to promote our values and ideas. I feel that that's important.

My dream has been to be able to establish on one side of the Bronx at least one hundred factories owned by the community that would provide jobs for local people who live on the other side of the Bronx—meaning the Hunts Point down to the Mott Haven area—while we built a good educational system, which we already have with the South Bronx High School and the Hostos, then at the same time to develop a good health delivery system, which we already have with the Lincoln and a network of community centers and mental health centers. So my dream is also one day to have a medical school next to Lincoln Hospital and next to Hostos that will provide an opportunity for our people to be educated in that particular field, with the educational complex of Hostos, Lincoln, a medical college and a law school and the high school in the same area, with a good commercial strip in the Third Avenue area, and a shopping mall in the old Lincoln Hospital site, with industry on the other side and housing in the middle.

That was my dream in the 1960s. That's my dream in the 1980s. It is closer in the 1980s. I feel that I have been able to show that if we put our shoulders to the wheel, we can move. Doing so, I know that I am going to be abused. I know that my credit is going to be stolen, I know that I am going to be denied my credit, and I know also that I am going to be denied everything by others that are in a better position or power—those in the media and the people at the top—because they will try to stop us one way or the other. Death is the only thing that can stop me.

I work with everybody in the whole city. I work in the Bronx, in Brooklyn, in Manhattan. I work with the other legislators in the Bronx, I work with the borough president and with Congressman Biaggi, who is my dear friend. I work with Senator D'Amato closely. I work with people in Manhattan and with people in Brooklyn. I work with anyone in any place because I feel that in order to build you must coordinate effectively and organize. I don't believe in destruction. That's why I believe in rehabilitation rather than tearing down a building.

My mind is constantly set in terms of projects. I have at least 150 projects going on right now at this very moment, whether they are housing, economic development and industry, whether they are physical or spiritual. I have them going, and some of them materialize. Soon we'll be opening a rehabilitated project in Beck Street. We just opened one in Avenue St. John, and we are about to begin building a new project in housing construction in Prospect Avenue and another one in Beck. So those are projects, it's something tangible, and you can see that it's here to stay. This building is something that's here to stay. It's been here already ten years. Lincoln is something tangible. Hostos is something tangible. So I feel that is the contribution that I have been able to give with the groups that have been helping me all these years. George Rodriguez was the head of the South Bronx Development program, Mike Nuñez—they have been working with me for twenty years—and Evelyn [Evelina] Antonetty, who headed United Bronx Parents organization,[11] Frank Lugoviña at LRF Management Corp., Louis Nine, who has just passed away, are people who have been working with me for twenty years. And these are just a few. I can name hundreds, and many of them are still around me in terms of work, but most of them are in the legislature or in better pastures. We coordinate our efforts, and we try to do the best we can.

PART FIVE
THE POLITICIANS

I. Stanley Friedman was born in the Bronx in 1936. His father, the eldest of thirteen children, had emigrated from Russia in 1911 when he was only three years old. Stanley's father encouraged him to be active in political clubs in order to make contacts and develop a network. He became an assistant district attorney, ran the city council, and in 1978 was county chairman, but never ran for a major office, preferring to be seen as the power behind the scenes, the patronage dispenser, the political operative. He was close to Mike Nuñez and Ramon Velez.

II. Jay Goldin's father, like Irma Fleck's, was a doctor. Born in the Bronx in 1936, Goldin's earliest introduction to different neighborhoods in the borough was accompanying his father on house calls to patients. A civil rights lawyer, he ran successfully for state senator in 1968 and was elected city comptroller in 1973. He helped plan for the Bathgate Industrial Park and encouraged economic development.

III. Robert Abrams was born in the Bronx in 1938. His family owned small businesses like candy stores, but one uncle was a lawyer, and this was what his parents wanted for him. His first move into politics was to help run Jonathan Bingham's campaign, then to be elected to the New York State Assembly, and then in 1969 elected borough president. His tenure as borough president saw many of the new institutions mentioned by Irma Fleck and Ray Velez: the Bronx Council on the Arts, the Bronx Museum, Hostos, and the South Bronx High School, and also major construction on the campus of Lehman College and a new stadium for the Yankees.

IV. Mario Biaggi, born in 1917 in Harlem, where his family was part of a large Italian neighborhood, didn't move to the Bronx until he married. Unlike Nuñez, Bick, Fleck, and others who struggled with English in schools, coming from families that spoke Spanish, Yiddish, and German, respectively, Biaggi's family—to his expressed regret—spoke English at home. He was an ardent supporter of the sometimes controversial bilingual programs devised to assist youngsters to master English while retaining their first languages. He had a series of blue-collar jobs and then entered the police force. A chance encounter with the then-dean of the New York Law School led to the offer of a full scholarship even though he had never been to college. He first ran for Congress in 1972. He recounted many stories of helping individual constituents with their needs, achieving the same satisfaction as Ada, Rae, Carmen, and Susan in helping their communities, and obviously enjoyed being able to talk one on one with U.S. presidents and to enlist their support for causes he believed in.

CHAPTER THIRTEEN
STANLEY

Stanley Friedman, Attorney, b. 1936
Interview: July 26, 1983

"I think that in the next twenty years the wheel is going to just keep turning around— as wheels generally do as long as they're round—and that the Bronx will be just as viable as Brooklyn and Queens will be."

My father was born in Minsk, Russia, in 1908, and came to this country with his thirteen brothers and sisters at the age of three. The oldest brother came first—he was twenty-five or thirty—and they came over a little at a time, including my parents, actually. My father was the youngest. As a matter of fact I have a photograph at home, hanging on the wall, of my father as a three-year-old with his eleven or twelve brothers and sisters and his mother and father. It's the old-fashioned portrait. My wife has one wall of her parents' wedding picture, my parents' wedding picture, us growing up, graduation, Bar Mitzvahs, and our kids in those same roles.

So my father came. They moved into Harlem, and my mother was born in Harlem of Greek immigrant parents who came to this country on their honeymoon in 1908 from Janina, Greece; came on the ship *The Martha Washington*, landed in Ellis Island in 1908, and never went back—never became citizens and never went back. And my grandmother, who is ninety-five, still lives in Hunts Point at 1291 Spofford Avenue, which is across the street from P.S. 48, the school I graduated from, and is still there and takes care of herself and won't move, although she's one of the few whites left in the neighborhood. She won't move because she says all the old people when they move, they die.

My parents got married in 1935 and moved to the Bronx just about that time. They may have moved a little earlier, but they both lived in Central Harlem around Madison or Lenox Avenue at 114th or 112th Street. Mount Morris Park is where they met. Neither had any formal education. My father was a taxi driver most of his life and then became a Teamster Local 802 employee and was a bakery truck driver. My mother was a housewife. She never had a formal education beyond probably grammar school. I'm not even sure she went to high school. She was a housewife, and they both died reasonably young. My mother died in 1970 of heart failure, my father died in 1971 of cancer of the throat, and I'm an only child.

I was born in the Bronx. I was born March eighteenth, 1936, in Bronx Hospital, which was on Fulton Street or Avenue near Third Avenue and 169th Street in the Bronx. Growing up in the Bronx was terrific. Hunts Point was the country. Before we moved to Hunts Point, which was in 1941, we lived in various different places in the Hunts Point neighborhood —which people call Hunts Point, which is not really Hunts Point. Hunts Point is the other side of Bruckner Boulevard, the peninsula starting with Bruckner Boulevard and then going down to the Hunts Point Terminal Market. Today the 41st Precinct, Simpson Street, Fox Street, Beck, Tiffany, Kelly, the newspapers of the world call Hunts Point, which of course is not true.

In 1941 when I was five we moved into 706 Faile Street, which is the corner of Spofford and Hunts Point Avenue. Before that we lived at 1161 Longfellow, which is near 167th. We lived on Hoe Avenue, 982 Hoe, and my father's family lived on Aldus Street, corner of Hoe Avenue, most of which is not there now. But we moved in 1941 to 706 Faile Street, and my grandmother moved into 1291 Spofford Avenue, where she still is now—she's in her forty-second year in that apartment—and her rent now is in the nineties. It's a lovely three-bedroom, high-ceilinged apartment. Not three bedrooms—three rooms, one bedroom. Our rent when we moved into 706 Faile Street, I recall, was thirty-six dollars. I don't think it was that much higher when we moved out.

It was a beautiful neighborhood. It was country. When we first moved in, I recall goats used to cross Hunts Point Avenue. There were goat farms that used to sell goat milk and cheese and all the other things. And then, like everything else, it changed. During the war it became commercial. It became a little Pittsburgh where all the steel companies and all the junkyards took over. Down on Spofford Avenue and Edgewater Road, where the Hunts Point Market is now, and all the streets heading toward Long Island Sound, were major junkyards where you could get a part for any car. I mean, if you went down to those junkyards, they had it. And there was a baseball field, Kelton Field, down at Oak Point Avenue, I believe, where they had semipro baseball. The playground across the street from P.S. 48, which is on Hunts Point Avenue, Spofford, and Faile Streets, surrounded by those three streets, was a hotbed of activity for all of us—the little guys, the medium-sized guys, and the big guys were fighting for the turf.

The neighborhood was mixed—Irish and Jewish and of course some Italian— and when we moved in in 1941 there already was one building there that was entirely black but there were never any problems. Its reputation was that they were there before any of us even came, and they were all basically civil service people—whether it was transit workers, conductors, bus drivers, postmen, policemen, teachers, firemen. It was a black building. There was no integration. Their children went to the same school, and they were just as friendly as anyone else, and we were just as friendly as anyone else. And then there were several Puerto Rican families. Most of them were homeowners. They lived basically in private houses on Faile Street, on Coster Street, on Bryant Avenue. They were native Hunts Point people.

Particularly, I'm thinking of a family that owned the grocery store. The Rivera family owned the grocery store at the corner. They bought the grocery store. The Teitelbaums owned it while I lived there, and then they bought it when the neighborhood became dominantly or predominantly Hispanic or Puerto Rican. It's in the building at 1291 Spofford—right on the corner—and the father, Rivera, was shot and killed in the store by a holdup man in Easter week in the mid-1960s. And then the sons took over the store. One son was a policeman; another son worked in the store full time. And then he had a couple of daughters. And now they're still there. And they own a lot of property now. They were the first ones in the neighborhood.

Most everyone in my graduating class of P.S. 48, in June of 1949, went on to high school. But I went to Stuyvesant High School. I graduated in 1953, and I would say 99 percent of that class went on to college. My neighborhood school—the zoning changed the year I graduated from public school. Up until 1949, anyone who lived in that community went to Monroe High School. In 1949 they changed the districts. If you lived on one side of the trolley tracks on Hunts Point Avenue, you'd go to Monroe, and on the other side, you'd go to Morris. I would have gone to Morris, and I took the test for Bronx Science, and they sent me to Stuyvesant.

I went to City College before it was City University, the College of the City of New York, commonly known as CCNY, on Convent Avenue and 139th Street, and I graduated from there in January of 1958, and then I went to Brooklyn Law School and graduated in June of 1961. I found an autobiography of mine when I cleaned out my parents' apartment that I wrote when I was in public school, and in it I said that I wanted to be a criminal attorney. No one in my immediate family—by immediate family, I'm talking about my mother's and father's brothers and sisters and their children—ever went to college. So I was one of two that ever went to college in a very large family. I can't say it was anything in particular that made me be a lawyer, but my father and my mother—but mostly my father—drove me to do my homework, stay in the room, study, go to school, and I don't know if it was fear or respect or both or a combination, or maybe it was the same thing, but that's really what got me through, including getting into politics.

Not having a family that was out there with any of the big business interests to take me in or with an established law practice, I had no idea what I was going to do, but I gravitated to politics and government, and that has brought me to this position. My father who came from Harlem and was, as I say, a cab driver, who was very well-read in spite of the fact that he didn't go to school, always drove into my head that "if you want to be successful as a lawyer, you've got to be in politics. You've got to be in politics. It's who you know, not what you know, that count." And made me join—and when I say "made me," I mean made me—a local political club, which was the Pondiac Democratic Club,[1] at 809 Westchester Avenue in the Bronx, which is right off Prospect Avenue, between Prospect and Union under the elevated tracks. In that club was Dave Ross, who was the city councilman, and there were other elected officials. They also lived at 720 Hunts Point, where we wound up living. And he used to say to me, "Do you know the councilmen? Do you know the assemblymen? Do you know the congressmen?" And "It's good, it's good."

I went to the club, and I kept going to the club, and it worked. I went to the club while I was in law school, and when I got out of law school, Kennedy had just become the president, and through the law school—it had nothing to do with politics—they put up notices. They were expanding the Federal Trade Commission. And I applied for a job. I was in the honors program at the law school, and I got the job. While I had the job I really didn't like it. I wanted to be involved in local politics. And in 1965 an opening came as an assistant district attorney in the Bronx. I was with the Federal Trade Commission from 1961 to 1964. In 1965 an opening came. My district leader asked me if I would be interested in going into the D.A.'s office, and I said yes, so I left the Federal Trade Commission and I went with the D.A.'s office. I took a cut in salary at the time. I was getting eight thousand dollars with the federal government, and the assistant district attorney was paying five thousand, seven hundred and fifty.

I took that, and I stayed there a year and a half, and on January 1, 1966, David Ross asked me if I wanted to go work with him. He was majority leader of the city council. He asked me if I wanted to come and work in his office as an associate counsel at eight thousand dollars, and I took that job January 1, 1966, and stayed there until Abe Beame was elected major in 1973. I stayed with Dave Ross and with his successor, Tom Cuite, who's the current majority leader. Dave left in 1969 to go on the Supreme Court. I ran the city council. I developed an ability to be able to relate to all the elected officials—the councilmen, the mayor's office, all the staff—and I actually set the agendas and to a great degree was responsible for handling and running the New York City Council. Lindsay was the mayor, and we were the loyal opposition. It was a Republican administration, even though he had switched in his second term. And Abe Beame then ran for mayor in 1973, was elected, and I became the mayor's legislative representative in Albany for one year.

One year I was the city's representative in Albany, and during that year Governor Carey ran for election and won. We were supporters of Governor Carey. I had traveled with him during his campaign, and we were friends, and when he got elected, he took one of the deputy mayors to be his counsel, and I got promoted from the mayor's legislative representative in Albany to deputy mayor, where I stayed for three years: 1975, 1976, and 1977. On January 1, 1978, we were kicked out of city hall, evicted, with notice. We were given notice on primary day by the voters, and I went into private practice. Came here with the firm of Saxe, Bacon & Bolan, and then three months later I ran for the county chairman. And at that point I had thought I was actually pretty much retired from politics.

This was the first time I was practicing law full time. I always had odds and ends at night—I'd have a client, a cousin, and do a little work, but nothing to speak of—a will, a real estate closing. And I came with the firm January 1, 1978, and then, three months later, my predecessor as the county chairman announced he was retiring and quitting. I said, "I would like to take your place." He said no, he had someone else in mind. Pat Cunningham said no, he had somebody else in mind for it, and I said, "That guy is not going to get it. I'm telling you, I'm going to try to put together the leaders"—a little pressure. And we were successful. We put a coalition together, and I was elected.

During my years from 1966 to 1978 I was very active in the party in Bronx County. I was secretary to the county chairman for many years and was recognized by most people in and out of government who were involved in the process, so that if you wanted something done in the Bronx, you wanted something done in city hall, call Stanley. He can get it done. And if he can't get it done, he'll tell you straight up front that it can't be done and usually why. The borough presidents—Stanley Simon is there now, Abrams was before him, Badillo was before him, and Periconi—the borough presidents in those years were all elected without the help and against the organization. So there was never really a relationship between my predecessor and those borough presidents. When I became the county chairman, it was the first time since Lyons that the organization was supportive of the candidate who ran for borough president. So our relation is singular, and as a result I think the Bronx is much better served.

I think to a great degree the neglect and decay of the Bronx, and I don't know over how many years—whether it started in the forties after the war with Moses and Wagner and it went to the fifties and the sixties—but at least in my political lifetime, part of the decay—social, economic, and physical—is the result of there being no strong political structure in the county, and therefore it became a dumping ground. Everybody had their own agenda. Everybody was too busy worrying about their own little world to really be cohesive. And I think that in spite of the fact that Badillo and Abrams were two of the most competent, qualified, articulate public officials, their heads were always somewhere else. They were always running for the next spot, and I don't think you can serve two masters. You need a bread-and-butter person. "Bread and butter" means paying attention to getting basic things and fighting that they don't put all their housing projects in one neighborhood. And maybe Co-op City was improperly planned and not well thought out to take people from the Concourse that could stabilize a particular neighborhood and put them all in one little area out in the swamps. You know, hindsight is always better than foresight, so we're not here to second-guess; we're here to try to correct.

The only direct connection I had with the antipoverty groups and leaders in the South Bronx was with the people I was close with politically, and that would be Mike Nuñez from Bronx Venture, Ray Velez from the Hunts Point Multi-Services Center, Carmen Arroyo, Frank Lugoviña. I'm still close to these men politically. At this end it's usually hit-and-run; they come and go. I could name some of them who were around then, but it really makes no point because they're gone. Some went to jail; some went to California. Victor Marrero was very active in the Model Cities program—was still a force and somebody who was dedicated to helping the rebuilding. And your elected officials today . . . we have a very young, bright, articulate group of legislators from the Bronx. I think if you'll look at our legislators now—and you get a book from fifteen years ago and look at their names and ages—I'm very proud of the people that we have: Joe Serrano, assemblyman, 73rd Assembly District; Hector Diaz, new assemblyman from the 74th—I'm just going to do the minorities for a minute—76th, Aurelia Green, she's second to none in being smart and pleasant and a character; 72nd, José Rivera, from a different walk of life, from a different school, but somebody who's out there and knows the street and can do a job; Gloria Davis. These are the minority Assembly people. Koppell [Oliver Koppell], he's not on the same wavelength as I am, but he's certainly an extremely bright, hardworking legislator; John Dearie, hardworking. We've got a very, very good bunch. And if we can ever get them all to work together, then they have ten votes to help or hurt a program. That's what I'd like to see some day.

Strangers are not welcome in old-line established clubs. I belonged because my father said I'd better belong. Mike Nuñez and I were both accepted because we made ourselves accepted. The same in a classroom or the same in a kindergarten, the same as a playground—perseverance pays off. Somebody goes into a club or a new neighborhood, a new house, a new apartment, a new job, and they walk in, and they go home the next day and they tell their wife or mother, "I'm quitting because nobody talks to me." Well, they're gone, they're never accepted. The one who stays and invites somebody for a drink and invites somebody for coffee and says, "I'll give you a hand in picking that box up," and when the floor is dirty at ten o'clock at night you see the people cleaning up and you pitch in. . . . Well, you don't get accepted by saying, by somebody saying, "Okay, Stanley, now we are going to accept you." You get accepted and liked by the opposite of attrition. I'm trying to say—by wearing people down. Nobody opened their arms and said, "You are accepted." When there came a problem and we filled a gap, we were accepted. And it doesn't matter what color you are, and I don't think it matters what part of the country you're in, I think it's the same. You've got to prove yourself.

As a matter of fact, when I played basketball at City College—I played for Nat Holman—after the first few tryouts I was cut from the team. I said to myself, "He won't know who's cut. There are still about thirty or forty guys still eligible." So the next day I went back even though I was cut, and I finally made the team, and in one year I was even in the first three. It was after the scandals, and the teams weren't as good. And then the college newspaper wrote a story where it said, "Perseverance pays off." That was the lead of the story, and it's true.

I fantasized from time to time about running for a major political office, but since I know I'm fantasizing, well, I guess that is the answer. I was brought up in a district in which I really couldn't run, because by the time I became of age and became viable enough, it no longer warranted a white Jewish public official. Then, as I got further entrenched in politics, my reputation—which is very important—is really not in the mold of someone running for office. Whether it was by design or by accident, I was always perceived and postured as a political operative, as the power behind the scenes, as the patronage dispenser—all the things that people want in terms of getting things done. I think that everybody, or at least the majority of people, look for strong leadership, look for direction. But if you're going to run for office, I don't think that the newspapers would look too favorably upon the political operative, the wheeler-dealer, the cigar-smoking, cynical, blah, blah, blah. So, yes, I've thought of it in the way of fantasizing, because I think I could do an excellent job in running a city or state, but no, I won't run for office. I also wouldn't want to subject myself and my family to the character assassination that takes place, which is disgraceful.

I'm very active in elections. I'm very active in the selection process where there's a vacancy. For example, the borough presidency, when it was vacant, Hector Diaz when Louis Nine passed away, and Joe Rivera and Aurelia Green getting there, and John Dearie running for comptroller. Even though we didn't win, I think under the circumstances we did a reasonably good job. I have a strong voice in selection and working, putting together a campaign. It's not just picking a person and saying, "Okay, you're going to run for the assembly," and then walking away. Then you try to help out in raising money and in organizing the campaign and making sure that the people work. You don't just say, "Okay, you're the candidate, go out there."

The first year I was the leader I think that did happen, and we lost the election. It was for the assembly race. I don't know if we would have won anyway, because we were going against an incumbent, but the point is, you just have to be involved, and I generally am involved—raising money, which is very important. I have an ability—I'm able to raise money and put people into positions where they can help the community and work together. You get the head of a Morris Park Association,[2] Pelham Bay or whatever, they have a particular problem that's important to them—they would call me direct. I try to include the local elected officials if I am going to be involved in helping them, so that if there's any credit to be had, they get it, because the assemblyman or the district leader should be able to go to that association to get reciprocity and votes or petitions or support when they need it. I mean, I don't run where Republicans will vote for me. My constituency is my leaders.

With respect to the decay, the severe deterioration, the arson, I think we have turned the corner—to a great degree because there's nothing left to burn, because the arson laws are getting tougher, because the insurance companies aren't paying, because half the property—and I'm only making up "half," I don't know what percentage it is that's left—is owned by the city, so there's no profiteering to be made by a landlord or somebody who has a vested interest. I think that businessmen who are in business to make a profit are realizing and will realize more that there's a better profit to be made in the Bronx because land values are cheaper, transportation is fantastic, public and rail and Major Deegan and Cross Bronx and New England Thruway. You can go from Long Island to Connecticut. You can go to Jersey or what have you—very easily accessible avenues of egress. And I think Manhattan is running out of land. The other boroughs are really running out of desirable land at normal prices. Where else are they going to go?

I don't think we are going to see residential of any magnitude for some time. We may see piecemeal. I think Father Gigante has done a fantastic job with SEBCO.[3] Aldus Green is a nice-looking area.[4] Roosevelt Gardens on the Concourse has been nicely done.[5] Piecemeal approaches like that. I don't think you're going to have a major middle-income-housing thing because I still think builders and developers say, when they're asked, "Why don't you build in the Bronx? Why everything in Manhattan?" "Because it costs just as much to build a building in the Bronx as it does in Manhattan, and you can't rent in the Bronx." The cost of construction is exactly the same. The land value is a little cheaper, but I've spoken to Resnick,[6] I've spoken to Trump,[7] I've spoken to major developers. They don't get enough of an incentive. When you mention the Bronx, if somebody could do a Rorschach test on their heads, when you say, "the Bronx," they're thinking of the South Bronx and burnout and muggings and rape. So they never get down to an analysis of, "Well, if I build up on 226th Street . . ."

I think Charlotte Gardens is a step in the right direction. I don't know if that's the best use of that type of land—I think I was an advocate for the high-rise housing on Charlotte Street, not being sure if that was the right use of that property either—but I thought that the perception (because so much of what we do, it's the perception that's more important than the reality) of the federal government, and everybody recognizing the need to do that, and if it was done, it would be a shot in the arm. I'm from the school that says, "Do something, even if it's wrong. Do it." And it was lying dormant. Ed Logue had an idea, so "let's do it." Nobody had a better idea. It's easy to criticize, but unless you're going to do something better, let the guy do what he wants to do, and they're moving along. I understand that the average or median income of the people that have applied for those houses is in the thirties, and one or two people are working in each of the families, and obviously they want a nice place to live.

I'm chairman of the Bronx Overall Economic Development Corporation, and we've had meetings with some of the banks and have had meetings with Howard Rubenstein and with a major advertising company where he gave me an outline of how to do a PR media effort, but we can't afford to do it. It's got to be repetitious. It's not something you can just do once. It's got to be a constant message day in and day out for a year or two years to show the positive. We can't afford it. So we from time to time put out a little booklet. It makes us feel good, but it's not going to sell General Motors to build a plant in the South Bronx.

Some students from Lehman worked last summer in a commercial strip survey—Julius Edelstein made that happen[8]—and they talked to many people who had stayed a long time in spite of the problems. They had good things to say, and when a news reporter only reported one negative "merchants fear crime" and nothing positive, that was a good lesson for the students. They have to learn that when somebody has something good to say it's not newsworthy, and it doesn't appear on the eleven o'clock news, and it doesn't appear in

Genevieve Brooks at Charlotte Gardens, 1987 (Susan Farley, *New York Times*, October 30, 1987)

the newspaper. You look at the newspapers, it's all the negative stories: who got mugged, who got killed, who got raped, who was burglarized. It doesn't talk about the five hundred families in the building that slept well during the night and woke up and took a shower and went to work. There's no story in that. There's no story about the politician who gets up in the morning and goes to four community meetings and then does his legislative duties and two more meetings at night. The only story in the paper is about the politician who went to bed with a seventeen-year-old boy or girl, not about the other 436 who were doing their job. There's no story there.

I really think the Bronx, although we now have over 1.1 million people and would be the seventh- or eighth-largest city in the United States, and we're all an ethnic mix, and we really are representative of the United States, more so than anybody I think in terms of ethnic breakdown—blacks, Hispanics, and then within the Hispanics all different ethnic breakdowns, Greek population, Italian, the Irish and the Jews—we're really representative. And we have always had a small-town mentality, whether it was doctors on the Concourse, lawyers, or what. I really believe there was always a small-town mentality, always a small club, small circle. I still feel that way. I still feel that there's a lot of pride in being from the Bronx. The Bronx has about 1.2 million people, and it's very close to being equally divided—say three hundred fifty to four hundred thousand Puerto Ricans, the same blacks, the same whites. It's pretty much a third, a third, a third.

I think that in the next twenty years the wheel is going to just keep turning around—as wheels generally do as long as they're round—and that the Bronx will be just as viable as Brooklyn and Queens will be. Manhattan is a different entity, different world. But the Bronx will have its appropriate share of good housing, and the economic development will come back. I believe that. A lot of people are putting the groundwork, I like to think, into the place now, and the work will continue.

I myself hope to stay as a political leader in the Bronx for a reasonable period of time—whether it's two, four, or six years. I like to think I do a good job. I like to think that I'm reasonably well regarded. And insofar as the minorities go, I like to think that if they can't agree on one of their own, then I'm the best one for them and to work with them, in the absence of getting one of their own. I firmly believe that, and that's how I got the job, that's how I've kept it up till now, and that's how I hope to keep it in the future. And I hope to develop a law practice and make a living like everyone else has, for my family and myself. The party job is a nonpaying job. You do get a car, and you can get reimbursed for actual expenses that you incur as a result of traveling. But it's unsalaried, and in a sixty-hour week I've spent at least half my time in politics and half my time in my business.

I live in Riverdale, the Bronx, and when people ask me, "Where do you live" I say, "In the Bronx." And when I write a letter I write, "Bronx, New York 10463," and my wife's stationery says,

"Bronx, New York 10463." And when we go traveling and people say, "Where do you live?" and when they insist, "Where do you live?" we say, "the Bronx." And they say, "Come on, you don't live in the Bronx." And I say, "Yes, we do." And my children were born in the Bronx. Even those who have left the Bronx are loyal to it. Well, the Bronx was good to all of us, so why shouldn't there be loyalty? We had good childhoods. We had a lot of fun. We got almost a free—if not a free—education, and many of the people have reached or achieved some modicum of success. So why shouldn't they be appreciative and pay something back, even if it's only good work and a spirit? I mean, it would be very ungrateful to bad-mouth a place that gave you your opportunity.

CHAPTER FOURTEEN
JAY

Harrison J. Goldin, Comptroller, City of New York, b. 1936
Interview: January 26, 1984

"You can't go home again in the sense that things are changed, they are different."

I was born in the Bronx Hospital, which stands to this day on Fulton Avenue. I was taken from there to our family's home on Rosedale Avenue. My father had come to the Bronx when he graduated from medical school to intern at Bronx Hospital—that was in 1924—and after he finished his internship he opened his practice on Rosedale Avenue, and my family continued to live there until 1937, when my father relocated both his office and his home to the Grand Concourse and 175th Street. His office was on the sixth floor, and we lived on the eleventh. He started in general practice. Thereafter, he began to specialize somewhat in gastroenterology, but he was what we would now today call a family practitioner.

I remember the neighborhood very well indeed. I lived in a very large apartment building. It was filled with physicians who maintained their offices there and lived there. Many names of many families I remember vividly. My father's associate for many years in his office was Dr. Charles Halberstam, who produced two famous sons—David Halberstam and Michael Halberstam, who unfortunately is no longer alive. Other doctors were Abe Jazer, who unfortunately just died earlier this week, and Jack Klar, and Jack Feierstein, and Eli Rubin, Paul Cohen—the list goes on and on. Most of them had children who were more or less contemporaries of mine, some of them older. And my parents remained friendly with many of these people for many, many years. My father continues to practice medicine. He will be eighty-six in July, and he goes to Montefiore Hospital every day.

I went to P.S. 70 to kindergarten, and then I went to a parochial school in Manhattan for the first nine years of my education, and then I went to the Bronx High School of Science. The school was a wonderful place. It was a highly charged and very competitive place, very stimulating. It was located on 184th Street and Creston Avenue, in the old building before the school moved. I graduated from the Bronx High School of Science in June of 1953, and then of course I went away to school. The high school had mostly Jewish students—a heavy preponderance of Jews. There were of course non-Jews, Asians, and some Catholics, Irish Catholics, a sprinkling of your ordinary garden-variety WASPs. We had some famous people at the school at the time—Walden Cassotto,[1] who ultimately became Bobby Darin.

I was always interested in public affairs and in what was going on around me and in current affairs. I have a vivid recollection of the war in that neighborhood. We were all very conscious of the war effort, and I remember collecting paper and taking it to depots over on 174th Street, not far from the Jerome Avenue El. If you lived on 175th Street it was easy.

In high school I was editor of the *Science Survey*, but I didn't have a particular interest in running for office. Indeed, it never occurred to me until much later when I was well out of school and was a civil rights lawyer for the Department of Justice in Washington, in Mississippi, and really until that point I never had the notion that I was actually going to be a full-time public official. That was much later; that was after I had come back, after having been away to school and with the government, away from the neighborhood essentially for ten years. I was away at college and law school for eight years, and then I was with the government for two. I would come back and forth, of course. I was in the Bronx often, at 1749 Grand Concourse. My parents did not leave there until the beginning of the decade of the 1970s, so my whole youth and young adulthood was spent at 1749. I came back to New York from the Justice Department in 1963, and I moved back into my parents' apartment, and I lived there until I was married in 1966, and then I moved from 175th Street and the Grand Concourse to 166th Street, where I lived until I was elected city comptroller.

Growing up in the Bronx I was in a very stable neighborhood, and a neighborhood that was a very comfortable place in which to be. I used to play outside, of course, right next to the Lewis Morris.[2] While I was young—very young—we had an undeveloped lot just to the south of the building on which an apartment house now stands, but it was a lot with a very steep grade going from the Concourse to Walton Avenue. It was a cliff, and we used to call it "the Rocks." We would play on the Rocks. On the other hand, when I started going to elementary school, I would leave early in the morning and have a very long day and would come back quite late in the afternoon—and then I had homework and so forth—so my life was not centered to the extent that it might have been if I'd been hanging around with other children in the neighborhood or belonging to clubs in the neighborhood or finding recreation in the neighborhood. I was away and had a very long day at school elsewhere.

My father had a large practice in the Bronx, going into what we used to call the East Bronx—by which we meant essentially the area to the east of Webster Avenue—from his early days of practice. I spent many, many hours waiting for him in the Parkchester and Rosedale Avenue area and elsewhere, where he would visit patients. I was an adult when the changing demographics really began to be noticeable, in the mid-to-late 1960s,[3] with the opening of Co-op City. Whether or not there had been a change in the West Bronx before then was not really very noticeable. There assuredly began to be a change in the East Bronx way before that, but in the area to the west of Webster Avenue the change was not perceptible until, as I say, Co-op City opened in the late 1960s, and then it was manifest. It was just about the time that I began to be active in politics, and Co-op City as I recollect opened in 1968, and I was already a New York State senator representing the West Bronx by the time Co-op City opened.

I became motivated to seek a career in elective public office during the time I was with the Justice Department. I spent the better part of two years as a civil rights lawyer, handling voting and education cases for the United States Department of Justice, a lot of my time spent in Mississippi. I had an extraordinary experience—including the better part of two weeks that I spent living with James Meredith[4] when he came onto the University of Mississippi campus in the fall of 1962. And I was deeply impressed that a country for all of its problems and for all of its need to change would nevertheless have a commitment to vindicating the law, to upholding the order of the court, that our great country evidenced during that episode in which we had nearly half as many troops in and around Oxford, Mississippi, as America had in Korea—simply to ensure that one American would be guaranteed his rights under the Constitution. And I saw that very close up, and it made a profound impact on my psyche, and I decided that such a country was one that I wanted to serve, and that it represented a phenomenon of which I wanted to be part, and I became inspired during that time to seek a career in public service. As I thought about how I'd want to go about that, I concluded that the way in which I would be able to have maximum impact would be to run for public office and be elected to a public position, so I came back to New York shortly thereafter, in January 1963, specifically with the idea of trying to get elected to public office and seeking a career in public service.

By June of 1964 I was a candidate for the New York State Senate, and by September of 1965 had been elected as the Democratic candidate for New York State senator from the West Bronx, so for a period of roughly a year, or a year and a half, I sought to make myself known in the community and got the opportunity to run, My first time around was aborted because my enrollment in the Democratic Party was found, as a result of a court action contesting the legitimacy of my registration, to be defective, and I was not able to complete my candidacy in 1964, but this was a period of rapid reapportionment, frequent reapportionment because of *Baker v. Carr*[5]—the one-man, one-vote decision of the United States Supreme Court—and there was a special election ordered in September of 1965, fourteen months after I was thrown off the ballot, and I ran again, and that time I was successful.

The kinds of issues that I emphasized

in my campaign were, first, that I would be an accessible and a visible elected official. I pledged that for the first time I would open a full-time district office that would be staffed and to which people could go with their problems. That was a novel idea in those days, virtually unheard of, certainly on the state legislative level, and it made, I think, a considerable impact on people as an important potential. I promised that I would be independent. I ran against the organization, against the machine, and I think that those were very important elements in my being elected. I also was a highly visible candidate and did the kinds of things that have become much more commonplace today, but that were novel in those days. I stood on subway platforms every morning for hours, rode around in an open car—in a convertible—standing up on the back seat with a microphone, speaking to people directly on the streets and in their apartments. They would come to the window and look out and see me, and I would talk to them as the windows opened. I had a large cadre of young friends with whom I had gone to school who came to the Bronx to help me, and volunteers—people who had never been active in politics before—from the neighborhood, friends of our family, who helped me to petition to get on the ballot. I had a substantial group of helpers from those kinds of sources.

In the eastern part of my district we had a large Hispanic and black community, and they were an important part of my constituency, and I campaigned there with equal vigor. My district ran considerably east; later on it was reapportioned, and it was extended north and a little east. The neighborhoods (which I had never heard of by these designations when I grew up) are today called University Heights and Morrisania, Highbridge, Fordham; those were the neighborhoods that I represented. Highbridge was heavily Irish; it changed dramatically only in the later years. I was in the state senate for five terms—for eight years—and assuredly when I was elected and reelected the first couple of times, Highbridge was overwhelmingly Irish, with some Jews, and very few blacks and Hispanics.

After I was elected, I kept my promises; I was a very visible and enormously active public official in the community, always accessible. I did, in fact, open a full-time district office, which I maintained, and I kept in touch with my district on a regular basis, which was novel, issued a newsletter and things of that kind. And because I was a junior member of a minority party in the state senate—and an independent member at that—I certainly didn't have much influence in ultimately shaping the course of legislation, but I was vocal and heard from, and my views were known. And from there I was elected city comptroller. I made an unsuccessful effort to be elected in 1969, ran in the Democratic primary unsuccessfully, and then I ran again in 1973, and of course I was elected.

I maintained my contacts with all parts of the city; I developed an extensive knowledge of the city and contacts all over the city, and I maintained them. It's a very big city, and I am visible and active all over the city. I feel a very special attachment and affection for the Bronx, but now my responsibility really transcends any one community or any one neighborhood, even the one that I started in, for which I have a special feeling. So I have emphasized really the broad responsibility I have to the city at large, rather than restricted it to any one community.

It was distressing to see the Bronx deteriorate in so many respects so quickly. The erosion was almost precipitous in the scope of history. It happened almost overnight, and it was distressing, it was sad. It was a wonderful neighborhood, although I was not as active as a lot of other children were in community types of activities because of where I went to school and the length of my school day. But otherwise I was there a lot. Weekends we would go over to the park on Mount Eden Avenue and Morris Avenue that was known as Claremont Park to play in the playground or walk. There was no library in the immediate vicinity in those days, and so not uncommonly my brother and I would walk over to the nearest branch, which was on Washington Avenue just south of Tremont, which is a very long walk—or at least was for a little boy—from where I lived. So I knew the neighborhood quite well, knew it intimately, knew the broader neighborhood because my father would make house calls and I would go with him on Sundays and travel about the larger Bronx community. And my parents had lots of friends and lots of associations. Our building was almost a community in itself—a very large building with lots of people in it.

I have been encouraged by recent signs that things are starting to turn around in the Bronx. Fortunately, despite the tremendous decline in population, many good people stayed, and they have been a kind of critical mass—keeping the faith, as it were—to begin to husband the resources that are necessary for the Bronx's revival, and you see the evidence around. As you begin to focus on the South Bronx, the area below Fordham Road, you see the rehabilitation of buildings. Of course, unfortunately, there are still many buildings that are boarded up and many others that have been torn down, but we are beginning to see some revitalization. The Bathgate Avenue industrial project was my idea. I recommended it to the mayor and urged that the city undertake that project, and I'm proud of its success. We've got a fair number of economic development grants that are going to the Bronx. There is recent evidence that a large supply of commercial structures that the city had taken back from owners because of nonpayment of taxes had now been able to be resold productively to developers and users, indicating that the Bronx is beginning again to be an attractive place to locate and expand a business.

I believe it will again become a desirable residential community; I don't have the slightest doubt about it. If you study the evolution of cities there is almost an organic pattern with respect to growth and deterioration and regeneration, and I don't have any doubt about that because of the Bronx's proximity to the central business district of Manhattan, and because of the availability of superb mass transit access—the mass transit isn't as good anywhere in the city, but the access is there—and because of other attractions that the Bronx has, the real estate is going to become very valuable again some time, and you are going to see major residential redevelopment. Now, I think that it will be a different kind in the beginning than it was, but I think that's desirable, and the Charlotte Street Housing Project represents the kind of development that I think is constructive for the Bronx. There was a proposal to replicate the dense, high-rise kind of development in Charlotte Street. I opposed that and successfully prevented the city from taking that course, which I considered to be very foolish. But I am satisfied that the current course of our residential redevelopment is appropriate and sensible and likely to succeed, and I believe that the emergence of that, together with the commercial reclamation of the Bronx, is a harbinger that is very exciting for the future.

Industrial parks with smokestacks and belching fumes are not pleasant places to live next to, but I've seen industrial parks in this country which are like campuses—very lovely, landscaped, and pretty—and that's what I had in mind for Bathgate. If there is one reservation I have about Bathgate it's that in executing the project the city and the Port Authority did not adequately vindicate the conception that I had, which was that it ought to be a very attractive setting, well landscaped, with lots of empty ground. I felt that would be very important. Unfortunately, in execution that notion was compromised.

Change is difficult. It's hard to go home again. I remember fondly as a little boy when I was good on a special occasion being taken to Ginsy's,[6] which was a large department store—the Bronx's equivalent of F.A.O. Schwartz—on Claremont Parkway. I can see it vividly. It was on the north side of Claremont Parkway right around the corner from Bathgate Avenue. Well, Ginsy's is no more. I remember being taken for a cherry Coke by my father, to the candy store on the north side of 174th Street just before you cross the bridge to go over into what I used to think of as the East Bronx. That's no more. Of course, the Cross Bronx Expressway took its place. 174th Street is the major way to get from the West to the East Bronx.

So you can't go home again in the sense that things are changed; they are different. Just to say you would go back to the same piece of real estate isn't to go home again, because everything is different, everything has changed. It doesn't mean that it's worse. I think it can be better some day, and I believe it will be. I say that not only because of what I said before about the inherent attractions of location, but also because I have already seen in my lifetime other areas that were similarly written off come back very smartly indeed and become enormously attractive places to live. I remember a time when you took your life in your hands to walk on side streets between Central Park and Columbus Avenue, and look at that neighborhood today. Brooklyn Heights—I remember it. Washington Heights is coming back, and I think the Bronx will, too.

I think that one of the strengths not only in New York but in this country in general is the multiplicity of cultural contributions. It seems to me that part of what makes America different and especially strong in the history of the world is that we are an amalgam of different cultures. Consciously and also subconsciously, the fabric of our civilization generally is rendered all the more vital by virtue of the preservation of these different cultural streams. So I consider it desirable that people from diverse backgrounds not only share a common acculturation as part of the American experience but also retain the traditions and the heritage and the customs of their forebears. So for me the phenomenon of people from varying groups, including the Hispanic background, who may come from families which are first-generation English-speaking, as they learn English and as they participate in the general American experience . . . to retain their ability to converse in their native tongue and their customs and traditions is not a sign of weakness but a sign of strength, and I try to do whatever I can to foster that. It's in the American tradition.

When I was a child, when you were in Highbridge you knew that you were in an Irish American neighborhood, and when you came to 170th Street and the Grand Concourse or Mount Eden Avenue you knew that you were largely in a Jewish neighborhood, and when you went up to Fordham or on the West you knew you were in an Irish neighborhood, and when you went on the East you knew you were in an Italian neighborhood. When I was asked as a child, "Where are you from?" I would say, "I am from the Bronx." It never would have occurred to me to say, "I am from Morrisania." Morrisania was a hospital; I didn't know that Morrisania was a neighborhood. And when I went down to Highbridge I was never aware that that neighborhood was called Highbridge. When I went up to NYU I was never aware that that neighborhood was University Heights. Or I would go up to Fordham Road to go to Krum's[7] to get a soda, or to a shop, or to go to Alexander's,[8] or to the movies, but I referred to it by the street, not by the section name. I knew when I left the ambit of my own community, but my own community ran roughly from Burnside Avenue on the north to 170th Street on the south, and from Walton Avenue and University Avenue on the west perhaps to Sheridan or Morris Avenue on the east. Now, it's true that that neighborhood was heavily Jewish (the periphery was heavily Jewish as well). Yet when I left that enclave where I lived, I was going into what seemed to be another neighborhood, not because the people who lived there were different, but because it was outside the ambit of my usual involvement and participation. So if I went to what we now know as Belmont, or to what we now know as Highbridge, I was going to another neighborhood—not because Irish Americans tended to predominate there or Italian Americans tended to predominate there—but because it was outside of the neighborhood where I spent most of my time when I went to the store, when I went to the movies. If I went to the movies I did not go to the movies in Parkchester, and I didn't go to the movies down on 161st Street. I didn't go to the movies up in Belmont. The furthest we would go to the movies was Fordham

Road, or 167th Street, and there were ten or fifteen movie houses where we went to the movies. Some of them no longer exist. The Surrey, on Mount Eden Avenue, just to the west of Walton Avenue, the Mount Eden, which is no more—my mother used to love to go there, and we used to love to go there—was torn down for the Cross Bronx Expressway. Or the Luxor on 170th Street; or the Kent on 167th; or the Ascot, which was a foreign-language movie house on 185th Street and the Grand Concourse; or the Devon or the Avalon, which were on Burnside and Tremont Avenue; or maybe occasionally to the Lido or the Valentine which were on Fordham Road; or the RKO on Fordham. Those were my movie theaters—every one of them—or the Paradise sometimes.

Then there were the schools and the churches. P.S. 70, Taft. The big synagogues, the Catholic churches, which I knew intimately. The churches in that neighborhood were Sacred Heart, Holy Spirit, Christ the King, St. Nicholas of Tolentine, St. Margaret Mary, and indeed young people who were Catholic and grew up in the neighborhood identified their geography by its parish. And when I meet people who grew up in the neighborhood who are Catholic, I always say to them when they tell me they grew up in the Bronx, "Where? Oh, that was St. Margaret Mary Parish," around Tremont on the Grand Concourse.

Mostly, you knew your neighborhood by where you walked. Of course, you didn't ordinarily walk to Fordham Road. That was the main shopping area; there were a lot of movie theaters there. The park, for example, was Claremont Park, but it was not the only park. Echo Park was within walking distance, but Echo Park was somehow or other a little bit to the north and a little bit to the east, and we tended not to go to Echo Park, and it wasn't as well-equipped a park. Claremont Park was a large and well-equipped park. There were several playgrounds, large playgrounds, in Claremont Park. And because in my family we were observant Jews and we didn't travel on Saturdays, since I tended to be around on Saturday I would go where I could walk. On Sundays we would generally get in the car and my father would make calls, and we'd go visiting. During the war we used to go a lot to the newsreels—that was always a great treat. My father liked to go to see the news, and so we would go down to the Trans-Lux, or we would go out to dinner downtown to an appropriate place where we could eat. And we didn't necessarily stay in the neighborhood; we would go to a museum, that kind of thing. My mother would go downtown to shop and meet people for lunch. On Wednesday she would often go to a matinée, and she always went to lectures and museums. In the Bronx we did not refer to Manhattan as "the city" the way they did in Brooklyn or in Queens. We called Manhattan "downtown." It was a comfortable and pleasant environment in which to grow up, and it would be nice to see that happen again.

CHAPTER FIFTEEN
BOBBY

The Honorable Robert Abrams, Former Bronx Borough President, b. 1938
Interview: March 17, 1983

"There had to be this delicate balance of showing pride—neighborhood pride, borough pride, borough strength, neighborhood strength—as well as documenting for the record the deprivation and the need for commitment of resources."

I was born in the Bronx in a place that I don't think any longer stands. I know it just by word of mouth from my folks. I was born in what was called the Bryant Sanitarium.[1] We lived first in the South Bronx at 1165 Simpson Street. I remember when I was borough president of the Bronx I once took a ride up Simpson Street to see where it was that I was born, and as I perhaps unfortunately suspected, the building was no longer standing. It was part of that whole area that has seen tremendous devastation and collapse.

My father was born on the Lower East Side, and I think my mother was born also in Manhattan. They came to live in the Bronx after they were married. I was born on Simpson Street—and then, when I was an infant, a year old, my folks moved to the place and the neighborhood where I really grew up, Pelham Parkway. My folks have lived in that same building on Holland Avenue in Pelham Parkway for forty-two years.

That was a defined community that I grew up in, a building that was on the same block as the school that I went to for the first six grades, P.S. 105. It had a very big schoolyard, and so my universe was that school and that schoolyard and the vacant lot across the street where we played king-on-the-rock. Somebody would stand up on this very big rock and protect the rock. There would be challengers who, with a thrust shoulder, would try to knock the king down. When the snow came there were a couple of little hills where we would go sleigh-riding, and of course we would go into Bronx Park. P.S. 105 went through the sixth grade, and so for seventh and eighth grade I left that neighborhood.

It was a very traumatic experience because I was going to have to go to a school in the adjacent neighborhood, and that was P.S. 34 in Morris Park, Van Nest section. Where I grew up was a very ethnic neighborhood—very heavily Jewish—and Van Nest and Morris Park was heavily Italian, so this was my first making a step out of the little *stetl*—the Yiddish word for the Eastern European communities where the Jewish population would be restricted. I remember there was a bit of fear and anxiety attached to it. As it turned out, it was wonderful for me. I made a lot of friends, and then from there I went to the neighborhood high school, Christopher Columbus High School.[2] Pelham Parkway was a good place to grow up for me, and as it turned out, it was the real springboard for my political life and career. It was my roots in Pelham Parkway that gave me the chance to develop the political base to run for the New York State Assembly, which was my first political office.

I went to college at Columbia, and for the first three quarters I didn't leave the Bronx because I would return home. College was a key turning point in my life, because I guess I had led a rather limited and restricted life since all of my education and socializing had been essentially tied to the neighborhood, and going to a rather cosmopolitan school that took a third of its student body from the world and another third from outside the New York metropolitan area, and then the third from the state of New York, I came in contact with a lot of different kinds of people who I had not really had a chance to meet in my previous years. And so that was a very important experience. It opened up my eyes and my horizons to a lot more of what the world was like. At the end of my first year, I got a room on campus. That even intensified the experience, because it gave me the chance to live among an interesting cross-section of people at Columbia.

I was always active in student government when I was going to school. In high school I ran for elected class officer. I was the class president, and the boy leader of the Arista—the junior and senior Arista—but I never really dreamt or anticipated that I would be doing that kind of thing in the real world. I had always heard in my family that I should go to college and go to law school and become a lawyer like my uncle Henry. My father had three brothers; there were four boys in the family. Three of the boys were in the candy store or luncheonette business. My father was included in those three. And they worked very hard; they had to get up very early in the morning—four or five o'clock in the morning—and go down and open the store, and they would come home late at night—eleven o'clock at night—six or seven days a week.

And so I was inculcated at a very early age that I should not subject myself to the kind of lifestyle that my father had, and I should go to school like my father's brother, like my uncle Henry. He was able to become a lawyer—go to college and become a lawyer—and be able to make his own unique contribution. I had never thought I would go to a school like Columbia. I had applied to the City Colleges. Lehman wasn't there as Lehman College, otherwise perhaps my aspirations would have been different. In my day, Lehman College was Hunter

College and restricted to women, so I was planning to apply to Queens College, and did, and was accepted at Queens College. A couple of my friends had older brothers who went to Columbia. All I kept hearing throughout my high school days from these two friends who I would walk to and from school with was Columbia, Columbia, and their brothers, and Columbia. So as a whim or a lark—because I think it was the year before Columbia had imposed a ten-dollar application fee—I was going to just make the application to Columbia. And I figured that I probably wouldn't get in, or if I did get in I couldn't afford it, and so I just didn't really think too much about it, and lo and behold I was able to get into Columbia, and that raised the issue with my family as to whether or not we could afford it. In those days tuition was not what it is today—I think it was about seven hundred fifty dollars—but that was still a lot of money for our family. But my parents encouraged me. They said, "Look, if you have the chance to go to a quality school like Columbia, you just don't turn your back on it." I was not a lazy teenager, and so I worked in the Catskill Mountains during the summertime—waiting on tables—and made enough money to cover the tuition, and when I got on campus I worked at several odd jobs that helped pay all the bills. I worked two meals a day in the dining room. That gave me my three meals. I delivered the Columbia *Daily Spectator* every morning. That gave me, I think, three dollars a day. I became a salesman for the Columbia Student Magazine Agency and hawked *Time* and the *New Yorker* and *Life* magazine and that kind of thing, and became the manager of the Student Magazine Agency, so, several jobs, and then on Saturdays I worked in my dad's store. Those kinds of jobs helped pay the bills. I've always said to my wife too that that experience, I thought, was very meaningful to me. I've got a daughter, and I would want to make sure that she knew something about hard work and sweat on a brow, and that it would be important for her to maybe be a waitress in the Catskill Mountains or some other place, because that's as much a part of learning about life and growing up as anything you might learn in the classroom.

I went to law school at NYU, also in New York City. When I was at Christopher Columbus High School we had an orientation class in the freshman year and we had to do a career book, and mine was all about my career in the law. I had interviewed Uncle Henry, and I put his stationery into my book, and I worked there as a summer clerk on a couple of occasions too. A couple of summers—I think during high school, or possibly it was even in between law school—I clerked there. And so I was gearing up and getting ready to get my law degree if I was able to pass the bar exam and join my uncle's law firm.

And, indeed, I had done that for a couple of years, but in between was a little foray into politics. It was my second year in law school that I had gotten an invitation to a cocktail party. It was extended by the former police commissioner of New York. He talked about the need for young lawyers to be involved in the civic affairs of their community and to be involved in politics, in political life. And there was a big fight emerging in the Democratic Party. Francis Adams and Eleanor Roosevelt and Herbert Lehman were leading the battle to open up the Democratic Party, and they were part of the reform wing of the party. And so they were encouraging people to get involved in that struggle. As a result, they sent my name to a local Reform Democratic Club in my neighborhood in Pelham Parkway. As a result of that, a phone call came to me, and I worked in a campaign in 1962—it was my second year in law school—in a campaign to unseat my congressman who was a long-term, very powerful congressman in the Bronx, Charles A. Buckley. He was the Bronx County chairman. He was a congressman for almost a quarter of a century, maybe thirty years. He was chairman of the Public Works Committee of the House. He was somebody who wielded enormous power governmentally and politically. He was chairman of the Democratic Party in the Bronx, chairman of a House committee, and actually the phone call—in terms of making a challenge to him—solidified some annoyance that I had experienced when I was at Columbia.

I was in my junior year when I had a very distinguished professor, David Truman, who taught a government course, and the assignment in that course was to do a term paper based upon an interview with your congressman and an analysis of the congressional district and the problems of that district. The core of that document was supposed to be the interview with the congressman and perceptions of that interview, and I was—I think—the only one in the class who couldn't get to see his congressman, and it was because Charlie Buckley, Congressman Buckley, was inaccessible to his constituents. So I got very angry. I think I only got a B or a B/B+ on that paper, and I really felt put out and deprived and alienated and annoyed. When that call came several years later that there was going to be somebody challenging him in a race based on issues of inaccessibility and no local office and no service really to the constituents in the district, I said, well, especially following that cocktail party, "I'm going to get involved in that race." That was my first foray into politics. That really started it all, because I worked for a man named David Levy, who is presently a Supreme Court judge in the Bronx, and he lost in that race against Buckley.

I went back to law school, finished law school, and I went to work in my uncle's firm. In the next two years I didn't do anything politically. Two years later I got another call from this local Reform Democratic Club saying that, "We're challenging Mr. Buckley again, and we'd like you to meet a very eminent and distinguished man. He's going to make the race, and we think we're going to win this time. His name is Jonathan Bingham." So I went to meet Mr. Bingham, and I thought he was a man of great stature and high character, and I decided to work for him. And, indeed, Jonathan Bingham beat Congressman Buckley in that primary in 1964, and then I was asked to be the campaign manager for this little club for the November election. After that campaign I was asked to become the president of the club. There was no one else willing to be president. I got it more or less unopposed. A few months later there was a United States Supreme Court decision declaring New York's legislative district lines to be unconstitutional, and so that opened up a race for the New York State Assembly. The club had urged me to run for the assembly. I made that race, and that really started it all because it turned out to be a winning effort. It was a very long-shot race because the assemblyman from that district was also very powerful, this time on the state or Albany scene. He was the chairman of the Ways and Means Committee. He was a seventeen-year incumbent. I was only twenty-seven years old and a kid—wet behind the ears. I didn't know that much about politics, and here I was running against a very powerful senior member of the state legislature, John T. Satriale.

The district was made up of three different parts. Pelham Parkway was a piece of it, Tremont was another part of it, and Belmont was the third part of it. Each part of the district had different ethnic communities. Belmont was a very heavily Italian section. It's interesting, because after that race I got to be very close to the people of Belmont, and I have developed to this very day the warmest possible feelings with the leaders there—with the parish, Our Lady of Mount Carmel parish. But that was John Satriale's strength at that time. And then there was the Tremont section, which had an elderly Jewish population and a black and Hispanic population. And so the race was really made up of different districts—election districts—that constituted the 89th Assembly District in those three communities.

I organized very heavily and leaned on, relied upon, grassroots volunteers, classmates of mine from high school and college and law school, neighbors, and my own family. My family worked very hard, my father and my mother. My grandmother wore a very big button and sat on a milk crate on Lydig and White Plains Road, which is the crossroads of that neighborhood. In a way it was a bit of a Horatio Alger story because I really wasn't that well known in the community as a leader. I'd just grown up there. My father was working in Smitty's luncheonette at that time, waiting on tables. My grandmother had lived on Bolton Street for decades, and we parlayed that kind of neighborhood association and organization into what amounted to a very significant political upset in the primary of that year.

My whole life was tied up with the Bronx until going to college, going to Columbia and living on the campus and then going to NYU. It was college and law school that was my bit of separation from the Bronx. I lived down in the Greenwich Village area attending law school. When I finished law school I returned home, back in the apartment with my folks. So, ironically, when I returned home and was in my first and second years of law practice, that's the time when I really presented myself as a candidate for the assembly.

A lot of changes were taking place while I was in public life, coming on the scene, and maybe those parts of the Bronx which were changing were not so immediate to my family because my folks were running for a long period of time a candy store and luncheonette in Pelham Parkway, and so that was really our anchor and our tie. It was when I got to be in public life that I became much more aware of the different parts of the Bronx—the kinds of sociological concerns and economic concerns that affected the Bronx, the kinds of demographic changes that were taking place, what was perhaps bringing that about. It was in that period that Co-op City was being planned and had unfortunately caused significant withdrawals from communities that caused precipitous change, so it was during the time from 1965 on that I personally became more aware of other parts of the Bronx, very frankly.

I remember when I ran for borough president in 1969. I think it was the very first time I had ever been to the community of Riverdale. I just never had the occasion to go to that community, so I guess I wasn't tied that much to other parts of the Bronx. The Bronx is a very large place. I had to constantly remind people about this when I was borough president of the Bronx for nine years. They wanted to paint the Bronx with a single brushstroke, and I tried to explain to them that the Bronx was an enormous place both in land mass—geographic size—and in population, and therefore had enormous diversity. The population has dropped according to the 1980 census, but at that time it was about one and a half million people, and that was a population larger than fifteen states in the union, larger than every single city in the country except four. Only Los Angeles, Detroit, Philadelphia, and Chicago were larger in population than the Bronx. Therefore, there were many different neighborhoods, and each of those areas or communities had different problems. Some were strong, some were weak, some were in transition, some were able to retain a strong economic base, others could not, and so you had to talk in much more sophisticated terms about the Bronx. I think too many people would refer and think of the Bronx only in terms of the problems of the South Bronx. They would think in pejorative or negative terms about the Bronx and think only of devastation and fires and decay and abandonment and high levels of unemployment and not realize that there were other parts of the Bronx. I could name fifteen communities that were as stable and as strong and as beautiful and as magnificent as major communities or cities in Connecticut: Silver Beach, Throggs Neck, Ferry Point, Eastchester, Pelham Bay, Pelham Parkway, Mosholu Parkway, Kingsbridge, Riverdale.

I was in my third term as assemblyman when I ran for borough president. Herman Badillo, who was the then-incumbent borough president, decided not to seek a second term and entered the mayoralty primary. I ran for borough president and had a vigorous primary fight. I had always been part of the reform wing or faction of the Democratic Party, and there were very strong battles between the regular Democratic organization and the reform wing, and so, for the assembly—the first time around, the second time around, and the third time when I ran—I had primary fights, and I had to fight a sitting judge who stepped down from the bench to run for the nomination for borough president. It was in that campaign that I had my first true feel and understanding for the borough of the Bronx, even though I had lived there my whole life.

As a result of four years in the state assembly—vigorously representing the parts of my assembly district—I began to get a better feel for different parts of the Bronx. So after my district changed—there was a reapportionment and after I won my first race they changed my district, and so I was moved south and west. The second district that I had, the 81st Assembly District, went as far west as Jerome Avenue, as far north as about 184th Street, as far south as Fulton Avenue and Crotona Park. And so it was a pretty diverse and cosmopolitan district taking in parts of five different assembly districts. It had black residents and Hispanic residents, Irish Catholics, Jews, and Italians, so it was a very cosmopolitan district. It touched on other neighborhoods, so I began to get an understanding of the problems of different neighborhoods. Then, as a candidate for borough president in 1969, I really got to know the borough quite extensively. That was a lot of fun for me because it was exciting, stimulating. I got to know the leaders of the various ethnic communities in the various parts of the borough—the Hub at 149th Street, the commercial leadership there—and how different they were from the homeowners of Throggs Neck and Pelham Bay, and how different were the concerns there as contrasted with the people on the lower end of the Grand Concourse, and how that was contrasted with people who were living in Norwood and Mosholu and the upper end of the Grand Concourse, how that was contrasted with Woodlawn and Wakefield and Riverdale, and so it was a fascinating as well as quite tiring experience just traveling through the borough and shaking hands and being very aggressive as a candidate.

Different communities may have had different kinds of concerns, but essentially they all wanted the same thing. They all wanted strong and stable communities, they wanted their fair share of city services, they wanted to make sure that the neighborhood was going to be safe, that the housing was going to be protected, so although when you really got down into the essence—the core—no matter where you were in the Bronx, people were really after the same thing. They wanted to live in a good-quality neighborhood, they wanted to be assured of safety, they wanted their parks to be free of drug pushers and to have the parks operable, so if there was a playground, they wanted to be sure that the benches were in good repair and that the swings were not broken.

It was at that point in time that a decentralization program for the school system in the city of New York was created, and so there was more opportunity for community involvement, and there was a great deal of concern on the local levels with respect to schools that the administration and teaching population bear greater resemblance to the student population in the area. One of the things that was most meaningful to me was the fact that I was able to win the confidence of the various groupings of people and areas in the borough even though they were very diverse and even though there might have been tension and friction from time to time. There would be perhaps at times racial tension and friction in some of the schools. In Lehman High School with the emergence of more and more nonwhite students there might have been a fight here and there, and we would have to come to grips with that and struggles within the school system, and some tensions between long-term older personnel and the newer people coming in, and I guess I worked very hard at the job, and I tried to be very fair and open-minded, and I saw that one of the functions that I had was being a safety valve for a borough that at times could have been a tinderbox because there was so much need, so much deprivation all over the borough, that there might have been the development of paranoia that, "Gee, the resources are certainly not coming to us, they're going *there*," and there might have been the development of jealousy that the next community board was getting more services, more sanitation commitment, more police resources than their own community.

So I saw my role as the liaison between the downtown city hall and the local communities, being a spokesperson, being a bridge, being a catalyst to try to bring about some of the needed changes, some of the additional resources, and, frankly, somebody who would be honest in listening to problems, in evaluating the merit or the worth of the issues that were being presented and then trying to do something about them. I guess all this was demonstrated by the kind of election results that emerged because I was challenged for reelection as borough president in 1973 by an incumbent assemblyman who replaced me in the assembly, and it was one of my proudest moments in public life because I scored the biggest vote in the history of the county, and I won big uniformly throughout the borough even though the communities and the politics of those communities were vastly different in the Bronx. The northeastern part of the Bronx had been represented by fairly conservative elected officials—the only Republicans in the county, in the state assembly, in the state senate. I would win as big there as I would in my old neighborhood, Pelham Parkway, as I would in Riverdale, as I would in the South Bronx in the midst of the black and Hispanic voting strength of the borough. I guess that was because I worked very hard at trying to be accessible, available to them, and working for each community, not to the detriment of the others, but we developed projects and programs for each community. And so, if the South Bronx felt that it needed a high school, we would work for a high school for the South Bronx, and that in no way would take away from the need of getting the resources to build a library in Riverdale or to open up Devoe Park in the northern Bronx or to get the park across the street from St. Nicholas of Tolentine rehabilitated and getting the seven hundred eighty thousand dollars that would be necessary to do that.

New York is a heavily centralized city government and especially on the expense budget side. The expense budget pays for all of the services. It pays for the salaries of the Police and the Fire Departments and for sanitation and education. The capital budget is the budget that funds the construction of buildings, the libraries and schools, the roads, the sewers, and so one of the things that we were struggling with in the sixties and seventies was a greater earmarking and definition of what would be allocated to boroughs and given communities. It was in that period that we had the emergence of the community boards and the development of community board budgets. So at least on the capital budget side we had to break out that way, and therefore people could see what they were getting and what other districts were getting, not only in their own borough but elsewhere in the city. The dispensation of the resources for services would still be done centrally by commissioners. The mayor would be appointing a sanitation commissioner, a police commissioner, a fire commissioner, and it was that commissioner centrally who would disburse the resources, where the manpower would go, how many firehouses there would be, how many people would be assigned to the police precincts, so all of that was a function of management decision centrally placed, but being pressured by the boroughs.

I tried to be an activist and vocal borough president and so would be constantly meeting with all these commissioners saying, "We need more, we're not being fairly treated, the Bronx doesn't have a museum, we need a museum" (we got a museum), "the Bronx has cultural strength, why do you give all your money to Manhattan? We just founded an entity called the Bronx Council on the Arts. You should be funding the Bronx Council on the Arts." (We got them to fund the Bronx Council on the Arts.) My job all the time was meeting with the housing and development administrator, saying, "Come on. Try to save some of this housing. Try to contain some of the blight. Give us some of the funds that the city is getting under federal programs." And I'd be doing that with each of the commissioners and the mayor himself. That would be a key part of my job, fighting, punching away to try to get more resources for the Bronx. And I guess by the time my term was over, I had gotten more capital projects in the budget than any preceding borough president in a comparable period. We were able to work with communities and have them understand the process and work within the system to create the pressure points. We developed local hearings in the community boards in the Bronx. I traveled into these communities to hold hearings at night, have local leadership come out. They would articulate what they felt were the priority needs. We would then compile a report based upon those twelve or fourteen hearings. We would submit it to the city planning commission, fight to have the city planning commission include in its capital budget these items. I would then bring them down to the city planning commission hearings and to the hearings of the board of estimate and the city council, so we would build a record, so that my colleagues on the board of estimate, the other borough presidents, the council president, the comptroller, and mayor would see that there were not only defined needs, but there would also be political pressure and muscle to try to justify and articulate those needs, and so we would get clergy involved, and educational leadership, and local block associations and community groups would come to testify, and as a result of that I think we began to be more and more successful in highlighting the various needs. I would be able to go into executive session and say, "Look, you heard those people from Soundview. They desperately need P.S. 152 and 182. The city planning commission did not provide for those two schools. We need it." They would come and fill the board of estimate chamber with three to five hundred people, speak hour after hour, and that gave me the muscle to go into private executive session and say, "Look, I can't leave this room until I have that line in the budget."

I had to walk what I felt in my own mind was a fine line because on the one hand nothing was going to be able to get done, you were not going to be able to get resources unless you were really on the front line fighting for them, and unless you were vocal, and unless you created the public pressure to bring about change. But, on the other hand, in my view, you couldn't be overly negative, consistently negative in articulating the needs, because that would be destructive of the morale of a significant portion of the Bronx, people living in neighborhoods who needed shoring up and confidence and hope, because there were lots of neighborhoods in transition, and if they felt that the only thing about their borough was negative, blight, horrendous fires and arson problems, then that would be a very dispiriting factor. And so there had to be this delicate balance of showing pride, neighborhood pride, borough pride, borough strength, neighborhood strength, as well as documenting for the record the deprivation and the need for commitment of resources. It was a velvet glove and a clenched fist at the same time, and we tried to do that in a variety of ways.

When I was borough president we instituted a Bronx Day that had been abandoned for decades.[3] It was my attempt at trying to bring to the surface something that I felt existed, namely, pride in the neighborhood and in the borough, and getting the various communities to know each other a little better and work better together. It became so successful that the Bronx Day merged into a Bronx Week,[4] and we would have literally hundreds of educational, cultural, and athletic programs throughout the various neighborhoods. The media would be brought to the borough, and they would focus on the positive, the various strengths that we had. Activities would take place in our great institutions of higher education. We would say that we had more educational facilities and institutions of higher education than half the countries in the world with the various colleges that we had. So that was done at the same time that you would be working at recognizing that there were needs in the community and that there would have to also be the attempt to talk about those and to document those. So it was a delicate balance that would have to be kept in mind all the time.

I came to the scene as borough president midway in the antipoverty efforts. They really began, I guess, during the term of my predecessor, maybe even before his term, but it was very interesting to me. I would always be amazed at the kind of indigenous leadership that existed in communities. What really amazed me was the kind of stalwart, courageous, true leadership and intelligent leadership that we found in even the most deprived communities. People without a formal education who were not as privileged as I, who did not have an opportunity to go to a college—and a fancy college—to get a degree, would be very articulate and very insightful and very committed to their cause and very proud about their neighborhood and very committed to their goal. I met some absolutely extraordinary people in my term as borough president; many of them became my personal friends and my allies, and we worked together on a variety of projects, many of them started through the antipoverty programs.[5] They would be community organizers. They would then emerge and ascend to other positions like head of day-care programs.

I just got an invitation this week, even though I'm in a new post and I have statewide responsibilities. I remember when I was in the assembly, I started a little block association in the Tremont section. It happened to be in the apartment of Cynthia Rowe, a black woman, who was very articulate. They were concerned about sanitation, and so I went to her apartment and said, "Cynthia, the only way I can work effectively with you as your assemblyman, the only way we're going to get anywhere, we've got to organize, so why don't we call ourselves the Monterey Block Association, a community association?[6] I'll buy the stationery." I laid out the twenty-seven dollars for the stationery, and from that emerged a viable group that got funding through the Tremont Community Corporation.[7] Cynthia formed the day-care center. She became a real leader in her community, and I saw lots of Cynthia Rowes emerge, some of whom went on to run for public office. Joe Serrano, I met—he's a distinguished assemblyman now from the South Bronx—I met him when he was attached to the South Bronx Community Action Theatre that was doing marvelous work for young people,[8] training them to learn to play classical guitar music. Yes, there was a lot of waste, and there were problems with those programs, but I saw them doing some very, very important things.

Federal funds came centrally to the city. Just like the other services, there would be a commissioner who would be in charge of the community development agency, and that agency would divvy up the money to the various community corporations. Then it would devolve down into various neighborhood structures, whether it would be to a rat-poisoning program, a day-care center, a hot-meal program for the elderly, or whatever. The problems were enormous; the resources were never adequate to meet the array of problems. There were also the signs of progress and enormous accomplishment.

Lehman College had a construction program, and there were master plans, blueprints drawn, and there was a groundbreaking, and steel was put up to build buildings. Then came the fiscal crisis and everything stopped, and then for a year and a half into the fiscal crisis, when we began to see the light of day, there was renewed focus on what would happen to Lehman College. There was actual talk that the fifteen or sixteen million dollars that was spent on the design and the structural steel should all be torn down and that we can't afford to go and give the additional twenty-two to twenty-five million to complete those buildings. And I thought that was repugnant and reprehensible, and so we mobilized. It was in my office that we brought together a consortium of the banks and the stalwart leader of Lehman, Dr. Leonard Lief, and the legislators from the county, and we said that the banks should purchase state dormitory authority bonds to complete the project. And that project was completed. It was a very exciting day to be with the wife of the vice president of the United States, Joan Mondale, when they opened up one of those beautiful concert halls—the Lehman Performing Arts Center—that's the Lincoln Center outside of Manhattan.[9]

You could see tangible progress and gains, such as the emergence of a Hostos Community College, that had never existed before. During the budget crisis it was threatened; there were proposals to close it down. We had to fight to make sure that it survived, and then we fought too to make sure that it would have a decent home, not just a converted factory building. We did see it obtain a very nice building just across the street, which added to its capacity in terms of physical facilities to serve its students, and one could trace this kind of thing all the way around.

Yankee Stadium was threatened; there was talk the Yankees were going to leave the Bronx and leave the city of New York. We mobilized forces to try to save the Yankees and keep them in New York and to rehabilitate the stadium. Indeed, that was done. So one could go from community to community, from project to project, and see a good deal of work. Maybe it took too much time, but the accomplishment brought about a positive and tangible result.

But at the same time one constantly saw all kinds of problems, decay extending beyond confined areas, the inability to retain younger people who had economic alternatives, who increasingly were exercising economic options to move to the suburbs, to Rockland County, to other places, and so it would never be a simple, placid day or week or a simple answer to a question like that. You'd see different dynamics at work all the time. You'd see the emergence of Co-op City, the world's largest single residential community, of 15,372 units[10]—a cooperative, planned community with resources available for the Little League and for the elderly and for whatever in terms of game rooms, etc. But then at the same time you'd see the way they tenanted Co-op City—and with the educational park, which was a magnificent structure, a $60 million facility, then you saw that that was a plus and a positive—but the way it was tenanted lent some negatives to other parts of the borough. It acted as a suction to too much of the West Bronx in depleting long-term residents of those communities, creating a real psychological problem for those who were left behind, and perhaps breaking the back of their confidence and causing them to leave and go to Co-op City, so instead of having gradual neighborhood change—absorption of newcomers, good quality integration in every sense of the word, of age, of race, and of ethnicity—you had precipitous change. My nine years as borough president constantly saw both of these things pulling and tugging at one another.

I tried to create goodwill between people and communities. I tried to do that by bringing them together as a unified family as much as possible. The borough of the Bronx is the Bronx, and that means all of us, and so we pulled together and united the county in a variety of ways. I tried to do that on the community board level, with the chairpersons of the community boards meeting together and understanding each other and being allies with one another in dealing with the problems. It's hard to single out one thing, but what I tried to do is create understanding and goodwill and communication, and I think a lot of that did emerge as more and more time went by.

There came a time for me as borough president where I was beginning to get frustrated because I knew so well the borough, I knew the problems, I knew the enormity of the needs, and yet I had so few direct powers to deal with it. The borough president was a sounding board, a cheerleader, if you will, and the real power was elsewhere. It was in city hall, it was in the hands of the commissioners, and it became increasingly difficult for me to drive to work and go down the Grand Concourse and see Roosevelt Gardens abandoned, and then we finally got the money to rebuild Roosevelt Gardens, but by the time Roosevelt Gardens gets rebuilt, the surrounding buildings get abandoned along the Grand Concourse. We see Bronx Community College emerge and try to help stabilize part of the borough, and then we see abandonment, and it was so difficult to get the city to respond to some of those housing problems that it became very tough for me as a feeling, thinking person.

I ran for the office of attorney general, and that job was very different in so many ways—with statewide responsibilities, running the law department of the state—not dealing with the same kind of problems. It's just running the litigation where the state is sued and has an interest, and shaping an affirmative litigation program where the attorney general has certain powers to enforce people's rights as consumers, in protecting them against the environmental perils, and to enhance their rights as citizens by bringing civil rights actions, etc. So on the one hand I was thrown into a new responsibility with significant power, and all that was satisfying, but I guess I've had moments when I've really felt cut off from a lot of the very wonderful and nice people who I worked with and knew, and worked with literally on a daily basis in the Bronx. I don't have as much contact as I would like with the variety of leadership in neighborhood organizations and groups that I did work with in the Bronx. My time is shared in Albany with offices found in fifteen separate locations: in Buffalo and Rochester and Syracuse and Watertown and Utica and Monticello and Poughkeepsie and Binghamton and Hauppauge and Garden City. It's a dispersed network of offices and responsibility, and I guess one of the things that saddens me a little bit is not seeing some of my old friends. I was on the elevator a few weeks ago, and I saw Xavier Rodriguez, who I worked with when he was chair of Community Board Number Three, and he was going to one of the agencies here, and he put in my hand a booklet all about the Bathgate Industrial Park. I came up to my office, and I thumbed through it, and it warmed my heart to see the implementation of a lot of things we had talked about and planned—building a new industrial facility that had the prospect for increased jobs—and so, I guess, as you go on in life there are changes, and there are plusses and minuses attached to them. I love what I'm doing, and I feel very fulfilled.

P.S. 8, 1949 (BRACHS Archives in Leonard Lief Library)

Boy in Melrose Branch, New York Public Library, 1983
Photograph by Georgeen Comerford

Schoolboys with yarmulkes, 1983
Photograph by Georgeen Comerford

Child in pew at Rapture Preparation Church, 1983
Photograph by Georgeen Comerford

Girl from Irish Dance Team, 1983
Photograph by Georgeen Comerford

Girl with cats, 1984
Photograph by Georgeen Comerford

Boy on branch: “The Bronx Is Up!”, 1984
Photograph by Georgeen Comerford

Boy on wall with Popeye graffiti, 1980
Photograph by Walter Rosenblum

CHAPTER SIXTEEN
MARIO

Mario Biaggi, Congressman, b. 1917
Interview: March 23, 1984

"You wonder what God had in mind because it was a miracle, just a miracle."

I moved to the Bronx when I married. My wife, who was born on the Albany Post Road, came down here as a child. I met her through a high school acquaintance when I was eighteen. I grew up in East Harlem in Manhattan—East Harlem and West Harlem, really—there was black Harlem and white Harlem. My parents were born in Italy, although my mother arrived here when she was three years of age. She met my father later. He came here when he was eighteen, a gallant-looking man with a mustache which was the fashion of the day, a bicycle rider, and a handsome-looking man. And my mother was attractive.

We spoke English at home. I kind of regret that. On the occasion when they would speak Italian it was a dialect from the northern part of Italy—Reggio Emilia—and I learned to understand it, but I never learned to use the language, regrettably, because we know now that the more languages you know, the better you are able to communicate.

There was a time in the evolution of immigrants who came to this country where, in an effort to embrace this country, we sought to be more American than the Americans at an accelerated pace, and that was pretty much the psychological state of mind across the board. My mother, however, spoke English. She was here since she was three. But she also spoke Italian well too, because she was in that whole milieu when she grew up. My father spoke English well, but he had a little bit of an accent, and that's the way it was.

There was a large Italian community in Harlem, and there was a special area where the people came from their area in Italy. It was almost a form of colonization. And that was New York City at that time. Yorkville had the Germans and also there was a segment there with the Irish, and you had the Italians and had Jewish groups down on the Lower East Side as well as Italians, Chinese, and blacks. We didn't have too many

Hispanics in those days. I was born in East Harlem, but I lived on the fringes. I lived on Lexington Avenue at 104th Street, and that was a mixture of Irish and Jewish and Italian. I guess it might have been mostly Jewish toward that area. It was a mixture pretty much where we lived. We never lived in areas where there was one predominant population, although I live on Mosholu Parkway now, and most of the people there are Jewish, but never in an area heavily populated by Italians anyway.

My father was a chef for a while in St. Augustine. I remember a postal card when the staff of the whole hotel was out in front with the palm trees and the like—it was a large staff—and there he was with his arms folded and his mustache, and he stood out. He told the story that when he was there he sent grapefruit to my mother, and she threw them away because she thought they were sour oranges. I don't know if that's true or not, but he had a sense of humor—it was wry—he would do that.

He was a marble setter. Most of his life he was a marble setter. He worked in churches. He used to construct altars. In those days the altars were constructed of marble made from Italy, and he would put them together. He worked for the McBride Brothers.[1] There's a story about that. He visited the catacombs once, and he went down into the bowels of the earth, and St. Theresa was lying down as a white marble statue, and part of the statue was contributed by the McBride Brothers. Why it was so important . . . during the Depression my father would go down to the office every day for work—it was the McBride Brothers—to see if there was any work. The McBride Brothers was a very important part of our family background. I thought the story was interesting. I got goose bumps on my head. Marble setting was heavy work. He wasn't a sculptor; he was putting it together. I helped him during the summers. I remember one summer there was a cross. That would be the final touch of an altar, and I brought that up. I was a young boy at the time. But then later, as he got older, he worked for the Parks Department. He came here alone. He left his family behind, and so did my mother. I don't know who she came with really. Obviously, she didn't come alone at that age. Her father visited us when he was seventy years of age and stayed with us for a while and went back.

I went to public school in East Harlem, P.S. 72 at 105th and 106th Streets, and then I went to Patrick Henry Junior High School, P.S. 171 at 103rd and 104th Streets at Madison and Fifth, and then I went to Haaren High School. I took a trade as well. I was learning automobile mechanics as well as general academics. From there I went to work and made eight dollars a week working in a braid factory. But before I took the job I'd been looking for a considerable time along Sixth Avenue. There was a whole series of employment agencies there, and they had little white slips, jobs for six or eight dollars a week. Once in a while you'd get a ten- or a twelve-dollar-a-week job. I reached a point where I was getting a little exasperated. I called my mother once. I said, "There's a job available for me washing glasses in a cafeteria. Should

I take it?" She said, "Hold out a little longer." And I did. I finally was employed in a braid factory, making eight dollars a week operating this machine. They also developed another department, handwork at home. I lived in East Harlem. There were many people happy to do homework. I had forty women working for me in short order. Really, I made a considerable amount of money. Then the minimum-wage law came into effect in Washington, and I didn't want to get involved with the law. I wasn't familiar with it because that wasn't a subject of discussion at home. Some families discuss business. In that period people weren't given to talking about public affairs too much. It was more concentrated on family and what was happening. I was fearful that I might get involved with the law, so I quit.

I took an exam for the post office, and I was appointed and served for five and a half years there. We got paid sixty-five cents an hour, nine cents for special delivery. In those times you didn't have much of either. I was a carrier, substitute carrier, but I learned how to play Ping-Pong a lot. In the swing room, that was the way you consumed your time. Then I became a regular. After five and a half years I took the police exam. I came out, I think, seventy-fourth out of some thirty-odd thousand. Police were making sixty dollars a week, and I was curious. Something was going on in the world that I knew nothing about—the night world. I started in 1942 during the war. The war started while I was still at the post office. I remember when it occurred, and I remember when I became a police officer. I had two brothers, and I was the eldest son, so I volunteered for officers' candidate school.

I was now in the Police Department. I was going to be sworn in when LaGuardia went to President Roosevelt and told him what was happening to the Police Department—we were down to about nine thousand members because they were all being drafted. So he halted the drafting of police officers. Otherwise I would have been in that. And I spent twenty-three years in the Police Department. I rose to the rank of detective lieutenant. I was injured ten times in the line of duty. I won the Medal of Honor, which is the highest award and the most coveted. I served on West 100th Street as a foot patrolman and East 126th as the second-in-command of the detective squad, then in Queens and Astoria as lieutenant in charge of the squad, and then in the Bronx, most of my time as a detective lieutenant in the Bronx. You were assigned, but you could express a preference. I really wanted 114—which was Astoria—and I received it. But you're studying all the time for the exams, and I received the Medal of Honor for an extraordinary incident that happened up here in front of the house, as a matter of fact.

I was in the car with a visitor who was staying at the house with us, in the apartment. It was about one o'clock in the morning, and a man approached me and put a gun to me. And to make a long story very short—because it was a traumatizing experience—he got in the back of the car, and I was able to take my gun out without him knowing it, and we fired eleven shots at each other with our guns almost touching—you could hear the metal—and I killed him. He didn't die immediately, though. I was shot, and miraculously I escaped alive, but as he was dying he said, "Jimmy, help me, help me," and I saw there was a car behind us with a fellow in it. He pulled up and came over and said, "What happened?" I told him what happened: "I'm a police officer; this fellow was trying to stick us up." And when the detectives came, people responded and wanted to take me to the hospital. I said, "Stop. See if that fellow's name is Jimmy." And it was. He was his accomplice. He had three or four guns in the car with him, a mask, and all that, and they were wanted. They were responsible for several deaths. But because of that I received the Medal of Honor.

Meanwhile, my friend had fled. I didn't know whether he was shot. I didn't know where he had gone. I know when I left the car I had a gun in each hand, because I went in the back seat after the shooting had ceased. I just assumed that no one else had bullets. I knew I was out. I thought he was, but he wasn't. He had one more, and happily two of those bullets went through the collar of my coat. I wouldn't reenact that scene with blanks. It was just frightening. It makes you think. You wonder what God had in mind, because it was a miracle, just a miracle.

That received a lot of press, and I received a number of awards from community groups. At one of those dinners there was a little man who was dean at New York Law School and who was a former counsel of Governor Harriman. He read my biography, heard me speak, and coached me and offered me a full scholarship at New York Law School. I had never attended college, but he suggested taking the state college equivalency exam, and I did, and I passed it. But in the interim the New York Bar Association passed a regulation that would prohibit admission on the basis of the college equivalency exam. He obviously wrote a persuasive letter, and they waived the rule, and I was in. I did it in two and a half years—days, nights, and summers. I had not been in school since 1935. But I was reading and studying, and outside of my own personal gratification, what this did, I think, was inspire my children: if it's that important to the old man to kill himself, it must be good. So my two sons, Richard and Mario, are attorneys, Jacqueline is a clinical psychologist, and Barbara is a nurse. And my wife received her degree a couple of years ago. And it was very significant because I think mine was the first degree in the whole family.

My brothers didn't go to college. Those were different days. If you completed high school, that was an achievement. And then you talked about economy, about living, really. My mother cleaned offices for eight dollars a week. I shined shoes for a nickel apiece, and on occasion I'd help my mother. But we put it all together. We were never on public assistance. We called it "relief" in those days. Of course some people did, and I understand it—they are not to be condemned. But there was a sense of shame associated with it. Even those who did tried to be as surreptitious as possible about it. We understood, but we were not inclined to do that. Things weren't good—were bad, as a matter of fact. It was a bitter experience, but one which

I think is addressed very profoundly by a statement my daughter Jacqueline made. She said, "Dad, you've given me everything but a Depression." It was a very important observation. I think that's profound. It makes us appreciate everything we have today, and we keep striving. I think psychologically we're trying to separate that period as much as possible from our present living, put as much distance between us and the past as possible.

I met my wife at Bryant Avenue. One of my former high school classmates, Jenny Zanaida—her father was superintendent of the building—invited me to a party at her home, and I did go, and my wife was there. She was the most beautiful. And we met, and nature took its course. I was twenty-three, and she's five years younger than I. That's a long time ago. She was also from an Italian family although her maiden name was Wassil. Her family suffered the experience that many Italian families—many European families—suffered when they came here. Their names were difficult to pronounce, and they were changed right in the official records when they came here. They were dealing with their own complexes in a strange land, and they were accepted, or shortened, changed, whatever. However, hers was a little different. The name was Vasile, and they lived up in that area which was predominantly Dutch, and the teachers changed it to Wassil, and it's been Wassil ever since, but they're of Italian origin. But her parents go back a ways. They tell me they were there when Schenectady burned, when the Indians burned Schenectady.

Immigrants used to try to Americanize as quickly as possible, but in the past fifteen years there's been a shift so that people are trying to maintain awareness of their dual identity and their pride as Italian Americans and others. When people started to talk in terms of their cultural background was when institutions got involved. The educational institutions started focusing attention on different ethnic groupings, and when they did it to one, others became involved, as with bilingual programs. Initially, that was intended to be a Hispanic program. "Well," they said, "what's its purpose?" Well, if you can justify it for the Hispanics, you can justify it for everyone. The Chinese in California got it by a Supreme Court decision. I'm on the Education and Labor Committee, and I believe in it. Either the theory is correct or it isn't, and if it's correct, then it should be universally applied. Well, what I did was amend the law, or make an effort to amend the law, in committee hearings to include all the people in my district. Now, I had Italians, I had Albanians, I had Greeks, and I had some Russians. I said, "Why shouldn't they be included?" That was almost heresy. My position was heresy. When I had the courage to do that, Congressman St. Germain said, "Well, I have French in my district and I have some Germans." So we had a whole litany. It became ridiculous. So then we eliminated the individual groups and used generic terms and also got after HEW to make sure that their people who were in charge of these programs really went out there to see that they were implemented.

Now, that didn't happen right away. They stayed with this mainly because the people in charge were predisposed in that direction. They didn't want to dilute the funding. But we took them to task in oversight hearings. We asked them to come by with a list of all of the programs, and clearly they were not responding to congressional intent, but we kind of prodded them a little bit, and they're responding. Now we have Greeks and whatever—Jewish and Italian—what the community requires. That's the way it should be if you're going to have it at all. Now, there's a school of thought that maybe we shouldn't have it. It's one thing teaching an additional language; it's another thing giving the substance in that language. And we found that many of the teachers in the bilingual Hispanic program couldn't speak English. I offered an amendment that's part of the law today that made that a requirement. To paraphrase it: a man with a crutch never really walks. And yet some of these Russian Jews come in and in short order—they're not here six months—they're speaking English. We used to do that when we were kids. If you want to learn how to swim, throw him into the water.

But there's been a change. It's no longer the melting-pot philosophy. We're not a homogenized group. We're all Americans, and we all have our own cultural background, and we're proud of it apparently. There's a focus on it. By the way, that process isn't universal. It's mostly in metropolitan areas, urban areas, that you'll find that process taking hold. People in the Midwest think that's kind of strange, and the South too, they think that's kind of strange. They recognize it, but they still think there should be a homogenizing process. But there's much more of an awareness than there was. I think it was sponsored really by the remarkable assertion of the black community and their advancement and what they advocated. What they advocated, really, was not bad, but it could be universally applied again. Now if it was confined to them alone, why then you'd say, "Well, if you feel there's inequity—if you're dealing with inequity with one group, why not deal with inequity in other groups?" And I think it was a reaction to the black movement. If blacks are getting parts of programs, then why shouldn't the others? Why shouldn't the others? It wasn't easy to implement because you were dealing with a very compelling tide. But it fell in place because the principle was correct. It fell in place, and the younger folks are out there. They're more conscious of it today in their own identity. Clearly, they are. Whether it's actual participation in that kind of identity, at least there's a feeling and a sense of pride. Whether it's in humor, in fashion, there's a realization. My daughter Jacqueline, she's an Italophile. She speaks Italian beautifully. During the winter she went to New Rochelle College, the College of New Rochelle, and during the summer she would go to Urbino in Italy. She studied there, and she speaks Italian beautifully. But my other children traveled more generally. She's more inclined. The others are aware and proud. Of course, my participation works by no other process than osmosis.

When I went to law school I was already in politics in a way, because when I was in the Police Department at twenty-nine years of age I was the first vice president of the Police Benevolent Association. Fourteen thousand people voted. Now, you're talking about a time when most of the members of the Police Department were Irish, I mean, old-time Irish. You had them there with the celluloid collars and the brogue, and they were very organization-minded. When I ran, I ran with another Bronxite, John Caron, with whom I was quite friendly. He was older than I. And they said, "Well, Biaggi, he's a fine officer, but he's too young to run." It was a two-day count. At the end of the first day I was far ahead of my opponent, and I knew I would win. But especially the old-timers, they were the greatest supporters. They were my greatest supporters, and I won. In that capacity, as first vice president of that organization, we dealt with political figures. We supported them, we had dialogue with them in our advocacy of our own causes, and we helped them in many different ways—I mean really all the way up to running for mayor and governor and things like that.

I spent my entire police career living in the Bronx. So politics and organizations weren't strange to me. I never was an aspirant myself. I helped the mayoralty campaign. I helped the Rockefeller campaign. As a matter of fact, Governor Rockefeller appointed me to his administration as a community relations specialist and later assistant to the secretary of state in New York State. And when I left

Mario Biaggi, 1980 (Georgeen Comerford)

him, I came back to the Police Department for a little while, and then I retired on disability. That was around 1965–66.

I first ran for elective office in 1968. I had become an attorney. I always had enjoyed a lot of publicity. As a police officer I was well known, very well known. I was especially well known by the Italian American community. I was their answer to the charges that Italian Americans were all involved in crime. I took on a special dimension at the point that I became the most decorated police officer in America. That kind of sticks out. I received a lot of publicity about it.

So I practiced law for about a year, and there was some movement in the Bronx, and then Thomas Paul Fino was talking about going to the bench if he could arrange it, and we helped him arrange it. I would have felt uncomfortable running against him because he and I were friendly—not dear friends, but friendly. At one time when I was still in the Police Department—and law enforcement was a critical issue in the city—I was his dark-horse candidate for mayor. It's amazing. I see him once in a while and say, "You might have been premature, but you had the idea," because I then ran for mayor in 1972–73. He was made a judge, and I ran for Congress, and that was a Republican district for sixteen years. I ran the same year President Nixon ran, and Nixon carried my district by sixty thousand votes. It was a Republican district. And I won it substantially, and I've been winning it ever since. The percentage rate has skyrocketed, 94 and 95 percent, but I work at it. I work at it in the same fashion Congressman Fino did, maybe even harder, because now there's a greater demand. And I like it.

Dealing with constituents is the most difficult, but it's gratifying. I'm in the office at least one day a week because I'm in Washington otherwise. If I'm not in Washington, I'm in my office, and that's where I am even on a Saturday. They come in with their burden, and offtimes they leave relieved of it. Just this last week I was talking to the staff. "What a day!" I said. "In the last two hours we had three people come in looking for jobs and needing desperately, and after they left, within an hour, I had them placed." One was a Russian engineer who had been let out of his present employment and was complaining about it. I said, "Well, let's not complain. Let's see if we can find you employment, because you'll go through a whole bureaucratic situation with frustration and the like, and you'll be without a job." And I made one call and found him a job. Another little Italian man who was a butcher came to my office on Windsor Road, had tried to be a butcher, couldn't make a living, said, "I'd like to be a porter." So I made two calls. There was one for four-fifty an hour and another one for seventeen thousand a year with full hospital benefits. He obviously took the one for seventeen thousand. He just couldn't believe it, and it makes me feel good. Then there was a woman who had some difficulty getting a job, and we found her a job. When we do it, especially one of the tough ones, when something like that happens, staff applauds because it's like "our team." And I get thank-you letters all the time. It's reached the point where when they have a problem they say, "Go see Biaggi." And that's good. And they come from all over.

During the war they came from all over the country because I was involved in the military. Especially in the brigs, they were badly treated. I'm not against the military—I'm pro-military, we need a national defense—but just because you cross a military threshold doesn't mean you've abandoned all human rights. This was the same time Jane Fonda was moving, but she was assailing the military—I was trying to correct the condition—and there was a time she'd call me every hour on the hour. And I wouldn't speak to her; I wouldn't be associated with her. But I had the ability of going into the camps and make inquiries. They knew I was a former police officer, and perhaps they thought there was a kinship, and there is, really. Sometimes they'd quietly tell me stories. We never punished anybody, but made sure the condition was straightened out. What we did in the end was a revision of the military justice code. We did that.

It was initiated by a black woman who came from out of my district whose husband joined the marines. He wanted to be a marine. And he went down to Parris Island, and the next thing she heard from him—she had written to him and there was some difficulty with some of the drill sergeants—and the next thing you knew she receives word that he drowned. I checked into it, and I found that he was an excellent swimmer, and no one had performed an autopsy, and the situation down there in South Carolina was . . . the pathologist didn't even see the body. He just put a tag on it. And he had been buried. I had his body exhumed and had Dr. Halperin up here perform the autopsy. But really there was too much decay to really find what we both wanted. That received a great deal of press, and the whole world focused in at that point.

I was just reading something about Jane Fonda. People asked her a question: "How do you account for all this unpopular reaction on the part of the public when you're going to appear?" The public calls the department store and complains, and they cancel the whole book signings and things. And she says, "Well, I guess what I wanted many other Americans wanted. I just went about it the wrong way." It's true. I said, "My God, had I spoken to her that time I might have guided her properly." But how do you make that connection?

A person would come into the office with a seemingly individual problem, and it could be the basis for legislation. For one example, I received a letter during the bicentennial. The bicentennial celebration was made up of tens of thousands of little things, and this one was from a legionnaire who said, "George Washington was only a lieutenant general," and he thought that his position should have been enhanced. We did some research. Ordinarily, I wouldn't have done it, but I thought the timing—because of the spirit throughout the nation—might warrant something. We did some research, and we found some interesting history. He was the commandant as well as commander-in-chief, but he really wanted to be a full-fledged, top-flight general. That was his love. And after he stepped down as president or in closing when he stepped down as president, the Congress authorized his successor to make him the general of the armies. His successor and he were feuding—John Adams—and he never would do it out of pique. So here you have this young kid from East Harlem crossing over two hundred years—not quite, but a long time—introducing legislation that was passed into law making Washington the only six-star general in the history of the United States. When you think of it! And I tell it to my grandchildren. It boggles your mind.

One of the things that I'm proudest of involves mass transit. I introduced language in the Urban Mass Transit Act of 1970. I offered it as an amendment on the House floor that created a national policy of accessibility for the seniors and handicapped. The kneeling bus that we have today, that's a direct result. The improved subways, the escalators, the elevators, that's a direct result. If you hear sounds, that's for the blind. If you find different services on the ground, that's also for the blind. For the deaf there are different lights. Accessibility to mass transit facilities . . . I think that would have to rank high in my consideration of my priorities. It was included in the big bill, but it was my language that established national policy. Much legislation has flowed from that, but that was important.

I'm on the Education and Labor Committee. Most of the social programs we have today come out of that committee. And there are so many, and they're so important and so massive that we almost regard them as commonplace, and yet the constituency out there knows how important they are. We're doing them all the time. You have to almost sit yourself back and have a clinical assessment. We did something for law enforcement. There are many places in this country, many police departments in this country, where policemen don't have any survivors' benefits. If they're killed, widows only get what the community would collect. We're not talking about New York City. In New York City if you get killed, you do get some pension. But how much is it? What do you pay for the loss of a breadwinner, a father? So our response in survivor benefits is fifty thousand dollars for every policeman and every fireman, nationwide.

I was on the select committee on narcotics. I'm also on the select committee on aging. I'm chairman of that subcommittee. I've been on it since it was organized. I'm next in line to be the full chairman. After Claude Pepper, I'm the number-one spokesman for the aging.[2] The chairman is preoccupied with appropriations. I understand that; it's demanding. After Claude Pepper, it's our committee that does the work. With narcotics, there was a situation in the Caribbean where there was drug smuggling, and there was a great deal of it. I was chairman of the Coast Guard subcommittee, and I asked the Coast Guard at a hearing whether or not interdicting drugs was one of their missions. They said no, they dealt with search and rescue. I said, "I don't understand that. Your job by the Constitution and the laws of the land is to enforce all the laws of the land on water." They didn't especially like it. And I said, "Well, I suggest that now you do make that one of your missions."

If I suggested it as chairman it was almost a mandate. Reluctantly, they got involved.

A very dramatic development, at that point they had just confiscated one vessel and about twenty thousand pounds of marijuana, and that was almost by accident. The vessel had lost power at sea, and they had towed it in. In four years they went from one vessel with twenty thousand pounds to 168 vessels and four million pounds!

Now a policy: You had President Reagan forming a task force, put Vice President Bush in charge, and now they know that the most important element in that area is the Coast Guard. We had another thing that developed. We found that after they were arrested there would be a turnstile process. The law was written in a fashion that you couldn't convict them unless you could prove intent. Now, the modus operandi—and I had been out with the Coast Guard when we did that—everyone on board would remain silent so you couldn't get any admissions from any one of them. They were generally all foreign nationals and one American. He was usually the captain. But they all sat on the deck and never resisted, in silence. No charts, no maps, because if you looked at a map you would see it was charted intending to come to the United States. So they could never prove intent. On occasion there was some mishap, but I think the convictions were only at a 10 percent rate. We found that out, and I had the law changed. My language changed the law, and conviction rates are now up to 80 or 90 percent.

I'm involved with child support, nonpayment of child support, a terrible situation; grandparents' visitation rights, a terrible situation. We have one out of two marriages dissolved today, more than a million children involved. When the principals—oftimes antagonistic—seek vengeance in any way, what happens? They'll strike out at anybody. They'll strike out at the grandparents. I say that even though the marriage may dissolve, when a child is born, a grandparent is created, that relationship. So we're moving in that direction. We had a resolution passed in the House, the Senate is going to deal with it, and we'll improve that situation. The grandparents will have a right to petition and a right to be considered in a more serious fashion than they are now when a marriage is dissolved.

Of course, whatever comes within your contemplation, at any stretch, that's how life unfolds itself. How could I have gone to law school? Who would think that I could go to law school and not college? As I say, God kept me alive for a reason. I really believe that. I should never be here today. That was an impossible situation. And what's the reason? I've been here sixteen years now, and I was a pretty well-known figure to begin with, and now after sixteen years I'm even more respected—on a personal basis and on pure, hard politics—and no one knows about tomorrow. That's always good. In politics people say, "Well, where will he go? Is it possible he'll be mayor? Is it possible he'll be governor?" Well, it's possible. And en route you help a lot of people who themselves move on into positions, so that when you call them, they're just happy to do something for you. And now what that has done is, I just pick up the phone: "This is Mario Biaggi, commissioner," and it's, "Yes, yes, yes," and "We'll get to it." Some letters too are just for information, for the record. But when a commissioner calls up the person in charge in that area, you know it's going to be given a hard look and generally be favorably disposed of. And we've become increasingly valuable to the constituency. I mean, I can call the mayor, the governor, and the president, and get them directly. It's a hell of an achievement. It dawned on me one day. I said, "Get me the president." I said, "What did I say?" But I realize I've been doing that, absolutely.

The president called me one time—President Reagan. President Ford and I served together, we're very friendly. President Carter . . . I was a strong advocate of President Carter because he was a great believer in human rights. He was the apostle really; in our time he was the apostle, almost too doctrinaire for reality, but important. But President Reagan called me one day. The call was precipitated by a question my staff put to his staff on his tax package, and they're smart, they're sensitive. They said, "If this man is inquiring intellectually, that means he's not bound yet by a party position." So they called the White House, and the president called. The minute the president calls, the staff withdraws. They understand. I said, "How are you, Mr. President?"

He said, "Fine. Mario, can I lobby you about the tax package?"

I said, "Before you do that, Mr. President, can I tell you something? I saw you last night at the gym supper," which is an annual event that all the members go to in the House. I said, "You look fantastic. I don't know what you're doing, but, please, if we can bottle it, we can become rich."

He said, "You know, you're beguiling. You're disarming." He said, "I'm calling you to lobby you."

I said, "I understand that, but you do look great." And he did. I said, "On this tax package, frankly, Mr. President, it came out yesterday. I didn't have a chance to thoroughly review it. I am not ironbound to any position, and I promise you I will deal with it on its merits and I'll weigh it."

He said, "That's fair. Can I get back to you?"

I said "Mr. President, I'm honored any time you call." Then I said, "Can I talk to you about another subject?"

"Sure."

I said, "We just passed the legislation that would cancel the minimum payment of one hundred twenty-two dollars to all the seniors that don't otherwise get anything," I said. "I really think that was ill thought-out. That would be an important factor in my consideration of this bill." I said, "I don't think it's doing you any good with them either, Mr. President, and I'm not sure how much money you are saving."

He said, "Let me look into that."

Okay, he called me back. That was a gentle quid pro quo. He called me back and we chatted a little bit. I said, "Mr. President, the bill is reasonable. I think it's time we started cutting taxes among the working people. But," I said, "have you made a determination on the seniors?"

"Yes," he said, "we're going to turn that around. New legislation will repeal it."

I said, "That's wonderful. Let me see if I understand you correctly, Mr. President. You said you're going to do this, this, and this."

He said, "Yes."

I said, "If that's going to happen, and you say it's going to happen, that's good enough for me. I will vote for your package." I was the only Democrat in the city that voted for his package, and I was subject to some criticism, but I'll still maintain my position, that I was correct. I don't know how many millions we were receiving in that one hundred twenty-two dollars. That's important to the seniors. In the end I live with it, and it was right. They did repeal it. That was carried in *Newsweek*. That was carried in a lot of other places.

I said, "While I have you, Mr. President, may I talk to you about another subject?"

He said, "Sure, what is it?"

I said, "On the Irish question, I was responsible for banning the sale of arms to the Royal Ulster Constabulary because they were in violation of our law. President Carter upheld that. I was wondering if you'd do the same unless they've amended their position and there's a new finding."

He said, "I'll get back to you." And he did, and he held up, and when Maggie Thatcher came here she gave him a whole list of things that she wanted to discuss, and he ticked them all off except the last one. The ban remains.

I've been here sixteen years, and it becomes a way of life. But if you remove yourself from the scene and look down, you see a little kid that shined shoes. We didn't have hot water in the house. The central heating was a coal stove. There was a gas wick for lighting. Happily, we had a bathroom in the apartment—many people didn't—and here we are dealing at this level. It could only happen in America.

AFTERWORD

This year, 2014, the Bronx celebrates its centennial, one hundred storied years since its designation in 1914 as the sixty-second and last county in New York State. The Bronx has come a long way since the 1980s when our oral histories were recorded. There are still good times and bad times, still areas of extreme poverty, something noted in June 2012 in the *New York Times* when it was observed that obesity—our national disease—is more pandemic in the Bronx than in any of New York's other boroughs.

But a handful of upbeat feature stories, also in the *Times* in 2012, 2013, and 2014, celebrate new commercial investment and even a rediscovery of the Bronx as prime residential real estate, progress that was worked for and dreamed of by Nuñez, Abrams, and indeed by all sixteen of the men and women whose voices make up this volume.

A feature article (February 21, 2012) announcing the upcoming building of a plant for Fresh Direct, the food-delivery company, was headlined, "In Bronx, Fresh Direct and Land of Great Promises." While this particular new investment has been controversial—how many jobs will actually be created for Bronx residents is unclear—it's one of a number of new moves. More upscale, its success unknown since completion is scheduled for 2014, is a new, huge 780,000-square-foot suburban-style mall announced in the *Times* (June 13, 2012) that will include an existing 150,000-square-foot J.C. Penney and a new 160,000-square-foot Macy's as anchors.

On the residential side, the *Times*, unwilling to let go of the old negative icon, headlined an article from March 26, 2012, "No Longer Burning, the South Bronx Gentrifies," and then reported on many middle-class professional people buying co-ops "with sunken living rooms and wraparound windows in Art Deco buildings" along the Grand Concourse—recently declared a historic district—at prices of $250,000, $300,000, and soon to be higher, but still reasonable by Manhattan standards.

On the cultural side, the Bronx Museum—Irma Fleck's dream forty years ago—announced in June 2012 a grant for $500,000 from the Ford Foundation in support of a $1 million campaign to permit acquisition of forty new works by artists with Bronx roots for the museum's permanent collection. The Bronx Museum hosted the U.S.

Pavilion at the 2013 Venice Biennale. In 2014, in honor of the centennial, the museum is bringing back Bronx-born celebrities like Alan Alda and Chazz Palminteri in an initiative called "Back in the Bronx." Irma would be proud but not surprised.

Plans for a new Hip Hop Museum were announced in the *Times* on March 13, 2014. If approved, the museum would occupy space in the Kingsbridge Armory, where 52,000 square feet of space is already dedicated to as yet unspecified community use. Other proposed community uses include a skating rink.

A *Times* article on October 3, 2013, announced a planned rezoning of a sixty-two-block area in the central Bronx, "an L-shaped area in the Tremont and Bathgate neighborhoods" where there are many vacant buildings allowing the development of new six- to eight-story apartment buildings and a full range of commercial and retail development, including shops and restaurants.

On October 23, 2013, the *Times* reported on progress in restoring access to the waterfront of the Harlem River. Long cut off by highways and train tracks, a dumping grounds on the Bronx side, the river now has advocates such as the Metropolitan Waterfront Alliance and the New York Restoration Project. The city has committed to a $62 million reconstruction of the High Bridge, built in 1848, fallen into disrepair and closed in the early 1970s. The bridge will provide access for Bronx residents to the 130-acre Highbridge Park on the other side of the river. The *Times* quoted Jennifer M. Hoppa, northern Manhattan Parks administrator, as saying, "It's really the centerpiece of the Harlem River corridor."

Finally, census data from 2010 showed an increase in the total population since 2000 of 3.9 percent to a total of 1,385,108 residents. What goes up can fall down, but what fell down starting in the 1960s held firm thanks to men and women like the ones whose stories are told here, and it's coming back to where, once again, "The Bronx is up."

EPILOGUE
THE INTERVIEWEES IN 2014

Morris (Moe) Greenstein died at home in January 2010, at age ninety-nine. In addition to his many years as an entrepreneurial and community-minded Realtor he had been awarded a Bronze Star and a Purple Heart during World War II, awards that he was too modest to talk about during our interview. He remained active as a broker, primarily of commercial and industrial properties, throughout the 1980s and 1990s. He also devoted many hours to creative pursuits as an artist, calligrapher, and puppet maker, and he even painted street signs for neighborhood associations. He was also an inventor of the first coin device for laundry machines (Greenbro Coin Meter), of an air heater for apartment house boilers known as "Little Devil," and of various other novel conceptions—a man of many parts! His name lives on in the Bronx—Morris Greenstein, Realtors—and his influence survives through his many contributions to other lives.

Irving Bick, now eighty-nine, and June, his wife of sixty-five years and a former real estate agent, live today where they lived thirty years ago, in a spacious third-floor apartment on a quiet street in Inwood. His insurance business had its office on the first floor of the same building. His son David lives across the street, his daughter Deborah lives one block away. After two heart attacks and a stroke—that last in 1995—Irving stopped working, but he helps out in his brother's real estate office. His memories of his childhood, first on the Lower East Side and later in the Bronx, are still crystal clear.

When **Ada Quiñones** sold her travel agency in the late 1990s she realized a dream held since early childhood, namely not to work. As a child she had helped her mother with sewing and from then on had never stopped working, often at multiple jobs. Now, finally, she could stay home and enjoy being a housewife while her husband engaged in community affairs. According to her daughter, staying home didn't lessen her commitment to helping others. She wrote letters, gave advice, and worked with government agencies so that the people in the community received whatever benefits were available to them. They moved back with their two daughters to her parents' homeland, to Loiza in Puerto Rico. In addition to her children and grandchildren Ada always cared for many "adopted" children who needed her as much as she needed them. In 2004 she moved to Florida to live near her daughter, Rafaella.

Raquel Flores retired from Phipps Housing in 1986 as a senior vice president. For the next decade she lived with her family in Spain, a property in Malaga she had bought many years earlier. Typically, she was active in her community. Now she is once more in New York, not in the Bronx, but upstate, living near her daughter, Michelle, in Saratoga.

Carmen Bermudez, for many years the executive director of NAPRA, died on May 15, 2001. After she retired from NAPRA she continued her volunteer work in her community all her life. In recognition of her service, two locations bear her name: Carmen B. Bermudez Place, at Bathgate Avenue between East 178th and East 179th Streets, and the Carmen B. Bermudez Residence at 2011 Hughes Avenue in the Belmont area, opened in 1999.

When **Susan Boyd** left community organizing, she worked for NBC News Europe as manager of finance, living one year in Moscow and three years in London, and was production manager for the Geneva Summit. She left NBC in 1990 to care for a friend with AIDS and subsequently moved to Pennsylvania, was executive director of Neighbors of Monroe County, and founded a major county initiative to recognize and care for people living with AIDS. In 2001 she moved to Florida, renewed her teaching license, and has been a social studies teacher at a charter junior high school. She also serves on the board of the Pelican Island Audubon Society and works to protect Florida's rich plant and animal life. While fighting to save Fordham Hospital—the story she shared with me back in the eighties—she met and adopted John Rivera, then a teenager, and this adopted son and her three grandchildren now live near her in Florida.

Father Robert Banome died in December 1992 from cancer, only sixty-two years old. After his nineteen years at St. Joseph's in the East Tremont neighborhood, he became pastor of St. Anthony's. He died in the rectory of St. Anthony's, still fighting for programs to aid drug addicts and to provide social services to the poor and elderly. The Fordham-Tremont Community Mental Health Program and the Tremont Community Council were part of his legacy.

Eae J. Mitchell's work on behalf of his community is commemorated in the park named for him, on 174th Street between Vyse and Boone Avenues. He purchased the property, at the time a "dust bowl," from the city for a dollar and developed it into a safe, clean park for community use. He died in April 1989, and four years later the city restored the park, gave it into the care of the Parks and Recreation Bureau, and changed its name from Mitchell Mall to Eae J. Mitchell Park.

Ernest Crooms, now eighty-eight, continues as the pastor at Rapture Preparation Church at 2015 Crotona Avenue, the building he bought so long ago from Moe

Greenstein. Father to sixteen children—twelve boys and four girls—he still lives in the apartment above his church, cared for by his youngest, Ernestine, and her husband. Parishioners still come in from Long Island. He still takes groups down to North Carolina. Sunday services, while smaller, are still filled with music and enthusiasm.

Irma Fleck died in 2004, age eighty-four, and received well-deserved tributes from former Bronx borough presidents Herman Badillo and Fernando Ferrer for her many initiatives to improve and enhance life in her beloved Bronx, including the Claremont Neighborhood Center, the Bronx Council on the Arts, the Bronx Museum, and Bronx Frontier.

Michael Nuñez died of a heart attack in June 2004, age seventy-four, still at the helm of Bronx Venture and the South Bronx Board of Trade. A former president of the Bronx Rotary, active in the chamber of commerce and the Bronx Overall Economic Development Corporation, Mike was tireless in his efforts to advance the Bronx up until the very day of his untimely death. Colleagues dubbed him "the Marathon Man" for his boundless energy and devotion.

Ramon Velez died in December 2008, age seventy-five, and his obituary in the *New York Times* called him "the one time pre-eminent antipoverty baron of the Bronx . . . a powerhouse figure . . . the political godfather to a number of Bronx politicians." He himself told me of the many times he was investigated and that, to his pride, he was never indicted, that he just kept on working for his community and for Puerto Rican pride.

Although **Stanley Friedman**, as he told me, never sought elected office, trying to avoid the scrutiny inflicted on public figures, he did not escape that scrutiny and spent four years in jail only a few years after I interviewed him. He was found guilty of charges of racketeering, conspiracy, and mail fraud in a scheme to defraud the city Parking Violations Bureau. In an interview in 1992 cited in the *New York Times* he said the following: "Because you justify you're doing a good job governmentally you rationalize that you are above the law." He left New York and is now living part-time in Miami Beach, Florida, where he has been the general manager of the Alexander Hotel since 2012, and part-time in the Bronx where he continues to maintain a home.

Harrison J. Goldin left public service in December 1989, after sixteen years as the longest-serving comptroller in New York City history, having previously been elected five times to the New York State Senate. Immediately thereafter he opened Goldin Associates, LLC, now a leading financial advisory and turnaround consulting firm that specializes in underperforming businesses, bankruptcies, and distressed situations. Industry publications consistently cite Goldin Associates as one of the country's top restructuring advisory firms.

Robert Abrams spent twenty-eight years in public life, including four terms as attorney general of the state of New York. He continues to be involved in leadership positions in not-for-profit organizations while maintaining an active law practice. The NYU School of Law has established an annual Attorney General Robert Abrams Public Service Lecture in his honor, and in 2009 Governor David Paterson renamed the Justice building at the Empire State Plaza in Albany as the Robert Abrams Building for Law and Justice.

At ninety-six, **Mario Biaggi** is a living legend, publicly celebrated by several hundreds of friends and admirers on the occasion of his ninetieth birthday in 2007. Italian American to the core, and proud of it, his tributes were numerous from Jewish, Irish, and Puerto Rican groups. True to what he had told me, he never defined himself by any one constituency, but sought to provide service wherever it was needed, whether locally or internationally, including working toward peace between the warring factions in Ireland.

CONTRIBUTORS

To permit the high-quality reproduction of the many images in the book is costly and was made possible by the generosity of the following angels: Hugh Calkins, Timothy Calkins, Virginia Calkins, Thelma Esteves, Ellen Hurwitz, Charles Jin, Joan Lipsitz, and Susan Van Dolsen, and by many contributors to Kickstarter on behalf of this project. I will never be able adequately to express my gratitude to them but hope the very beauty of the book will justify their faith in me and in *Bronx Faces and Voices.*

This book owes more than I can say to the staff at Texas Tech University Press: Kasey McBeath, gifted designer; Bob Land, a sensitive and meticulous editor; Joanna Conrad, Karen Clark, and Amanda Werts, who together oversaw and guided the process from beginning to end; and Robert Mandel and Dr. Peggy Miller, whose belief in this project over the long haul made it possible. These wonderful individuals at TTUP skillfully and tactfully helped transform what had been a personal vision into a finished work. I and my colleagues in this enterprise are deeply grateful.

Emita Brady Hill
January 2014

APPENDIX A
DISTRIBUTION OF ALL INTERVIEWS IN BRACHS BY NEIGHBORHOOD

BRACHS INTERVIEWS /
NEIGHBORHOOD COVERAGE
January 1982 Through December 1986

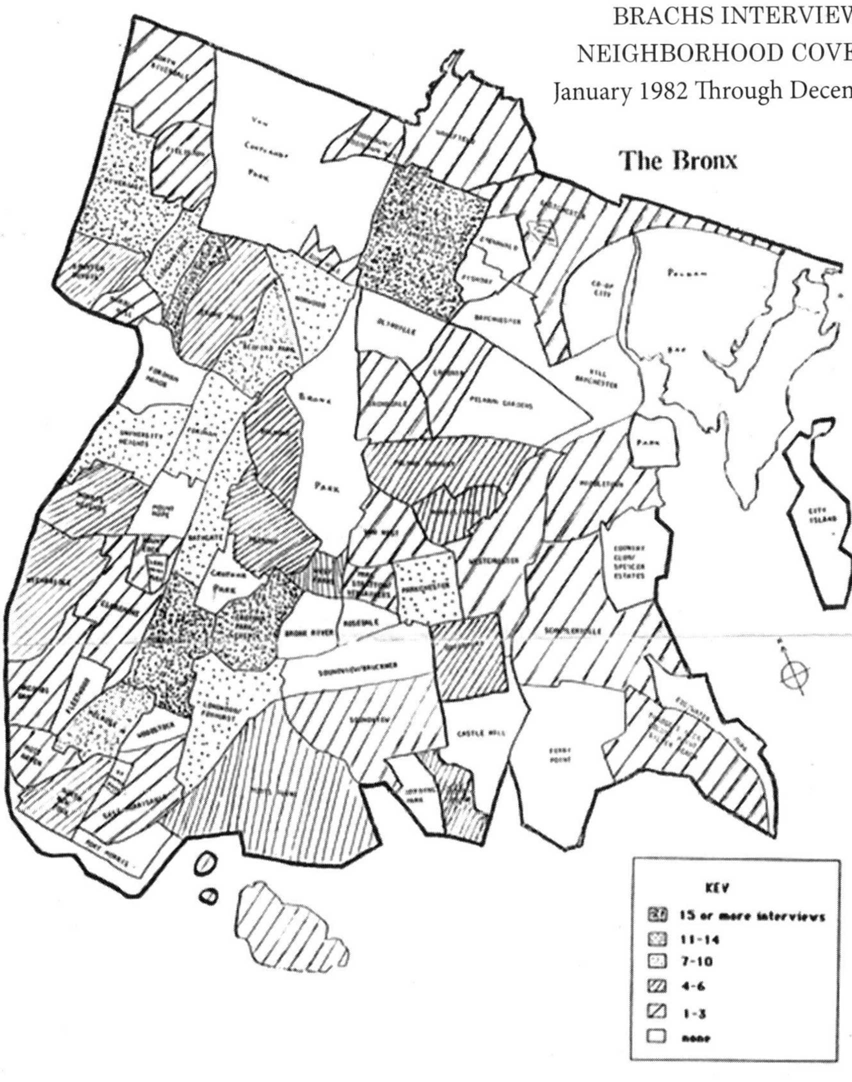

APPENDIX B
CHRONOLOGY OF ELECTED OFFICIALS: 1930–PRESENT

Bronx Borough Presidents, New York City Mayors, and New York State Governors

Bronx Borough President (1934–present)	Mayor (1934–present)	Governor (1928–present)
James Lyons, 1934–62	Fiorello La Guardia, 1934–45	Franklin Roosevelt, 1928–32
Joseph F. Periconi, 1962–66	William O'Dwyer, 1946–50	Herbert H. Lehman, 1933–42
Herman Badillo, 1966–70	Vincent Impellitteri, 1950–53	Charles Poletti, 1943
Robert Abrams, 1970–79	Robert Wagner, Jr., 1954–65	Thomas Dewey, 1943–54
Stanley Simon, 1979–87	John V. Lindsay, 1966–73	Averell Harriman, 1954–58
Fernando Ferrer, 1987–2002	Abraham D. Beame, 1974–77	Nelson Rockefeller, 1959–73
Adolfo Carrión, Jr., 2002–09	Edward I. Koch, 1978–89	Malcolm Wilson, 1973–74
Ruben Diaz, Jr., 2009–	David N. Dinkins, 1990–93	Hugh Carey, 1975–82
	Rudolph W. Giuliani, 1994–2001	Mario Cuomo, 1983–94
	Michael R. Bloomberg, 2002–13	George Pataki, 1995–2006
	Bill de Blasio, 2014–	Eliot Spitzer, 2007–08
		David Paterson, 2008–10
		Andrew Cuomo, 2011–

NOTES

Preface

1. The second, revised, and expanded edition of the book was retitled *South Bronx Rising: The Rise, Fall, and Resurrection of an American City.*
2. Population data are derived from the Community District statistics presented in City of New York, Department of City Planning, *Community District Needs*, comparing totals for Districts 1–6 (the South Bronx) with Districts 7–12 (the North and East Bronx).
3. Movie with the same name, 1990 (dir. De Palma).
4. Examples of such New York–centric writing are Caro, *Power Broker*; Starr, *Rise and Fall of New York City*; and Fitch, *Assassination of New York*. These three books concentrated on the extraordinary dimensions of New York City and powerful New Yorkers, largely ignoring national and international trends, or simply assuming that the world follows New York. For a critique of Caro's treatment of the Bronx, see Bromley, "Not So Simple!" For a contrasting perspective putting the Bronx in national comparative context, see Vergara, *New American Ghetto*.
5. The most plausible explanation is that Jonas Bronck was the first European settler in the area, and that the area became associated with Bronck's family. In turn, the river through the middle of the area became known as Bronck's River, and rivers are usually accompanied by a definite article, as the Hudson, the Mississippi, and the Bronx.
6. Data on population and land area are derived from boroughwide statistics and from City of New York, Department of City Planning, *Community District Needs*.
7. The seminal work is Gottmann, *Megalopolis*.
8. E.g., Bronx Museum of the Arts and Robert Jensen, *Devastation/Resurrection*; Glazer, "The South Bronx Story"; Rooney, *Organizing the South Bronx*; Rosenthal, *In the South Bronx of America*; Gonzalez, *The Bronx*; Su, *Streetwise for Book Smarts*.

Chapter 1

1. "Fort Apache" was a pejorative nickname for the 41st Police Precinct station house in the Bronx. Located at 1086 Simpson Street, the precinct became a metaphor for urban crime, gangs, and drugs in the 1960s and 1970s. The 1981 movie *Fort Apache, the Bronx*, starring Paul Newman, gave notoriety to the area, much to the chagrin of area residents who condemned the film as racist. See "Committee Against Fort Apache," in *Diana Caballero Papers* in Centro de Estudios Puertorriqueños; Walker, *Fort Apache*;

Fisher, "Pulling Out of Fort Apache, the Bronx."

2. St. Barnabas Hospital, at 183rd Street and Third Avenue, in the central Bronx, was not then serving as a general community hospital. The reference to Fairfield Nursing Home is actually the Fairfield Division of the Hebrew Home for the Aged in the Riverdale section of the Bronx.
3. The peak period of the Bronx real estate boom was October through December 1904, following the completion of the subway line to West Farms, according to auctioneer and real estate agent J. Clarence Davies. See Coates, "Profiles King of the Bronx."
4. "Dumbbell building" refers to the nineteenth-century tenement-style building plan enforced under the Tenement House Act of 1879. It was characterized by its pinched, dumbbell-like shape at its center and was criticized for its narrow airshafts, darkness, and poor ventilation (Plunz, "Legislating the Tenement," in *History of Housing*).
5. Ibid.
6. New York State's ten-year real estate tax exemption law spurred a construction boom in new housing despite the trebling of building costs. See "Gov. Smith Urged to Aid Tax Exemption," *New York Times*.
7. Henry Morgenthau (1856–1946) developed real estate in northern Manhattan and the Bronx (Morgenthau, *Mostly Morgenthaus*, 77, 88–89, 91).
8. During the 1920s, guaranty companies were selling mortgage certificates to guarantee property titles and the validity of mortgage loans. Backing by the New York State Insurance Department gave investors confidence in their certificates. Cheating on the underwriting requirements, however, destabilized the system when the real estate market collapsed (Posner, "The Lesson of Guaranteed Mortgage Certificates").
9. The Benenson Theater, built by Isidor Benenson, originally opened in 1921 as the Miracle. It had also been known as the Fenway and was located at 1546 Washington Avenue, north of Claremont Parkway. The theater was demolished in the 1990s. The Benenson Family has long been active in New York City real estate.
10. Sam Minskoff (1884–1950) founded the Sam Minskoff & Sons real estate concern in 1908. The firm dealt in apartment houses, office buildings, retail, and shopping centers in New York City and beyond. The business was managed, following the father's death, by his sons. Their obituaries appeared in the *New York Times*: "Sam Minskoff Dies," *New York Times*; "Henry H. Minskoff," *New York Times*; "Jerome Minskoff," *New York Times*.
11. Two-fare zones were sections of the city where residents had to pay an extra full fare when they transferred to a subway from a bus, or vice versa. In some cases there was a small charge for a paper transfer used to change from one bus to another connecting bus en route. On July 4, 1997, two-fare zones were eliminated, and a new policy allowed customers to transfer for free when using their Metro Card within a two-hour period, from bus to bus, bus to subway, or subway to bus. See New York City Transit Authority, *Elimination of Two-fare Zones*.
12. Someone who blocks (shapes) or cuts might work in the clothing or millinery industry.
13. The Great Depression of the 1930s

was a time of severe economic crisis in which one-third of the nation's labor force was unemployed. For a good overview of how the Bronx was affected by the Depression years, see Jonnes, *South Bronx Rising*, 75; Gonzalez, *The Bronx*, 102–4, and "Great Humanitarian Work."

14. The State Mortgage Commission was created under the Joseph-Pack Bill, and its three-member board was appointed by Governor Herbert H. Lehman ("Mortgage Board Voted at Albany," *New York Times*). At the urging of the commission, early New York mortgage moratorium legislation enacted in 1933 was extended in 1943 (Meyer, *History of the New York Court of Appeals*, 135–37).
15. Noxon is a commercial polish used to clean and shine such metals as stainless steel, aluminum, chrome, pewter, brass, and copper.
16. The art deco style began in France and flourished in the United States in the 1920s and 1930s. Its features could include geometric, zigzag patterns, polychrome ornamentation, contrasting wood veneers, and colored marble. The style drew inspiration from such early cultures as Egyptian, Aztec, Mayan, etc. The West Bronx has a heavy concentration of art deco buildings, notably along the Grand Concourse and its surrounding streets. (Sullivan, *Bronx Art Deco Architecture*).
17. Lehman College was established on July 1, 1968, as the only Bronx senior college in the City University of New York. The site had originally served, since 1931, as the uptown campus of Hunter College. Lehman College is named for Herbert H. Lehman (1878–1963), former four-term New York governor, U.S. senator, and first director-general of the United Nations Relief and Rehabilitation Administration (UNRRA).
18. WAVES is an acronym for Women Accepted for Volunteer Emergency Service. Established during World War II as a volunteer women's reserve unit in the U.S. Navy, the WAVES took over the uptown Bronx campus of Hunter College (now Lehman College) from 1943 to 1946 as their boot camp. Some eighty-six thousand women trained in eight-week rotations and were housed at nearby apartment buildings vacated by former residents (Munch, "Making Waves in the Bronx").
19. For background on the Astor's early real estate deals, see Thomas, *Lords of the Land*, 40–46. When plans for a union-sponsored cooperative failed, John D. Rockefeller, Jr., funded construction in 1927–28 at 840 Grand Concourse. Known as Thomas Garden Apartments, this five-story complex was named for its architect, Andrew J. Thomas, and was a rental property, restricted to middle-income whites. It was notable for its interior Japanese courtyard. See Rosenblum, *Boulevard of Dreams*, 53–54.
20. Astor Concourse Garden Apartment, named for the Astor Family, was built in 1927 and is at the southeast corner of the Grand Concourse at 171st Street ("Bronx House Bought from Vincent Astor," *New York Times*).
21. William Howard Taft High School opened at Sheridan Avenue and East 172nd Street in 1941. It closed in June 2008, and the building is now occupied by six small specialty high schools. Morris High School, named for early landowner and U.S. Constitution signer Gouverneur Morris, began in 1897 and occupied the building at 1110 Boston Road in 1904. The high school closed in 2002, becoming the Morris Annex and home to five small specialty high

schools. James Monroe High School, at 1300 Boynton Avenue, opened in 1924 and closed in 1994. It is now home to seven small specialty high schools.

22. Franklin Armory, located at 1122 Franklin Avenue, was built from 1908 to 1911 and was the first permanent armory built in the Bronx. Originally called the Second Battery Armory, it was later known as the 105th Artillery Armory (Ultan, "Franklin Avenue Armory").
23. *The Winds of War* was a 1983 ABC television network miniseries based on Herman Wouk's 1971 bestselling novel. It explored historical events leading up to the United States' entry into World War II, through the perspective of a fictional naval officer and his family. See "Winds of War," *Movies Made for Television*, 398. For the U.S. airplane buildup, see Kluckhorn, "Big Defense Program Is Launched."
24. The Bronx manufactured many products during World War II, especially aircraft instrumentation (Walton, *Miracle of World War II*, 435). Triboro Brass Foundry was located at 234 Rider Avenue during the 1940s. During the busy war years, the company placed a *New York Post* job advertisement for experienced bench moulders, offering the "highest wages" and "plenty of overtime" ("Bench Moulders," *New York Post*). Ex-Cell-O, a Detroit-based company, established a location in New York in 1929 as Ex-Cell-O Aircraft and Tool Corporation. By 1937 its name was changed to Ex-Cell-O Corporation.
25. R. Hoe & Co. was, at one time, the world's largest manufacturer of printing equipment. The firm moved to the Bronx in 1929, where its plant was in proximity to rail and dock facilities at East 138th Street and the East River. During World War II the company converted its plant to manufacture ordnance material under contract to the U.S. Army. R. Hoe & Co. thrived until going into bankruptcy proceedings in 1969, from which it emerged ten years later. It then moved away from manufacturing printing presses to focus on its profitable industrial woodcutting products. Later R. Hoe & Co. sold its saw-making division, becoming Pacific/Hoe Saw and Knife Co. (Auer, "R. Hoe & Co., Inc."; Sloane, "Chief Officer Is Named").
26. The American Bank Note Company opened its factory in the Hunts Point section of the Bronx in 1911 on the old Faile Estate. The company produced fine engravings of international currency, stamps, and bond and stock certificates. The firm operated until 1985 and was purchased by the U.S. Bank Note Co. in 1990. Its massive factory, at 841 Barreto Street, became the Bronx Apparel Center and foundered. It then became home to BAAD! (the Bronx Academy of Arts and Dance), featuring artists' studios as well as performance and theater spaces (Griffiths, *Story of the American Bank Note Company*; Sheftell, "Banking on It"); Gonzales, "In New Home."
27. Fort Dix, south of Trenton, New Jersey, was established as Camp Dix in 1917 as an army training and staging site for troops. By 1939 it was a permanent garrison and renamed Fort Dix. During World War II, it became the army's major basic combat training center in the Northeast. The site is now a unit of the Joint Base McGuire-Dix-Lakehurst in Burlington County, New Jersey (Rubenstein, "Fort Dix").
28. Camp Rucker is located some ninety

miles south of Montgomery, Alabama, and was originally called Ozark Triangle Division Camp. During World War II it was used for army aviation training and maintenance. See Turner, "Fort Rucker"; "Alabama Had Vital War Role," *Tuscaloosa News.*

29. The Kingsbridge Armory at 29 West Kingsbridge Road was the official home of the 258th Field Artillery. See Bady, "Kingsbridge Armory."
30. Quonset huts were originally created during World War I as prefabricated shelters for troops. Constructed of galvanized steel in a cylindrical shape, they were portable and useful in any climate. Following World War II, Quonset huts were sold for commercial and emergency housing use. Castle Hill and Bruckner Houses were two notable Bronx Quonset hut developments. See "2,000 Houses Given to the City," *New York Times*; Decker and Chief, *Quonset Hut.*
31. Levittown, in Long Island's Nassau County, was a suburban housing development constructed from 1947 to 1951. Initial home purchase was limited to World War II veterans. Many Bronx residents took advantage of low-interest G.I. Loans, under the Serviceman's Readjustment Act of 1943, to buy their houses. Levittown was a model for many postwar American suburban communities. More about Levittown is found at the Levittown Historical Society's website.
32. Stuyvesant Town was constructed as a seventy-two-acre middle-income housing development in Manhattan on a tract north of 14th Street between First Avenue and East River Drive. It was the first such development created under the 1941 Urban Corporation Law, by which the city cleared slum areas and rehoused former tenants. Metropolitan Life Insurance Company purchased the site from the city and created housing with affordable rents for white middle-income tenants; it opened in 1947. Metropolitan received a twenty-five-year tax exemption for constructing the apartment buildings and maintaining the property (Simon, *Stuyvesant Town U.S.A.*).
33. At 15,372 units on 320 acres, Co-op City was the largest cooperative housing development in the world when it was constructed in the Baychester section of the Bronx from 1966 to 1973 (Farrell, "Vast Co-op City Is Dedicated"). Co-op City drew many West Bronx residents away when the development opened (Linton, Mields & Coston, *Apparent Effect of Co-op City*).
34. "Heat and Hot Water," *New York City Charter.*
35. Memoirs about drug problems in the Bronx are discussed in Jones and Naison, *Rat That Got Away*; LeBlanc, *Random Family.*
36. "South Bronx" is a term that came into vogue during the 1960s to connote urban blight, high crime, and poverty. It was never a neighborhood term, and the difficulty of defining its boundaries is problematic (Onshi, "Neighborhood Report: South Bronx").

Chapter 2

1. Once located in a working-class Bronx neighborhood, Charlotte Street fell prey to drugs, crime, building abandonment, and arson in the 1960s and 1970s. President Jimmy Carter brought national attention to its physical deterioration during his October 5, 1977, tour of the street and surrounding neighborhood. For an idea of what everyday life on

Charlotte Street was like from the 1930s through the 1970s, see Rosen, "Glory That Was Charlotte Street"; Jonnes, *South Bronx Rising*, chapters 19–21 and 31.

2. Early local labor unions in the garment trade competed for workers' allegiance. The Amalgamated Clothing Workers of America (ACWA) emerged in 1914 from an array of diverse local groups that splintered from the United Garment Workers Union. No records of Sam Spector and his partner are found among the *Amalgamated Clothing Workers of America Records, 1914–1980.* The relationship of Sidney Hillman (1887–1946), first ACWA president, and the cloakmakers was characterized by friction. They thought of him as a "complete outsider" unable to deal with "ordinary workers" (Stolberg, *Tailor's Progress*, 88). Under Hillman the ACWA sought collective bargaining and arbitration, tried to avoid strikes, offered union members insurance and banking services, and even funded construction in 1927 of the Amalgamated Housing Cooperative in the Bronx (Fraser, *Labor Will Rule*).
3. The International Ladies' Garment Workers Union (ILGWU) was founded in 1900. In 1902 the Amalgamated Ladies Garment Cutters' Union Local 10 was formed in New York (Stolberg, *Tailor's Progress*, 88); the *International Ladies Garment Workers Union Records, 1884–2006*; *Amalgamated Clothing Workers of America Records, 1914–1980.*
4. The Dale Carnegie Training Program was founded in 1912 and focuses on developing effective human relations, self-improvement, public speaking, and salesmanship. Millions in the United States and abroad have participated in Carnegie's courses, and his book *How to Win Friends and Influence People* (1936) remains widely translated and read around the world.

Chapter 3

1. Federation of Puerto Rican Volunteers was established in 1967 and focused on personnel issues. As an agency of the Tremont Community Corporation, it was cut under President Reagan. Its programs were later funded under the Puerto Rican Community Development Program.
2. Bess Myerson was commissioner of the New York City Department of Consumer Affairs from 1969 to 1973, during the administration of Mayor John Lindsay. In 1945 she won the Miss America Pageant, the first Jewish woman to receive this honor. See Leson, "Bess Meyerson."
3. Herman Badillo was Bronx borough president from 1965 to 1970.
4. PAL, or Police Athletic League, is a private agency sponsored by the New York City Police Department. It offers recreational, social, educational, and cultural activities for children and evening programs for teens. PAL's Webster Giannone Center is located at 2255 Webster Avenue and helps foster friendly relations between the police and youth.
5. The Puerto Rican Day Parade has been held annually in New York City since 1958. It began in Spanish Harlem, El Barrio, and then moved to Fifth Avenue. The parade has colorful floats to help celebrate and promote Puerto Rican cultural awareness and pride. See Alicea, *50 Years of the Puerto Rican Day Parade*. During the 1980s the Bronx also held Puerto Rican Day parades. In 1988 the Bronx Puerto Rican Day Parade was

formally established (Serrano, "Tribute to the Bronx Puerto Rican Day Parade").

Chapter 4

1. Brooklyn College was established in 1930 and is a senior college in the City University of New York (CUNY).
2. City College of New York (CCNY) is a senior college and the oldest of the twenty-three higher education institutions in the City University of New York (CUNY).
3. "Albanians for Foreign Nationals" was the Albanian Association for Foreign Nationals. It provided counseling and referral services on citizenship and jobs Siegal, "Change Creeps into World of Bronx Albanians." For a better sense of why the Albanians settled in the Belmont community and what everyday life was like for them, see Jordan, "Albanians of the Bronx."
4. Council of Belmont Organizations (COBO) was established in 1970 as a nonprofit organization. It serves as an umbrella organization for a number of community groups and advocates for seniors, families, and immigrants. It provides general social services, helps residents secure government benefits, and assists with vocational counseling, translations, housing, and health information. The Albanian Association for Foreign Nationals shared space with COBO. See Siegal, "Change Creeps into World of Bronx Albanians," and Maida, "Belmont," 154–57.
5. Bronx 2000 was a grassroots group created in 1979 by Phipps Houses as a privately funded local development organization. During its nearly twenty years of operation, Bronx 2000 promoted economic renewal and business revitalization, housing stabilization, development, and renovation. See Smothers, "Fire Fails to Daunt Merchant."
6. Phipps Houses is New York City's oldest not-for-profit developer and sponsor of housing for low-to-moderate income families. It also provides property management and social services. Its website is www.phippsny.org.
7. T.I.P. Neighborhood House, or the Tremont Improvement Program, was developed by Susan Boyd in 1972 under the auspices of Phipps Houses. T.I.P. created sports and recreational programs for East Tremont community youth to help combat gang violence. They encouraged school dropouts to complete high school and offered counseling for students to attend college, or vocational or technical schools. T.I.P. also sought older adults as volunteers for community gardening and greening initiatives. See Bronx Museum and Jensen, *Devastation/Resurrection*, 100–101.
8. Tremont Health Planning Council was founded in 1974 as a domestic, not-for-profit corporation. Fr. Robert Banome was the founder and first director.
9. Bronx Developmental Center opened in 1978 as part of Bronx State Hospital. It provided total residential services for the severely retarded and handicapped. Its Waterbury Place building, by architect Richard Meier, was later demolished, and the center's mission was expanded.
10. Tremont Crisis Center started in 1969 on East Burnside Avenue. From 1972 to 1975 it was part of the Tremont Residency Training Program for Albert Einstein College of Medicine and Bronx State Hospital. As part of the community health movement, it functioned as a storefront clinic for patients released

from Bronx State; the Washington Avenue site was supplemented with other aftercare satellite clinics. See Clurman, "Patients Can Walk Out at Any Time."

11. Misericordia Hospital moved from Manhattan to the Bronx in 1958. Renamed Our Lady of Mercy Hospital in 1984, it was sold by the Archdiocese of New York to Montefiore Hospital in 2008. Located at 600 East 233rd Street, it is now the Wakefield Campus of Montefiore Hospital and is non-sectarian.
12. Community Action Agencies were nonprofit, public organizations established under the Economic Opportunity Act of 1964. They were meant to help America's war on poverty and generally funded initiatives on housing, health care, economic development, training, and development. For an early history of the Tremont community action programs, see Pollinger and Pollinger, *Community Action and the Poor*, 10–11.
13. CETA, Pub. L. 93–203.

Chapter 5

1. Founded in 1963, the Upper Bronx Neighborhood Association for Puerto Rican Affairs (NAPRA) offered a daycare center for special-needs community children, youth programs, and job training and placement services. For her role as leader of NAPRA, Carmen B. Bermudez was honored by the New York City Council in 1978 with her own street name. Carmen B. Bermudez Place is at Bathgate Avenue between East 178th Street and East 179th Streets. Another honor came in 1999 with the opening of the Carmen B. Bermudez Residence at 2111 Hughes Avenue in the Tremont area. For photographs and an architectural description of the building, see Meltzer and Paganelli, *Marvin H. Meltzer*, 41–43.
2. East Tremont Action Committee, founded in 1968, was concerned with community block organizing, building rehabilitation, and new housing development.
3. For Federation of Puerto Rican Volunteers, see chapter 3, note 1.
4. "Community Council" refers to the Tremont Community Council. All of the "team members" cited were agencies of the Tremont Community Corporation. Agencies having a manpower outreach mandate from the corporation included the Tremont Community Council (not Community Council), the Federation of Puerto Rican Volunteers, the Monterey Community Association, and the National Association of Puerto Rican Affairs. Neither West Bronx Villagers, nor Bronco (Bronco-Self Improvement Association), nor United Bronx Parents provided manpower outreach. See Pollinger and Pollinger, *Community Action and the Poor*, 60 (Table 3.4).
5. United Bronx Parents was founded in 1965 by Evelina Antonetty as a voluntary self-help organization primarily for Puerto Rican parents, but also for blacks. Parents were encouraged to protest minority discrimination in the public school system and advocate for the children. These efforts led to the establishment of community school boards, after-school and summer lunch programs, drug prevention education, and high school equivalency classes. See Antonetty, "History of United Bronx Parents."
6. West Farms Projects was originally proposed by the West Farms Neighborhood Housing Development Fund Company

Inc. as the Bronx Parks South Urban Renewal Project. See "City of New York Housing and Development Administration: Public Notice"; D'Avanzo, *South Bronx*; and Daly, "Project That Transformed a Bronx Neighborhood."

Chapter 6

1. East Tremont Housing was under the Tremont Community Corp. While there Susan Boyd founded the Tremont Housing Clinic (sponsored by the Tremont Little League) to focus on tenant housing issues. An earlier housing clinic started in 1963, by the Robert F. Wagner Association, kept evening hours to advise tenants and landlords of their rights and responsibilities. See "Robert F. Wagner Association."
2. Twin Parks is a large-scale scatter site public housing development built by the New York State Urban Development Corporation in 1973 and 1975. The housing encompasses thirteen parcels across four areas and has some two thousand units for low- and moderate-income residents. The development takes its names, Twin Parks East and Twin Parks West, from its proximity to the nearby Bronx and Crotona Parks in the Belmont and Tremont neighborhoods. See Keifetz, *Decade of Service*, 91–95.
3. Tremont Community Corporation was the administrative coordinator of the then-functioning neighborhood antipoverty delegate agencies. These agencies focused on welfare, housing, education, recreation, and manpower issues. For development and structure of the Tremont corporation, see Pollinger and Pollinger, *Community Action and the Poor*, 50–61.
4. Dennis Lane Apartments, located at 2141 Crotona Avenue, opened in 1959 as a Mitchell-Lama cooperative housing development. It was sponsored by the Amalgamated Meat Cutters and Butcher Workmen of the AFL-CIO. See New York City Office of the Comptroller, "Dennis Lane Apartments."
5. Antipoverty initiatives proposed by President Lyndon Johnson in 1964 resulted in the Economic Opportunity Act of 1964. Its Office of Economic Opportunity (OEO) administered the federal funds on the local level. Ten years later the law was repealed and funds were reallocated. See Arnold, "Good War That Might Have Been."
6. The Urban Development Corporation (UDC) was created in 1968 by the New York State Urban Development Corporation Act. The UDC had unprecedented legal and economic powers, and could issue bonds and override local zoning. Its primary mission was initially urban renewal through the building of state-subsidized low-income housing, primarily in New York City. By the mid-1970s, their focus shifted from housing to economic development.
7. Robert Abrams was Bronx borough president from 1970 to 1979.
8. Patrick J. Cunningham (1928–2002) was leader of the Bronx County Democratic Party (1967–79) and chairman of the New York State Democratic Party (1974–77). He played a major role in bringing the Democratic National Convention to New York City in 1976 and 1980.
9. Tremont Housing Clinic's full name was the East Tremont Housing Clinic.
10. Both Bird S. Coler Memorial Hospital, on Roosevelt Island, and Bellevue Hospital in Manhattan are located in New York City.

11. Brooklyn's Greenpoint Hospital is now closed. Woodhull Hospital is still operating in Brooklyn as Woodhull Medical Center.
12. Stanley Simon was Bronx borough president from 1979 to 1987.
13. "Tremont Health Council" refers to the Tremont Community Health Council chaired by Fr. Robert Banome.
14. Anthony Bouza rose to the rank of Bronx commander of the New York City Police Department and served in this capacity until 1976 when he moved to the New York City Transit Authority.
15. Peter Peyser represented the Bronx in New York's 25th Congressional District, U.S. House of Representatives, from 1971 to 1973; and New York's 23rd Congressional District in the House from 1973 to 1977 and 1979 to 1983.

Chapter 7

1. Arthur F. Murphy Houses are at the northern edge of Crotona Park and east of Crotona Avenue. Opened in 1964, the project's two buildings were completed in 1967 and have 281 low-income apartments. The project was named, at the request of Borough President James J. Lyons, for a former board of aldermen member who was instrumental in the creation of Bronx County. See "Bronx Houses Change Name," *New York Times.*
2. Mario Merola (1922–87) was Bronx district attorney for fifteen years. After his death, the Bronx County Building on the Grand Concourse was named for him by Mayor Ed Koch. See Munch, "Mario Merola Building." A grove of white pine trees in Van Cortlandt Park also bears his name—"Mario Merola Grove"—and is marked with a historic sign describing his accomplishments (see New York City Parks and Recreation Department, http://www.nycgovparks.org/parks/X092/highlights/11625). The Bronx arson period is described in Merola and Giordano, *Big City D.A.*, 77–92; and "Arson," in Jonnes Papers.
3. Starr, "Making New York Smaller," *New York Times.*
4. Vocational Instruction Program (VIP) was begun in 1974 by Fr. Robert Banome. This agency offered counseling, rehabilitation, and drug treatment to recovering substance abusers; residential programs for homeless women and men; and a methadone treatment program especially for residents of the East Tremont and Crotona Park neighborhoods.
5. "Bathgate Corridor," anchored by Bathgate Avenue, referred to the area between Tremont and Belmont that was hard-hit by blight.
6. Bathgate Industrial Park is a twenty-one-acre business zone covering eight blocks on Bathgate Avenue between Claremont Parkway and the Cross Bronx Expressway. The site was formerly occupied by blighted buildings that had to be demolished. When rising square-footage costs in Manhattan forced business to look elsewhere, lower cost at the industrial park encouraged owners to relocate to the industrial park when it opened in 1982.
7. Edward Logue (1921–2000) was an experienced urban developer when he was asked by Herman Badillo to come work on redeveloping blighted Bronx neighborhoods. Redevelopment work in Boston, New Haven, and New York City's Roosevelt Island secured Logue's reputation. Logue directed the South Bronx Development Organization, established in 1978, that linked the com-

munity to all levels of government for housing, economic development, and construction. Charlotte Gardens was spearheaded by Logue. See the Edward Joseph Logue Papers.

Chapter 8

1. The Corps of Army Engineers is the U.S. Army Corps of Engineers.
2. Parkchester, in the East Bronx, was one of three housing developments owned by Metropolitan Life Insurance Company. Under a 1968 agreement between Metropolitan and the City Commission on Human Rights, the company agreed to admit Negroes and Puerto Ricans. See Shipler, "Negroes Say Pact on Housing Lags," *New York Times.*
3. "HRA" stands for the New York City Human Resources Administration. This agency is responsible for managing the city's social services.
4. The Togetherness Tenants' League evolved into Togetherness Housing, which has been variously described at different times as Togetherness Housing Development Fund Corp. (est. 1974); Togetherness, Hope, and Deliverance Fund Corp. (THDF; est. 1980); and Togetherness Management Inc. (1982). Other names used have been Togetherness Management Realty Corp. and TRM (Togetherness Realty Management).
5. Morrisania Community Corporation coordinated the activities of its local antipoverty agencies dealing with community development and redevelopment, counseling and training for employment, and providing information and referral for mental health, addictions, consumer education, and small business support.
6. "Concerned Citizens" refers to the Concerned Citizens of East 174th Street, founded in 1971. This community organizing group worked with city agencies to secure services and protection for area residents. They advocated for housing rehabilitation and development and worked to unite the community with recreational programs for all ages.
7. Under New York City Local Law 45 of 1977, in-rem meant that the city could foreclose on owners whose buildings were in tax arrears for one year versus the original three years. In trying to get owners to pay up and reduce decay, the city unintentionally became the owner of thousands of dilapidated residential properties. Encouraged by housing activists, the city sold some buildings to tenants. See Lawson and Naison, *Tenant Movement in New York City*, 239–42.
8. "Association of Neighborhood Houses" may have been a reference to the Association of Neighborhood Housing Developers, formed in 1974, to coordinate lobbying and fundraising efforts. Their work is discussed in Katz and Mayer, "Gimme Shelter." A later honor accorded to Eae Mitchell was the naming of "Eae J. Mitchell Terrace," a low-income housing project at 945 East 174th Street. See "76 Units in the Bronx," *New York Times*; Logue, "Charlotte Gardens."
9. The planned industrial park, called the Mid Bronx Industrial, actually ran north to East 176th Street, south to East 174th Street, west to Vyse Avenue, and east to Boone Avenue. See Jonnes, *South Bronx Rising*, 385.
10. South Bronx Overall Economic Development Corp. (SBOEDC) was established in 1972 in response to the designation of the Bronx as a federal Special Impact Area. The goal of SBOEDC, now SoBRO, is to provide manpower

training and development and technical assistance to promote economic improvements.

11. SEBCO (South East Bronx Community Organization), established under Fr. Louis Gigante in 1968, grew out of earlier coalition building among neighborhood businesses, churches, and organizations. Securing private and public grants, low-interest loans, and subsidies, by 1980 SEBCO had rehabilitated and managed some two thousand Hunts Point housing units in eight building complexes. It also encouraged small business investment along the 163rd Street shopping district. See Sahd, "Community Development Corporations and Social Capital"; Bronx Museum and Jensen, *Devastation/Resurrection*, 94, 96.
12. Mid-Bronx Development, formerly known as Mid-Bronx Desperadoes, was incorporated in 1974. It was formed from a coalition of individuals from associations, service organizations, and community churches in Community Planning Board Number Three and the Crotona Park area. MBD tried to stabilize their neighborhood and make it economically viable. Fr. William J. Smith and Genevieve Brooks co-led the group. See Von Hoffman, *House by House*, 31–34.
13. When President Jimmy Carter toured Charlotte Street in 1977, his visit focused national attention on an urban area of abandoned apartment buildings. By 1984, Charlotte Gardens rose on the ruins as owner-occupied ranch-style houses complete with backyards and white picket fences. With federal, state, and foundation financing, the development became a source of owner pride and stability. See Jonnes, *South Bronx Rising*; Logue, "Charlotte Gardens."

Chapter 9

1. Institution Security involves credit or loans to individuals or businesses that may have insufficient resources to secure traditional bank loans.
2. The Apostolic Church is a Pentecostal Christian denomination that can trace its origins back to the 1904–5 Welsh Revival.

Part Four

1. See chapter 13, this volume.

Chapter 10

1. Claremont Village is a large public housing complex located from 169th to 172nd Streets between Webster and Third Avenues. It consists of thirty buildings that rise either thirteen or twenty-one stories high. This housing development opened in 1964 and was a $76 million slum clearance project, creating housing for seventeen thousand residents.
2. Castle Hill Bathing Park at 355 Castle Hill Avenue in the East Bronx was owned and operated by Castle Hill Estate Inc. The bathing park became the Castle Hill Beach Club. See Twomey, *Bronx in Bits and Pieces*, 60–61.
3. When Irma Fleck and her physician husband, Henry, were apart during World War II, their letters helped them survive the separation. See Fleck, Fleck, and Stevens, *Letters from the Front*.
4. Forest Houses is a public housing complex located at Trinity Avenue and East 163rd Street. It opened in 1954 and has some 1,350 rental apartments.
5. Irma Fleck founded the Claremont Neighborhood Center at East 169th

Street in 1956. It provides recreational and educational programs for youth as well as day-care and after-school services for working parents.

6. Queens College was established in 1937 and is a senior college in the City University of New York (CUNY).
7. William Kalaidjian was active in Bronx civic affairs and is perhaps best remembered as the long-serving minister of the Bedford Park Congregational Church and as chaplain of the New York City Police Department. Irma Fleck's 2004 obituary notes that the Bronx Committee on the Arts merged with Gerald Klot's Bronx Council on the Arts and that he had been involved in arts in the Bronx since 1945. This strongly suggests that the individual she was actually referring to was not Kalaidjian but Klot. See Marten, "Irma Fleck, 84, Who Battled Decay."
8. Bronx Community College, a community college in CUNY, was established in 1957 and acquired the fifty-five-acre University Heights campus of New York University in 1973. NYU operated its uptown campus from 1894 to 1973.
9. Irma Fleck was executive director of the new Bronx Council on the Arts, founded in 1971. The council coordinated events and sought funding for such cultural offerings as opera, theater, poetry, and the visual arts.
10. The nationally known Chuck Davis Dance Company was founded in 1967 by its artistic director of the same name. Davis bridged traditional and contemporary African dance with African American dance. While on the faculty of Bronx Community College, Davis generated interest and a high profile for his dance style. See Patrick, "Chuck Davis and DanceAfrica."
11. Bronx Opera Company was founded in 1967 and is the only such company whose musical productions are only in English. The company is regularly featured at Lehman College's Lovinger Theatre. The Bronx Opera Company has no relationship to the old Bronx Opera House on East 149th Street that featured vaudeville, drama, and musicals.
12. Irma Fleck began the Bronx Museum of the Arts in 1971, under the auspices of its parent body, the Bronx Council on the Arts. The museum was housed in the rotunda of the Bronx County Courthouse on 161st Street until it moved up the Grand Concourse in 1980 to occupy the former Temple Emmanuel.
13. The New York State Council on the Arts was established in 1971.
14. Irma Fleck and former New York City detective Jack Flanigan established the Bronx Frontier Development Corporation in 1976 in response to open Bronx space resulting from loss of housing. Using Hunts Point Market fruit and vegetable waste, they created compost as fertilizer for community gardens. This beautified the area, improved resident diets, and created jobs. Government and foundation support helped Bronx Frontier implement further initiatives such as the creation of topsoil for some nine local mini-parks and the use of efficient alternative energy sources.
15. ZooDoo, a composted organic material product, was produced from animal manure donated by the Bronx Zoo to Bronx Frontier Development. An odorless soil additive, it was originally sold in two-pound plastic bags at the Zoo, the Botanical Garden, and at area nurseries and garden centers (Faust, "Community Project Produces Fertilizer"). ZooDoo Gold is the newer version of the product.

16. For CETA, see chapter 4, note 13.

Chapter 11

1. The Prospect Theatre was located at 851 Prospect Avenue and is thought to have been constructed prior to World War I. Later converted to the Olympic Theater, it closed in 2006.
2. The Robert F. Wagner Association was a political club founded in 1961 in reaction to long-serving Bronx County Democratic leader Charles Buckley's opposition to the renomination of Mayor Wagner for reelection. See "Wagner Assails Buckley in Bronx," *New York Times*. The association's founders were the Puerto Rican judge Frank Torres and the African American lawyer Joseph M'Lemore. See also "Robert F. Wagner Association," in Frank Torres Papers; "Joseph M'Lemore, Lawyer, 72, Dead," *New York Times*. The association tried to bring 4th Assembly District minorities into party politics.
3. Ace Spray Finishing Corp., an industrial paint finisher, was acquired in 1974 by Bronx Venture. With the help of Bronx Venture, a community development agency, Ace grew and developed. When Bronx Venture invested four hundred thousand dollars and secured matching loans from banks and other financial institutions for Ace, the company made impressive gains. Within five years Ace had exponential growth in sales, space, and the number of its skilled employees. Ace was able to pay back all its loans and taxes. This successful business helped stabilize and rebuild the economic base in what was considered a redlined community. See "Statement of Michael Nuñez, President, Bronx Venture Corp.," in *United States, The Urban Jobs and Enterprise Zone Act*.
4. Carol Bellamy was president of the New York City Council from 1978 to 1985.

Chapter 12

1. The Puerto Rican–born Leoncia Rosado Rousseau (Mamma Leo) (1912–2006), and her husband, Rev. Francisco Rosado, started the Iglesia Christiana Damascus in the Bronx. When her husband was drafted into the military, Mamma Leo became what is thought to be the first Latina Pentecostal pastor in New York City. Her ministry included gang members, drug addicts, and prostitutes, and later the couple established the Damascus Youth Crusade, an inner-city drug outreach program. See Espinosa, "Pentecostalism," 431.
2. WHOM was a Spanish-language radio station featuring music and news about the Hispanic community. Velez worked at WHOM and used it to promote his agenda, according to Jill Jonnes, *South Bronx Rising*, 166.
3. South Bronx Neighborhood Orientation Center was established in 1964 to help substance abusers and those dealing with housing and consumer fraud issues. The center lost its funding in 1966 after an embezzlement scandal. See Jonnes, *South Bronx Rising*, 166, 168.
4. Hunts Point Market construction was halted in 1964 because blacks and Hispanics were not being hired. See "Plumbers Agree to a Wagner Plan," *New York Times*. The Hunts Point Market, opened in 1967, has long supplied more than half of the produce consumed in the city.
5. For further information about ASPIRA, see Pantoja, *Memoir of a Visionary*. Both Records of ASPIRA of New York, Inc. and the Antonia Pantoja Papers are in Centro de Estudios Puertorriqueños.
6. Nelson Rockefeller (1908–79) was governor of New York State from 1959 to

1973 and served as vice president of the United States (1974–77). He established the New York State Urban Development Corporation to create low-income housing with "moral obligation" bonds. Under Rockefeller, the state built a new and expanded Lincoln Hospital in the Bronx. See "State Will Build 4 Hospitals Here," *New York Times*.

7. The South Bronx Community Housing Corporation (SBCHC) was established in 1972 and focused on community development, housing management services, planning, and construction.
8. Voter's Crusade, or La Cruzada Civica del Voto, was an initiative that helped swell Puerto Rican voter registration in 1972. See Estades, *Patrones de Participación Política*, 63–65, 69–72; and Sanchez, "Puerto Ricans and the Door of Participation," 120.
9. South Bronx High School at 701 St. Ann's Avenue opened in 1977 for some one thousand students. When the school closed in 2005 the site was renamed South Bronx Educational Complex and serves two small high schools.
10. Hostos Community College is named for Eugenio Maria de Hostos and opened in 1968 as part of the City University of New York. It is located at 475 Grand Concourse and pioneered bilingual education.
11. United Bronx Parents. See chapter 5, note 5.

Chapter 13

1. Pondiac Democratic Club was founded in 1921 at the urging of county boss Edward J. Flynn (1891–1953). The naming of the club was meant to honor American Indian Chief Pontiac, but a registrar's misspelling changed that intent. The club was known for its ability to secure a high voter turnout and supporting Hispanics for elected office as early as the 1950s. Extortion sullied the club's reputation in 1967, and in 1972 it finally disbanded. See "Pondiac Democratic Club" in the Felipe N. Torres Papers.
2. Morris Park Association is a membership community association that provides recreational activities for seniors, softball leagues, after-school programs, and referrals for services. It has neighborhood civilian patrols and sponsors holiday parties and parades.
3. For SEBCO (South East Bronx Community Organization), see chapter 8, note 11.
4. Aldus Green at 996 Aldus Street was SEBCO's first housing project. Developer Hy Kraus offered to partner with SEBCO if they could find tenants supportive of redevelopment. Fr. Gigante secured financial subsidies for moderate-income residents, and the project was completed in 1977. It has eleven buildings with a total of 395 apartments. See Silverman, *Community-Based Organizations*, 103.
5. Roosevelt Gardens, now Roosevelt Court, is at 1455–1499 Grand Concourse between East 171st and 172nd Streets. This block-sized complex had been made up of stable apartment buildings. However, it became the first abandoned property on the Concourse and a case study of the building abandonment process replicated many times over around the Bronx. While rehabilitated in 1981 and thriving today, Roosevelt Gardens is described at its lowest point in Stevenson, "Abandonment of Roosevelt Gardens," 72–75.
6. Jack Resnick began his real estate business in 1928 in the Bronx and developed Jack Resnick and Sons into one of New York City's top real estate firms. See "Jack Resnick, 83; He Helped

Shape," *New York Times*. Albert Einstein College of Medicine, in the Morris Park section of the Bronx, named its twenty-three-acre campus for Jack and Pearl Resnick. The Jack Resnick building at the Hebrew Home for the Aged, in the Riverdale section of the Bronx, additionally honors the Realtor and philanthropist.

7. Donald Trump is one of the best-known real estate developers in the country. For insights into his real estate deals, see his autobiography, *Trump: The Art of the Deal.*
8. Karen Arenson, "Julius Edelstein, 93, Dies."

Chapter 14

1. Walden Cassotto (1936–73) was better known as the Bronx-born singer and songwriter Bobby Darin. See Evanier, *Roman Candle.*
2. Lewis Morris Apartments was an elite address at 1749 Grand Concourse, which had professional offices and was home to many Bronx physicians, attorneys, and businessmen. See Rosenblum, *Boulevard of Dreams*, 55–56.
3. At 15,372 units on 320 acres, Co-op City was the largest cooperative housing development in the world when it was constructed in the Baychester section of the Bronx from 1966 to 1973. See Farrell, "Vast Co-op City Is Dedicated in Bronx." Co-op City drew many West Bronx residents away when the development opened. See Linton, Mields & Coston, *Apparent Effect of Co-op City.*
4. James Meredith, civil rights activist, was the first black student admitted to the University of Mississippi following a lawsuit that went all the way to the U.S. Supreme Court. He was the university's first African American graduate in 1963. See McGee, *James Meredith.*
5. *Baker v. Carr*, 369 U.S. 186 (1962), was a Supreme Court case establishing that apportionment of seats in state legislatures is not a political matter and is subject to the judicial authority of federal courts. The ruling affirmed that district constituents are entitled to equal protection of the law. See Lewis, "Decision Is 6 to 2." *New York Times.*
6. Ginsy's Toy Shop had been at 485 Claremont Parkway, around the corner from the Benenson Theater. It sold games, dolls, doll carriages, bicycles, Lionel trains and accessories, and stationery. See *Bronx New York City Yellow Pages.* Ginsy's was named for its owner, Barnett Ginsberg.
7. Krum's was a chocolatier, ice cream parlor, and eatery at 188th Street and the Grand Concourse. It was a favorite stop after viewing a double feature at the nearby Paradise Theatre. See photo in Ultan and Hermalyn, *The Bronx*, 112.
8. Alexander's was a department store known to all Bronxites who shopped at its Third Avenue and 152nd Street location, and its uptown site at Fordham Road and the Grand Concourse. The store outfitted the entire family at affordable prices, and could be relied on for linens, housewares, jewelry, games, and gifts. By 1992, Alexander's filed for bankruptcy and closed its eleven retail outlets. For a shopper's personal account of Alexander's and store photos, see Greenbaum, "Alexander's," 16–17.

Chapter 15

1. Bryant Sanitarium is no longer operating, though its building at 1214 Hoe Avenue still exists.
2. Columbus High School at 925 Astor Avenue, in the Pelham Parkway section,

was constructed in 1936 and first occupied in 1939. Its student enrollment was over 2,750. The school closed in 2004 and was reorganized as four small high schools.

3. Bronx Day, begun in 1971, was inspired by the earlier Bronx Borough Day celebrated from 1912 to 1928. The 1971 celebration had a full day of activities, including a parade on the Grand Concourse, a fair at the Bronx Zoo, a concert at Bronx High School of Science, and a rock concert at the Paradise Theatre. Bronx Day grew into Bronx Week the following year, with an expanded range of activities. See Ultan, "Bronx Pride."
4. Ibid.
5. For antipoverty initiatives, see chapter 6, note 5.
6. Monterey Block Association provided referrals for social services, child welfare, housing, and educational training programs.
7. Tremont Community Corporation. See chapter 6, no. 3.
8. South Bronx Community Action Theatre established the Performing Arts and Creative Arts Workshop Series and exposed thousands of children to dance, drama, music, fine arts, film, and photography. They helped students think of the possibilities of careers in the arts and helped prepare interested students for auditions to specialty high schools.
9. Lehman Center for the Performing Arts has a 2,310-seat concert hall that features classical and popular music, as well as dance and theater companies from around the world, in addition to hosting public programs and debates. See Blair, "Lehman College Opens New Cultural Complex."
10. For Co-op City, see chapter 14, note 3.

Chapter 16

1. McBride Studios dealt in marble for altars, shrines, statues, pulpits, and communion railings. They maintained offices variously at Park Row and Barclay Street, in lower Manhattan, and employed skilled sculptors and carvers at the company's Italian Studios in Pietrasanta-Carrara, near Milan. For a company advertisement, see "McBride's Studios" [advertisement], *American Catholic Quarterly Review. See also* "Paul H. McBride, 54, Expert on Marble," *New York Times.*
2. Claude Pepper (1900–1989) served as a U.S. senator from Florida (1936–51), was a member of the U.S. House of Representatives (1963–83), and served as chairman of the House Aging Committee (1977–83).

BIBLIOGRAPHY

Books

Alicea, John. *50 Years of the Puerto Rican Day Parade*. New York: Galos Publishing, 2007.

Bronx Museum of the Arts and Robert Jensen. *Devastation/Resurrection: The South Bronx, November 9–January 13, 1980*. Bronx: The Museum, 1980. Exhibition catalog.

The Bronx New York City Yellow Pages Classified Telephone Directory, 1955. New York: New York Telephone Co., 1955.

Carnegie, Dale. *How to Win Friends and Influence People*. New York: Simon & Schuster, 2009. [Originally published 1936; revised edition 1981.]

Caro, Robert A. *The Power Broker: Robert Moses and the Fall of New York*. New York: Alfred A. Knopf, 1974.

City of New York, Department of City Planning. *Community District Needs: Fiscal Year 1991: Bronx*. New York: DCP # 89-66, 1989.

D'Avanzo, Albert N. *South Bronx: West Farms Area Development*. Prepared for Neighborhood Community Renewal Corp., New York, 1979.

Decker, Julie, and Chris Chief, eds. *Quonset Hut: Metal Living for a Modern Age*. New York: Princeton Architectural Press, 2005.

Espinosa, Gaston. "Pentecostalism." In *Hispanic American Religious Cultures*, vol. 2., ed. Miguel A. De La Torre, 423–36. Santa Barbara, CA: ABC-CLIO, 2009.

Estades, Rosa. *Patrones de Participación Política de los Puertorriqueños en la Ciudad de Nueva York*. Río Piedras: Editorial Universitaria, Universidad de Puerto Rico, 1978.

Evanier, David. *Roman Candle: The Life of Bobby Darin*. Albany, NY: SUNY Press, 2010.

Fitch, Robert. *The Assassination of New York*. London: Verso, 1993.

Fleck, Irma, and Capt. Henry Fleck with Marcia Stevens, comp. and ed. *Letters from the Front: A Love Story*. Lexington, KY: Create Space, 2003.

Fraser, Steven. *Labor Will Rule: Sidney Hillman and the Rise of American Labor*. New York: Free Press, 1991.

Gonzalez, Evelyn. *The Bronx*. New York: Columbia University Press, 2004.

Gottmann, Jean. *Megalopolis: The Urbanized Northeastern Seaboard of the United States*. New York: Twentieth-Century Fund, 1961.

Greenbaum, Marilyn. "Alexander's: Goodbye & Thank You." In *Back in the Bronx, Celebrating the Experience of Growing Up in the Bronx*, ed. Stephen M. and Susan J. Samtur. Scarsdale, NY: S. M. Samtur, 1995.

Griffiths, William H. *The Story of the American Bank Note Company*. New York: American Bank Note Co., 1960.

"Heat and Hot Water." In *New York City Charter and Administrative Code Annotated*, Title 17, Article 8, Section 2027–29. Guilderland, NY: New York Legal Publishing Corp, 1993.

Jones, Allen, and Mark Naison. *The Rat That Got Away: A Bronx Memoir.* New York: Fordham University Press, 2009.

Jonnes, Jill. *South Bronx Rising: The Rise, Fall, and Resurrection of an American City*. New York: Fordham University Press, 2002.

Jonnes, Jill. *We're Still Here: The Rise, Fall and Resurrection of the South Bronx*. Boston: Atlantic Monthly Press, 1986.

Lawson, Ronald, ed., and Mark Naison. *The Tenant Movement in New York City, 1904–1984*. New Brunswick, NJ: Rutgers University Press, 1986.

LeBlanc, Adrian Nicole. *Random Family: Love, Drugs, Trouble, and Coming of Age in the Bronx*. New York: Scribner, 2004.

Linton, Mields & Coston, Inc. *The Apparent Effect of Co-op City on Mobility within the Bronx and on Neighborhood Conditions*. Washington, DC: Litton, Mields & Coston, 1972.

McGee, Meredith Coleman. *James Meredith: Warrior and the America That Created Him*. New York: Praeger, 2013.

Meltzer, Marvin H., and Carlo Paganelli. *Marvin H. Meltzer: City as Poetry*. Milan: L'Arca, 2002.

Merola, Mario, with Mary Ann Giordano. *Big City D.A.* New York: Random House, 1988.

Meyer, Bernard, et al. *History of the New York Court of Appeals: 1932–2003*. New York: Columbia University Press, 2006.

Morgenthau, Henry, III. *Mostly Morgenthaus: A Family History.* New York: Ticknor & Fields, 1991.

Pantoja, Antonia. *Memoir of a Visionary: Antonia Pantoja*. Houston: Arte Público Press, 2002.

Plunz, Richard. *A History of Housing in New York City: Dwelling Type and Social Change in the American Metropolis*. New York: Columbia University Press, 1990.

Pollinger, Kenneth J., and Annette C. Pollinger. *Community Action and the Poor: Influence vs. Social Control in a New York City Community.* New York: Praeger Publishing, 1972.

Rooney, Jim. *Organizing the South Bronx*. Albany, NY: SUNY Press, 1995.

Rosenblum, Constance. *Boulevard of Dreams: Heady Times, Heartbreak, and Hope along the Grand Concourse in the Bronx*. New York: New York University Press, 2009.

Rosenblum, Walter. *Walter Rosenblum Photographer*. Dresden: Verlag der Kunst, 1990.

Rosenthal, Mel. *In the South Bronx of America*. Willimantic, CT: Curbstone Press, 2000.

Rubenstein, David. "Fort Dix." In *Historical Dictionary of the U.S. Army,* ed. Jerold E. Brown, 184. Westport, CT: Greenwood Press, 2001.

Sahd, Brian. "Community Development Corporations and Social Capital: Lessons from the South Bronx." In *Community Based Organizations: The Intersection of Social Capital and Local Context in Contemporary Urban Society*, ed. Robert Mark Silverman, 85–121. Detroit: Wayne State University, 2004.

Sanchez, Jose Ramon. "Puerto Ricans and the Door of Participation in U.S. Politics." In *Handbook of Hispanic Cultures in the United States: Sociology*, ed. Nicolas Kanellos and Claudio Esteva

Fabregat, 110–32. Houston: Arte Público Press, 1999.

Silverman, Robert Mark. *Community-Based Organizations: The Intersection of Social Capital and Local Context in Contemporary Urban Society*. Detroit: Wayne State University Press, 2004.

Simon, Arthur. *Stuyvesant Town U.S.A.: Pattern for Two Americas*. New York: New York University Press, 1970.

Starr, Roger. *The Rise and Fall of New York City*. New York: Basic Books, 1985.

Stevenson, Gelvin. "The Abandonment of Roosevelt Gardens." In Bronx Museum of the Arts and Robert Jensen, *Devastation/Resurrection: The South Bronx, November 9–January 13, 1980*, ed. Robert Jensen, 72–80. Bronx: The Museum, 1980. Exhibition catalog.

Stolberg, Benjamin. *Tailor's Progress: The Story of a Famous Union and the Men Who Made It*. Garden City, NY: Doubleday, Doran, 1944.

Su, Celina. *Streetwise for Book Smarts: Grassroots Organizing and Education Reform in the Bronx*. Ithaca, NY: Cornell University Press, 2009.

Sullivan, Donald G. *Bronx Art Deco Architecture: An Exposition*. New York: West Bronx Restoration Committee, Graduate Program in Urban Planning, Hunter College, City University of New York (CUNY), 1976.

Thomas, Dana Lee. *Lords of the Land: The Triumphs and Scandals of America's Real Estate Barons from Early Times to the Present*. New York: G. P. Putnam's Sons, 1977.

Trump, Donald. *Trump: The Art of the Deal*. New York: Random House, 1988.

Turner, Kenneth. "Fort Rucker." In *Historical Dictionary of the U.S. Army*, ed. Jerold E. Brown, 197–98. Westport, CT: Greenwood Press, 2001.

Twomey, Bill. *The Bronx in Bits and Pieces*. Bloomington, IN: Rooftop Publishing, 2007.

Ultan, Lloyd, and Gary Hermalyn. *The Bronx: It Was Only Yesterday, 1935–1965*. Bronx, NY: Bronx County Historical Society, 1992.

Vergara, Camilo José. *The New American Ghetto*. New Brunswick, NJ: Rutgers University Press, 1995.

Von Hoffman, Alexander. *House by House, Block by Block: The Rebirth of America's Urban Neighborhoods*. New York: Oxford University Press, 2003.

Walker, Tom. *Fort Apache: New York's Most Violent Precinct*. New York: iUniverse Star, 2009.

Walton, Francis. *Miracle of World War II: How American Industry Made Victory Possible*. New York: Macmillan, 1956.

"The Winds of War." In *Movies Made for Television: 1964–2004*. Vol. 2, *1980–1989*, ed. Alvin H. Marill, 398–99. Lanham, MD: Scarecrow Press, 2005.

Wolfe, Tom. *The Bonfire of the Vanities*. New York: Farrar, Strauss and Giroux, 1987.

Articles

Auer, Joseph L. "R. Hoe & Co., Inc." *Bronxboro* 25 (February–March 1948): 11–12.

Bromley, Ray. "Not So Simple! Caro, Moses, and the Impact of the Cross-Bronx Expressway." *Bronx County Historical Society Journal* 35, no. 1 (Spring 1998): 5–29.

Coates, Robert M. "Profiles King of the Bronx [J. Clarence Davies]." *New Yorker*, December 7, 1929, 33–35.

Glazer, Nathan. "The South Bronx Story: An Extreme Case of Neighborhood Decline." *Policy Studies Journal* 16, no. 2 (Winter 1987): 269–76.

"Great Humanitarian Work Carried on in

the Bronx," *Bronxboro* 8 (January 1931): 7–8.

Katz, Steven, and Margit Mayer. "Gimme Shelter: Self-Help Housing Struggles within and against the State in New York City and West Berlin." *International Journal of Urban and Regional Research* 9, no. 1 (March 1985): 15–46.

Logue, Edward J. "Charlotte Gardens: Is There a Future for Single-Family Homes in New York?" *The Assessor* 3, no. 1 (April 5, 1985): 1–11.

"McBride Studios" [company advertisement]. *American Catholic Quarterly Review* 36, no. 144 (October 1911).

Munch, Janet Butler. "Making Waves in the Bronx: The Story of the U.S. Naval Training School (WR) at Hunter College." *Bronx County Historical Society Journal* 30, no. 1 (Spring 1993): 1–15.

Patrick, K. C. "Chuck Davis and Dance Africa." *Dance Magazine* 78 no. 4 (April 2004): 44–46.

Posner, Louis S. "The Lesson of Guaranteed Mortgage Certificates." *Harvard Business Review* 26, no. 5 (September 1948): 560–71.

Archival Material

Amalgamated Clothing Workers of America Records, 5619. Kheel Center for Labor-Management Documentation and Archives. Cornell University Library, Ithaca, NY.

Antonetty, Evelina. "History of United Bronx Parents," undated. Jill Jonnes Papers, United Bronx Parents file, Special Collections, Leonard Lief Library, Lehman College, City University of New York, Bronx, NY.

Antonia Pantoja Papers. Centro de Estudios Puertorriqueños, Hunter College, City University of New York, New York, NY.

"Arson." Jill Jonnes Papers, Special Collections, Leonard Lief Library, Lehman College, City University of New York, Bronx, NY.

"Committee against Fort Apache, 1980–1981." Diana Caballero Papers, Box 4, Files 1–2. Centro de Estudios Puertorriqueños, Hunter College, City University of New York, New York, NY.

Congressman Mario Biaggi Papers. The Bronx County Historical Society, Bronx, NY.

Edward Joseph Logue Papers. MS 959. Manuscripts and Archives, Yale University Library, New Haven, CT.

International Ladies Garment Workers Union Records, 5780. Kheel Center for Labor-Management Documentation and Archives. Cornell University Library, Ithaca, NY.

New York City Office of the Comptroller, Mortgage Banking & Housing Unit. "Dennis Lane Apartments, Borough of the Bronx," 1957. Item 1992-6-25*. Special Collections, Leonard Lief Library, Lehman College, City University of New York, Bronx, NY.

Oral History Collection of the Bronx Institute Archives, 1981–1991. Special Collections, Leonard Lief Library, Lehman College, City University of New York, Bronx, NY.

"Pondiac Democratic Club, 1953–1964." Felipe N. Torres Papers, Box 30, File 2. Centro de Estudios Puertorriqueños, Hunter College, City University of New York, New York, NY.

Records of ASPIRA of New York Inc. Centro de Estudios Puertorriqueños, Hunter College, City University of New York, New York, NY.

Records of United Bronx Parents Inc., 1966–1989. Centro de Estudios Puertorriqueños, Hunter College, City University of New York, New York, NY.

"Robert F. Wagner Association." Frank Torres Papers, Box 23, Folder 7. Centro de Estudios Puertorriqueños, Hunter College, City University of New York, New York.

Internet

Bady, David. "Kingsbridge Armory." Bronx Architecture, 2006, http://www.lehman.edu/vpadvance/artgallery/arch/buildings/armory.html.

Leson, Lisa. "Bess Myerson." *Jewish Women: A Comprehensive Encyclopedia*, http://jwa.org/thisweek/sep/08/1945/bess-myerson.

Levittown Historical Society. http://www.levittownhistoricalsociety.org.

Munch, Janet Butler. Childhood in the Bronx: Contemporary Photographs by Georgeen Comerford & Vintage Photographs from the Collections of the Bronx Institute Archives, 2009, http://www.lehman.edu/library/childhood-bronx/home.htm.

Munch, Janet Butler. "Mario Merola Building, Formerly Bronx County Building." Bronx Architecture, 2006, http://www.lehman.edu/vpadvance/artgallery/arch/buildings/BCBuilding.html.

New York City Department of Parks and Recreation, "Mario Merola Grove." http://www.nycgovparks.org/parks/VanCortlandtPark/highlights/11625.

Phipps Houses. www.phippsny.org.

Ultan, Lloyd. "Franklin Avenue Armory." Lehman College Art Gallery. Bronx Architecture, 2006, http://www.lehman.edu/vpadvance/artgallery/arch/buildings/Franklin_Armory.html.

Theses and Dissertations

Jordan, Cecko N. "The Albanians of the Bronx, A New Ethnic Community in New York City; a Survey." MA thesis, City College of New York, City University of New York, 1982.

Maida, Lori M. "Belmont: A Community Fighting to Survive." PhD diss., Fordham University, 1987.

Government Documents

Keifetz, Harry (Chairman). *A Decade of Service, Community Board Six—The Bronx*. Bronx, NY: City Planning Commission, May 18, 1974.

New York City Transit Authority. *The Elimination of Two-Fare Zones and Other Fare-Policy Changes: Proposed Tariff Revision and MetroCard Gold Roll Out*. New York: MTA Finance Committee, Metropolitan Transportation Authority, 1997.

Serrano, Jose E. "Tribute to the Bronx Puerto Rican Day Parade." *Congressional Record* 144, no. 104 (July 29, 1998), E. 1458.

"Statement of Michael Nuñez, President, Bronx Venture Corp., South Bronx, N.Y." *Hearing before the Subcommittee on Economic Stabilization of the Committee on Banking, Finance, and Urban Affairs, House of Representatives, Ninety-Seventh Congress, First Session, on H.R. 3824. New York, N.Y., July 8, 1981*, 140–43. Washington, DC: U.S. Government Printing Office, 1981.

Newspapers

"Alabama Had Vital War Role, Became Munitions Center of South." *Tuscaloosa News*, August 16, 1945, 6.

Arenson, Karen. "Julius Edelstein, 93, Dies; Devised CUNY's Open Admissions." *New York Times*, November 19, 2005, B18.

Arnold, Mark R. "The Good War That

Might Have Been: Ten Years Ago, President Johnson Called for a Total Victory over Poverty, 'Because It Is Right, Because It Is Wise, and Because It Is Possible', What Happened?" *New York Times*, September 29, 1974, 56+.

"Bench Moulders" [advertisement]. *New York Post*, April 3, 1943, 34.

Blair, Eleanor. "Lehman College Opens New Cultural Complex: 40 Minutes from Broadway." *New York Times*, September 26, 1980, C4.

"Bronx House Bought from Vincent Astor: 6-Story 'Walk-Up' on Concourse Cost $900,000 in 1927." *New York Times*, August 11, 1942, 32.

"Bronx Houses Change Name." *New York Times*, April 29, 1961, 25.

"The City of New York Housing and Development Administration: Public Notice." *New York Times*, August 10, 1970, 10.

Clurman, Robert. "The Patients Can Walk Out at Any Time at Bronx State Mental Hospital." *New York Times*, April 2, 1972, SM14.

Daly, Stephen. "The Project That Transformed a Bronx Neighborhood: Lambert Houses, Marking Decade, Provide Stability." *New York Times*, May 15, 1983, 7.

Farrell, William E. "Vast Co-op City Is Dedicated in Bronx." *New York Times*, November 25, 1968, 1+.

Faust, Joan Lee. "Community Project Produces Fertilizer." *New York Times*, March 24, 1983, C7.

Fisher, Ian. "Pulling Out of Fort Apache, the Bronx." *New York Times*, June 23, 1993, B1.

Gonzales, David. "In New Home, Bronx Dance Academy Seeks to Step Up Its Presence." *New York Times*, April 28, 2014, A19.

"Gov. Smith Urged to Aid Tax Exemption. Joseph P. Day Sends Letter Asking Extension of the Law." *New York Times*, February 4, 1923, RE1.

"Henry H. Minskoff, 73, Head of Major Building Company." *New York Times*, August 15, 1984, B24.

"Jack Resnick, 83; He Helped Shape New York Skyline." *New York Times*, June 10, 1991, B11.

"Jerome Minskoff, 78, a Producer and Developer." *New York Times*, August 16, 1994, B10.

"Joseph M'Lemore, Lawyer, 72, Dead." *New York Times*, November 28, 1971, 73.

Kluckhom, Frank L. "Big Defense Program Is Launched: Defense Planner." *New York Times*, May 19, 1940, 73.

Lewis, Anthony. "Decision Is 6 to 2: Many States Likely to Be Affected by Landmark Case." *New York Times*, March 27, 1962, 1+.

"Low-Income Housing: 76 Units in the Bronx." *New York Times*, October 27, 1991, Sec. R1.

Marten, Douglas. "Irma Fleck, 84, Who Battled Decay in the Bronx, Is Dead." *New York Times*, February 26, 2004, 10.

"Mortgage Board Voted at Albany; Lehman Fight Won: Bill Is Finally Passed to Create Commission to Direct $800,000,000 Rehabilitation." *New York Times*, January 31, 1935, 1+.

Onshi, Normitsu. "Neighborhood Report: South Bronx; Mapping the Lower Bronx: It's South, but South of What?" *New York Times*, February 19, 1995, CY9.

"Paul H. McBride, 54, Expert on Marble, Retired Head of Studios Long Operated by Family Dies at Home in Brooklyn." *New York Times*, January 1, 1942, 25.

"Plumbers Agree to a Wagner Plan to End Walkout." *New York Times*, May 16, 1964, 1+.

Rosen, Ira. "The Glory That Was Charlotte Street." *New York Times*, October 7, 1979, SM11.

"Sam Minskoff Dies; Noted Builder, 66: Constructor of Hotels, De Luxe Apartment Houses, Hospitals Came from Russia in Youth." *New York Times*, December 27, 1950, 34.

Sheftell, Jason. "Banking on It. Will a Giant South Bronx Building Change a Neighborhood?" *New York Daily News*, December 5, 2008, 6.

Shipler, David. "Negroes Say Pact on Housing Lags: Accuse Metropolitan Life of Stalling on Apartments." *New York Times*, July 28, 1968, 27.

Siegal, Allan M. "Change Creeps into World of Bronx Albanians: Changes Noticed." *New York Times*, January 24, 1974, 31.

Sloane, Leonard. "Chief Officer Is Named by R. Hoe & Co." *New York Times*, January 30, 1981, D2.

Smothers, Ronald. "Fire Fails to Daunt Merchant." *New York Times*, February 9, 1982. B3.

Starr, Roger. "Making New York Smaller: The City's Economic Outlook Remains Grim. Shrinkage Is Inevitable, the Author Argues, and the Time Has Come to Plan for It." *New York Times*, November 14, 1976, 32+.

"State Will Build 4 Hospitals Here: City to Run Them—8 Health Centers and 2 Housing Projects Planned." *New York Times*, November 1, 1968, 1.

"2,000 Houses Given to the City by U.S. for Emergency Use." *New York Times*, January 17, 1946, 1+.

Ultan, Lloyd. "Bronx Pride." *New York Daily News*, May 12, 2011, 21.

"Wagner Assails Buckley in Bronx: Republicans in Legislature Also Draw Mayor's Fire." *New York Times*, October 14, 1961, 24.

INDEX

Numbers in italics type refer to illustrations.

ABOUT THE EDITORS

Emita Brady Hill is the former chancellor of Indiana University Kokomo and spent twenty years at Lehman College, the Bronx campus of CUNY, in various roles including department chair, dean, vice president, and professor of French language and literature, and was the program director for two NEH funded programs, The City and the Humanities and the Bronx Regional History Project. She lives in New Rochelle, New York.

Janet Butler Munch is an associate professor and special collections librarian at Lehman College, CUNY. For the past twenty years, she has worked with Bronx researchers and collections including Lehman's Bronx Institute Archives of community oral histories, books, documents, maps, and photographs.